W. B. YEATS

Literary Lives
General Editor: Richard Dutton, Professor of English
Lancaster University

This series offers stimulating accounts of the literary careers of the most admired and influential English-language authors. Volumes follow the outline of writers' working lives, not in the spirit of traditional biography, but aiming to trace the professional, publishing and social contexts which shaped their writing. The role and status of 'the author' as the creator of literary texts is a vexed issue in current critical theory, where a variety of social, linguistic and psychological approaches have challenged the old concentration on writers as specially gifted individuals. Yet reports of 'the death of the author' in literary studies are (as Mark Twain said of a premature obituary) an exaggeration. This series aims to demonstrate how an understanding of writers' careers can promote, for students and general readers alike, a more informed historical reading of their works.

W. B. Yeats

A Literary Life

Alasdair D. F. Macrae
Senior Lecturer in English Studies
University of Stirling

St. Martin's Press   New York

First published in the United States of America in 1995

Printed in Great Britain

ISBN 0-312-12310-8

Library of Congress Cataloging-in-Publication Data
Macrae, Alasdair D. F., 1939–
W. B. Yeats : a literary life / Alasdair D. F. Macrae.
p. cm. — (Literary lives)
Includes bibliographical references and index.
ISBN 0-312-12310-8
1. Yeats, W. B. (William Butler), 1865–1939. 2. Poets,
Irish—19th century—Biography. 3. Poets, Irish—20th century–
–Biography. 4. Ireland—In literature. I. Title. II. Series:
Literary lives (New York, N.Y.)
PR5906.M276 1995
821' .8—dc20
[B]   94–20524
                                                          CIP

In memory of my parents
and for
Elise, Calum and Brendan

Contents

Preface

A word is needed on the organisation of this book. I have not written a straightforward or chronological narrative of Yeats's career; there are a number of excellent, detailed biographies of him already. I have chosen to approach him from a number of angles, to locate him in relation to the people, ideas and events with which he was involved, so that the complexity of his literary personality might emerge. For this complexity to emerge, the book needs to be taken as a whole, with whatever overlaps, developments and contradictions occur. A preliminary but substantial chronology of Yeats and contingent happenings is provided, to which the reader can return for support and gradually fill out.

Acknowledgements

Yeats is often a difficult writer and I have been greatly helped over the years by many of the books written on him. In attempting to write an accessible literary life I have had to find my way through vast amounts of material by and on the poet. My students in seminars have helped to keep my excitement fresh and one of the real privileges of my life has been the opportunity to teach several times at the annual Yeats Summer School in Sligo. There I have been stimulated, informed and entertained in a very special way, and many fellow teachers and students have become close friends. I have learned much from Augustine Martin, Brendan Kennelly, Seamus Heaney, Helen Vendler and Declan Kiberd, to name only the most striking. Eoghan O'Neill has helped me to understand something of Ireland's history, particularly the Gaelic side of Irish culture. For over twenty years I have enjoyed a friendship with A. Norman Jeffares, and his gusto, acuteness and generosity have been invaluable: I owe an unrepayable debt to Derry and Jeanne Jeffares. Margaret Walshe has been a wonderful typist and reader between the lines. My wife, Elise, has sustained me, proofread and advised with patience and insight.

Quotations from Yeats are taken from the works by him listed in the Select Bibliography.

The poem 'The Artist' by William Carlos Williams is reprinted by kind permission of The Carcanet Press from *Selected Poems*. In the United States and Canada permission has been granted as follows: William Carlos Williams: *The Collected Poems of William Carlos Williams, 1939–1962, vol. II*. Copyright © 1962 by William Carlos Williams. Reprinted by permission of New Directions Publishing Corp.

Chronology: Yeats's Life and Contemporary Events

1865	William Butler Yeats born in Dublin.	Salvation Army founded. End of American Civil War. Assassination of Lincoln.
1866		Dostoevsky, *Crime and Punishment*.
1867	Family moves to London.	Attempted Fenian Rising. Marx, *Capital*. Arnold, *On the Study of Celtic Literature*.
1869		Church of Ireland disestablished by Gladstone's Government. Suez Canal opened.
1870		First Irish Land Act passed. Dickens dies. Ruskin, *Lectures in Art*. D. G. Rossetti, *Poems, 1870*.
1873		Pater, *The Renaissance*.
1874	Family moves house in London.	First Impressionist Exhibition in Paris.
1876	Family moves to Bedford Park.	First telephone message transmitted. Wagner, *The Ring*, completed. Ibsen, *Peer Gynt*.
1877–81	Attends the Godolphin School in London.	Tolstoy, *Anna Karenina*. Standish O'Grady, *History of Ireland: The Heroic Period* (completed 1880). Court case between Whistler and Ruskin.

1879		Irish National Land League founded. Ibsen, *A Doll's House*. Electric light bulb first used successfully.
1880		Gladstone becomes Prime Minister for the second time. Parnell elected leader of Irish Parliamentary Party. Dostoevsky, *The Brothers Karamazov*.
1881	Family moves back to Dublin.	Death of Carlyle.
1881–83	Attends the Erasmus Smith High School, Dublin.	Wilde, *Poems*. Second Irish Land Act passed.
1882	Family moves house in Dublin.	Chief Secretary and Under-Secretary in Ireland assassinated in Dublin. Childe, *The English and Scottish Popular Ballads* (Vol. I). R. L. Stevenson, *Treasure Island*.
1883		Bombings by Irish Fenians in London.
1884–86	Attends classes at Metropolitan School of Art, Dublin. Meets Russell (AE).	Gaelic Athletic Association founded. Morris founds the Socialist League.
1885	Family moves house in Dublin. Chairs first meeting of Dublin Hermetic Society. Meets O'Leary, Hyde and Katharine Tynan. First poems published.	Zola, *Germinal*.

1886	Meets Morris. Begins *The Wanderings of Oisin*. *Mosada* published.	Gladstone's Home Rule Bill for Ireland defeated. Death of Ferguson. Hardy, *The Mayor of Casterbridge*. James, *The Bostonians*.
1887	Family moves to London. Joins Madame Blavatsky's Theosophical Society in London. Mother suffers strokes.	Queen Victoria's Golden Jubilee. Strindberg, *The Father*. Mallarmé, *Poésies*.
1888	Family moves house in London. Meets Shaw, Lady Wilde, Davidson, Oscar Wilde. *Fairy and Folk Tales of the Irish Peasantry*. Composes 'The Lake Isle of Innisfree'	Arnold dies.
1889	Meets Maud Gonne. *The Wanderings of Oisin* and *Other Poems*. *Stories from Carleton* (ed.).	Death of Hopkins, Browning and Allingham. Pater, *Appreciations*. Shaw, *Fabian Essays*.
1890	Co-founds Rhymers' Club. Initiated into the Hermetic Order of the Golden Dawn. Meets Florence Farr.	Frazer, *The Golden Bough* (Vol. I). Downfall of Parnell. G. B. Shaw, *Quintessence of Ibsenism*.
1891	*Representative Irish Tales* (ed.). *John Sherman and Dhoya*. Friendly with Johnson and Dowson. Writes poem on Parnell.	Ibsen, *Ghosts* performed in London. Death of Parnell. Morris, *News from Nowhere*. Wilde, *The Picture of Dorian Gray*.

1892	Co-founded Irish Literary Society, London and Dublin. *Irish Fairy Tales. The Countess Kathleen and Various Legends and Lyrics.*	Death of Tennyson, Whitman. Nietzsche completes *Thus Spake Zarathustra.* Kipling, *Barrack-Room Ballads.*
1893	*The Works of William Blake* (ed. with Ellis). *The Celtic Twilight.*	Second Home Rule Bill passed by the Commons, defeated by the Lords. Dvořák, *Symphony No. 9 (From the New World).* Gaelic League founded. Hyde, *Love Songs of Connacht.* Wilde, *Salomé.*
1894	Attends Villiers de l'Isle Adam's *Axel* in Paris. *The Land of Heart's Desire* performed in London, then published. Meets Olivia Shakespear. Stays in Sligo and Lissadell. Collects folklore.	Stevenson dies. Larminie, *West Irish Folk Tales.* Moore, *Esther Waters.* Somerville and Ross, *The Real Charlotte.* Wilde, *Salomé* (translated into English).
1895	Moves out of the family home in London, shares flat with Symons. *A Book of Irish Verse* (ed.). *Poems.*	Wilde, *The Importance of Being Earnest.* Wilde's trial and imprisonment. Hyde, *The Story of Early Gaelic Literature.* Wells, *The Time Machine.* X-rays discovered.

1896	Rents rooms in Woburn Buildings, London. Affair with Olivia Shakespear. Visits Aran Islands with Symons. Becomes acquainted with Lady Gregory. Meets Synge in Paris. Member of Irish Republican Brotherhood.	Morris, *The Well at the World's End*. Morris dies. Housman, *A Shropshire Lad*.
1897	First summer at Coole Park. *The Secret Rose*. *The Adoration of the Magi*.	Havelock Ellis, *Sexual Inversion*. Bram Stoker, *Dracula*.
1898	Much time spent travelling and organising. Active in celebrations of the centenary of the Rising of 1798.	Shaw, *Plays Pleasant and Unpleasant*. Rodin, *The Kiss*.
1899	*The Wind Among the Reeds*. *The Countess Cathleen* performed, first production of the Irish Literary Theatre co-founded by Yeats.	Outbreak of Second Boer War. Palace at Knossos discovered. Somerville and Ross, *Some Experiences of an Irish R.M.* A. Symons, *The Symbolist Movement in Literature*. Sibelius, *Finlandia*.
1900	Mother dies. Succeeds MacGregor Mathers as head of Golden Dawn in London. *The Shadowy Waters* (poem version).	Protests against visit of Queen Victoria to Dublin. Boxer Rising in China suppressed by European army. Freud, *The Interpretation of Dreams*. Death of Nietzsche, Wilde and Ruskin.

1901   Resigns from Irish   Death of Queen Victoria.
        Literary Society.   Chekhov, *Three Sisters*.
        Meets Gordon Craig
        and Fay brothers.
        Diarmuid and Grania
        (written with George
        Moore) produced in
        Dublin.
        Experiments with
        psaltery.

1902   *Cathleen ni Houlihan*   End of Second Boer War.
        produced with AE's   Conrad, *The Heart of Darkness*.
        Deirdre.   William James, *The Varieties of*
        Meets John Quinn,   *Religious Experience*.
        James Joyce.   Gregory, *Cuchulain of*
        Co-founds Irish National   *Muirthemne*.
        Theatre Company.
        First reads books by
        Nietzsche.

1903   Maud Gonne marries   Wyndham's Land Purchase Act.
        John MacBride.   Butler, *The Way of All Flesh*.
        Ideas of Good and Evil.   Synge, *In the Shadow of the Glen*.
        In the Seven Woods.   Moore, *The Untilled Field*.
        Lecture tour in North   Shaw, *Man and Superman*.
        America.
        Dun Emer Press
        established.
        The King's Threshold
        performed.

1904   Returns from United   Puccini, *Madame Butterfly*.
        States.   Shaw, *John Bull's Other Island*.
        Where There is Nothing   Synge, *Riders to the Sea*.
        produced.   Barrie, *Peter Pan*.
        The Shadowy Waters   Bradley, *Shakespearean Tragedy*.
        (play) produced.   Chekhov, *The Cherry Orchard*.
        Abbey Theatre granted   Gregory, *Gods and Fighting Men*.
        patent, opens in Decem-
        ber. *On Baile's Strand*
        performed.

1905	*Stories of Red Hanrahan.* Abbey Theatre's first tour in England.	Sinn Fein Party founded. Futurist Manifesto issued in Italy by Marinetti. First cinema opens in USA. debussy, *La Mer*. Einstein, *Special Theory of Relativity*. First Underground lines in London opened.
1906	*The Poems of Spenser* (ed.). *Poems 1899–1905. Deirdre* produced.	Samuel Beckett born. Ibsen dies. de la Mare, *Poems*. Doughty, *The Dawn in Britain*.
1907	Rows related to opening of Synge's *The Playboy of the Western World*. Visits Italy with Lady Gregory and her son. His father sails to America (never to return to Ireland). *Discoveries*.	John O'Leary dies. Joyce, *Chamber Music*. Gosse, *Father and Son*. Service, *Songs of a Sourdough*. Picasso, *Les Desmoiselles d'Avignon*. First Cubist exhibition in Paris.
1908	Affair with Mabel Dickinson begins. *Collected Works* in eight volumes. Meets Ezra Pound.	Forster, *A Room with a View*. The first Ford Model T produced.
1909	Quarrels with John Quinn. In dispute with authorities in Dublin Castle over production of *Blanco Posnet* by Shaw.	Swinburne, Meredith, Synge die. Ballet Russe brought by Diaghilev for first visit to Paris. Blériot flies across the English Channel. Pound, *Personae*. Galsworthy, *Strife*.

1910	*The Green Helmet and Other Poems.* Awarded Civil List pension (£150 annually). Disputes with Miss Horniman over policy at the Abbey. His uncle, George Pollexfen, dies.	King George V succeeds Edward VII. Masefield, *Ballads and Poems.* Tolstoy dies. Post-Impressionist exhibition held in London.
1911	Miss Horniman terminates her financial support of the Abbey. Accompanies Abbey Company to USA. Meets Georgie Hyde-Lees.	Moore, *Hail and Farewell*, Vol. I (completed 1914). Brooke, *Poems.* Strauss, *Der Rosenkavalier.*
1912	Trouble in USA caused by performances of Synge's *Playboy. The Cutting of an Agate* published in USA. Meets Rabindranath Tagore, for whose poems he writes an introduction.	First volume of *Georgian Poetry.* Third Home Rule Bill introduced by Asquith. *Poetry: A Magazine of Verse* founded in Chicago. Scott reaches South Pole. *Titanic* sinks on her maiden voyage.
1913	Experiments with automatic writing. Shares house in Sussex with Pound who acts as his secretary. *Poems Written in Discouragement* Ends affair with Mabel Dickinson.	Home Rule Bill rejected by House of Lords. Formation of militant groups: Ulster Volunteer Force, Irish Citizens' Army, and Irish (National) Volunteers. Strikes in Dublin and lock-out of workers. Lawrence, *Sons and Lovers.* First volume of Proust, *A la Recherche du Temps Perdu.* Frost, *A Boy's Will.* Freud, *Totem and Taboo.* Stravinsky, *The Rite of Spring.*

1914	American lecture tour. *Responsibilities* published. *Reveries over Childhood and Youth*, first part of his autobiography written.	Outbreak of First World War. Home Rule Act for Ireland passed, but suspended for the duration of the War. Joyce, *Dubliners*. Panama Canal opened.
1915	Declines the offer of a knighthood.	*Lusitania* sunk by German navy: Sir Hugh Lane drowned. Buchan, *The Thirty-Nine Steps*. Brooke, *1914, and Other Poems*. Pound, *Cathay*. Einstein's General Theory of Relativity.
1916	*At the Hawk's Well* produced in Lady Cunard's house in London. *Reveries over Childhood and Youth* published by his new publisher, Macmillan. Summer in France with Maud and Iseult Gonne. Proposes to both.	Easter Rising in Dublin and execution of the leaders. Battles of Verdun and the Somme. Joyce, *A Portrait of the Artist as a Young Man*. Jung, *Psychology of the Unconscious*.
1917	Buys tower house at Ballylee. Marries Georgie Hyde-Lees at Registry Office in London. Wife begins automatic writing. *The Wild Swans at Coole*.	Zeppelin attacks on England. Bread rationed in Britain. US declares war on Germany. Russian Revolution and rise of Lenin and Trotsky. Eliot, *Prufrock and Other Observations*. Edward Thomas, *Poems*. Valéry, *La Jeune Parque*.

1918	Lives in several different places while Thoor Ballylee is restored. *Per Amica Silentia Lunae.*	End of First World War. General Election in which women (over 30) allowed to vote for the first time. Constance Markiewicz (Gore-Booth) elected for Sinn Fein, first female MP. Hopkins, *Poems* published. Strachey, *Eminent Victorians.* Worldwide influenza epidemic: over 20 million die by 1920.
1919	Daughter, Anne Butler Yeats, born. *The Player Queen* produced. *Two Plays for Dancers.*	Mussolini founds Italian Fascist Party. League of Nations founded. Sassoon, *The War Poems.* Eliot, `Tradition and the Individual Talent'.
1920	Lecture tour in America. Last visit to his father.	Government of Ireland Act passed, granting independence to Southern Ireland but partitioning the North from the South: martial law declared, fighting intensifies. Jung, *Psychological Types.* Eliot, *Poems.* Pound, *Hugh Selwyn Mauberley.* Edward Thomas, *Collected Poems.* Wells, *The Outline of History.*
1921	Condemns British action in Ireland at a debate in the Oxford Union. Son, Michael Butler Yeats, born. *Michael Robartes and the Dancer. Four Plays for Dancers.* Lectures in Scotland.	Fighting in Ireland continues. Anglo-Irish Treaty signed in December. Pirandello, *Six Characters in Search of an Author.* Lawrence, *Women in Love.* BBC founded.

1922	Father dies in New York.	Irish Dáil ratifies the Treaty: civil war results, Collins murdered.
	Buys house in Merrion Square, Dublin.	Mussolini comes to power in Italy.
	Honorary Degree from Trinity College, Dublin and Queen's University, Belfast.	Tutankhamun's tomb discovered in Egypt.
		Joyce, *Ulysses*.
		Eliot, *The Waste Land*.
	Meets T. S. Eliot in London.	Sitwell, *Façade*.
		Pirandello, *Henry IV*.
	Becomes a Senator in new Irish Free State.	Death of Proust.
	The Trembling of the Veil.	
	Later Poems.	
1923	Nobel Prize for literature awarded to him in Stockholm.	O'Casey, *The Shadow of a Gunman*.
	Plays and Controversies.	Shaw, *Saint Joan*.
	The Gift of Harun al Rashid.	Wallace Stevens, *Harmonium*.
1924	Honorary Degree at Aberdeen.	First Labour Government in Britain.
	Holiday because of illness in Southern Italy, including Sicily.	Death of Lenin, arrival of Stalin.
		Forster, *A Passage to India*.
		Death of Kafka.
	The Cat and the Moon.	O'Casey, *Juno and the Paycock*.
		O'Neill, *Desire under the Elms*.
1925	Opposes anti-divorce legislation in Senate.	Fitzgerald, *The Great Gatsby*.
	Visits Switzerland and Milan.	Whitehead, *Science and the Modern World*.
		MacDiarmid, *Sangshaw*.
		Pound, *A Draft of XVI Cantos*.
		e. e. cummings, *XLI Poems*.
		Eisenstein, *The Battleship Potemkin*.
		Chaplin, *The Gold Rush*.

1926   *A Vision* (dated 1925).   General Strike in Britain.
        Chairman of the   O'Casey, *The Plough and the Stars.*
        Senate committee   T. E. Lawrence, *The Seven Pillars*
        on design of coinage.   *of Wisdom.*
        Riots at the Abbey   MacDiarmid, *A Drunk Man*
        caused by *The Plough*   *Looks at the Thistle.*
        and The Stars.
        Autobiographies
        published (containing
        Reveries over Childhood
        and Youth and *The*
        Trembling of the Veil).

1927   Health breaks down   Kevin O'Higgins assassinated.
        with congestion of the   Woolf, *To the Lighthouse.*
        lungs. Doctors order
        complete rest.
        Lengthy stay in Southern
        Spain and later Cannes.

1928   Yeats and the Abbey   Penicillin discovered.
        reject O'Casey's   Hardy dies.
        The Silver Tassie.   Huxley, *Point Counter Point.*
        Changes houses in   Brecht/Weill, *The Threepenny*
        Dublin.   *Opera.*
        Resigns from the   Lawrence, *Lady Chatterley's*
        Senate.   *Lover.*
        Spends the winter at
        Rapallo in Italy.
        The Tower.

1929   Returns to Ireland for   Censorship of publications
        the summer, last stay   tightened in Ireland.
        in Ballylee.   Stock-market collapse in New
        Seriously ill with Malta   York.
        fever in Rapallo.   Faulkner, *The Sound and the Fury.*
        The Winding Stair.   Graves, *Goodbye to All That.*
        A Packet for Ezra Pound.   Bridges, *The Testament of Beauty.*
        Fighting the Waves
        produced at the Abbey
        with choreography by
        Ninette de Valois and
        music by George Antheil.

1930	Returns to Ireland in the summer. Meets Virginia Woolf and Walter de la Mare in England. *The Words upon the Window-Pane* produced.	Gandhi leads passive resistance to British rule in India. Eliot, *Ash Wednesday.* Auden, *Poems.* Hart Crane, *The Bridge.*
1931	Spends first half of year at Killiney, south of Dublin. Has to rescue (financially) Cuala Industries, run by his sisters. Works hard on a new edition of his work proposed by Macmillan. Spends several months at Coole where Lady Gregory is terminally ill. Reads eighteenth-century Irish writers and modern Italian philosophers. First broadcast (from Belfast).	Economic depression in Britain with three million unemployed; National Government formed. IRA is banned in Ireland. Edmund Wilson, *Axel's Castle.*
1932	Death of Lady Gregory. Irish Academy of Letters founded with his leadership and support. Moves house to Rathfarnham, County Dublin. Lecture tour of United States and Canada. *Words for Music Perhaps and Other Poems.*	Eamon de Valera becomes President of Ireland. Roosevelt becomes President of USA. Leavis, *New Bearings in English Poetry.* Huxley, *Brave New World.*

1933	Meets de Valera to discuss politics. Involved for several months with O'Duffy's Fascist Blueshirt movement. *The Winding Stair and Other Poems.* *Collected Poems.*	Hitler becomes Chancellor. First concentration camps built. Books by Jews and non-Nazis burned in Germany. George Moore dies. Lorca, *Blood Wedding.* Day-Lewis, *The Magnetic Mountain.* Spender, *Poems.*
1934	Undergoes Steinach operation in London. Visits to Italy include a lecture in Rome. Commences friendships with Margot Collis and Ethel Mannin. *Wheels and Butterflies.* *Collected Plays.*	Nazi campaigns of murder and intimidation in Germany. Struggle for power in China between Communists and Chiang Kai-shek. Pound, *ABC of Reading.* Toynbee, *A Study of History,* Vol. I. Muir, *Variations on a Time Theme.* Dylan Thomas, *Eighteen Poems.*
1935	Seriously ill with congestion of the lungs. First meets Dorothy Wellesley. Travels to Majorca for his health and helps Shri Purohit Swami to translate the *Upanishads.* *Dramatis Personae.* *A Full Moon in March.*	Sale of contraceptives banned in Ireland. George Russell (AE) dies. Italy invades Abyssinia. Show trials take place in USSR. Eliot, *Murder in the Cathedral.* MacNeice, *Poems.* Stevens, *Ideas of Order.* George Barker, *Poems.*
1936	Winter and spring: very ill in Majorca. Margot Collis arrives in mad condition; Yeats tries to help her. Broadcasts with the BBC on *modern poetry.* *Oxford Book of Modern Verse.*	Hunger marches in Britain. Civil War begins in Spain. Hitler and Mussolini enter an alliance. Penguin Books commence business. Dylan Thomas, *Twenty-Five Poems.* Auden, *Look, Stranger!* Deaths of Pirandello, Lorca, Chesterton, Kipling, Housman.

1937	Becomes friendly with Edith Shackleton Heald. Delivers several radio broadcasts. *Broadsides*. *A Vision* (Revised Edition). *Essays 1931–1936*.	Spanish Civil War intensifies. War between Japan and China. Picasso's mural *Guernica*. Auden and Isherwood, *The Ascent of F6*. Sartre, *Nausea*. Muir, *Journeys and Places*. David Jones, *In Parenthesis*.
1938	Early months in south of France. Final public appearance at the Abbey Theatre for opening of his *Purgatory*. Leaves Ireland in October and travels on to France. *New Poems*.	Olivia Shakespear dies. Germany annexes Austria and enters Czechoslovakia. Beckett, *Murphy*. Jeffers, *Selected Poems*.
1939	Yeats dies, 28 January, in South of France (body reinterred at Drumcliff Churchyard near Sligo, 1948). *Last Poems and Two Plays*. *On the Boiler*.	Outbreak of the Second World War. Franco's Nationalists win the Spanish Civil War. Irish Government declares Ireland neutral. Joyce, *Finnegans Wake*. O'Brien, *At Swim-Two-Birds*. Eliot, *Old Possum's Book of Practical Cats*. MacNeice, *Autumn Journal*. Frost, *Collected Poems*. Fleming, *Gone with the Wind* (the film of Margaret Mitchell's 1936 novel).

Introduction

It may not be surprising that in F. S. L. Lyons's *Culture and Anarchy in Ireland, 1890–1939* the name of W. B. Yeats has more entries in the index than any other person. After all, the book is partly concerned with culture, and the period covered is the period of Yeats's writing career. He is, however, also the most-cited name in the index of *The Oxford Illustrated History of Ireland*, edited by R. F. Foster, which covers the period from prehistory to 1987. It is unlikely that anywhere else in the world in the twentieth century have a poet's career and a nation's development been so intertwined. There were specific actions and proposals, such as his chairing of the committee to supervise the design of the new Irish coinage in 1926 and his special committee's recommendation to the Senate in 1924 that a programme should be instigated to catalogue, translate and distribute all surviving texts in Irish. And there were particular involvements in many political actions and debates. His influence, however, was and remains much more pervasive in Ireland's images of itself and the images of Ireland held by outsiders. It is difficult to conceive of a brochure on the country issued by its Tourist Board which does not seek to market an aspect of Ireland nurtured by the attention of Yeats. Not only does the poet (or his spirit) enjoy one of the longest-running Summer Schools dedicated to a single author, but its success has led to an extraordinary and lucrative business in Irish authors and culture. He, more than any individual in Ireland, challenged and dislodged some of the pejorative nineteenth-century stereotypes of the Irish, created in England but sometimes internalised by the Irish themselves. It may be true that, as some have argued, he was actually in Ireland for a smaller proportion of his life than James Joyce was of his; Joyce lived abroad for more than thirty years. It may be that, although to the English he always seemed utterly Irish, to many Irish people he seemed rather English. Nonetheless, no writer has had a more passionate involvement with his or her country in his writing and his actions.

With a person who wrote so much over such a long career, who was so active in so many spheres beyond writing, who had working or social relationships with so many people, any kind of literary biographer faces a problem: should the literary work be approached from a context of activities, ideas and contacts outside

1

the individual works; or, should the work cast a light on, and suggest readings of the wider context? In this book I have, with painful awareness of the dilemma, moved back and forth between the two. In Yeats's case there are two other major complicating factors.

First, of all writers, he must be one of the most elaborately intertextual. His work abounds in cross-references and, because of his compulsive revising of earlier pieces, the reader without a variorum edition may sometimes assume that early works anticipate very late works in a most remarkable manner. And, of course, sometimes an unrevised piece, in a turn of phrase or an image, does re-emerge in very different surroundings. One example must suffice. In the introduction to *Fairy and Folk Tales of the Irish Peasantry,* published in 1888, Yeats describes a certain Paddy Flynn, a traditional storyteller in County Sligo:

> Nor seems his own cheerfulness quite earthly – though a very palpable cheerfulness. The first time I saw him he was cooking mushrooms for himself; the next time he was asleep under a hedge, smiling in his sleep. Assuredly some joy not quite of the steadfast earth lightens in those eyes – swift as the eyes of a rabbit – among so many wrinkles, for Paddy Flynn is very old. A melancholy there is in the midst of their cheerfulness – a melancholy that is almost a portion of their joy, the visionary melancholy of purely instinctive natures and of all animals.

Move ahead fifty years to the poem 'Lapis Lazuli' written in 1936 and published in 1938. At the end of the poem Yeats is describing two Chinese pilgrims climbing a mountain with a servant carrying a musical instrument:

and I,

> Delight to imagine them seated there;
> There, on the mountain and the sky,
> On all the tragic scene they stare.
> One asks for mournful melodies;
> Accomplished fingers begin to play.
> Their eyes mid many wrinkles, their eyes,
> Their ancient, glittering eyes, are gay.

In 'Lapis Lazuli' he has moved from 'joy' to one of the specially favoured words of his late poetry, 'gay', but the consistency of thought is apparent. This example has no great significance except to illustrate the point of continuities in the poet. His expectation generally seemed to be that a serious reader of his poetry would read everything else published by him. A symbol or name could be introduced and later developed or referred to on some assumption that the reader would already be familiar with and remember its introduction. This notion of planting and propagating and grafting symbols is one factor in the careful arrangement of individual poems in a collection. It bothers some readers that the poet presumes that they come to a poem with such a memory-bank of names, symbols and personal references.

The second complicating factor is that Yeats wrote so much (outside the poems) about himself. He wrote thousands of letters which have survived and been published, or are in the process of being published, large autobiographical accounts, essays, introductions to his own work, explanatory notes, radio talks and Senate speeches. How far should we trust him as a reporter on his own life or should we consider all his autobiographical writings as ancillary parts in the self-construction of a public figure and, therefore, lacking in any objective reliability? Again I see the problem but do not have a categorical solution to it. Yeats himself has various views on what he thinks he is doing and on what he wishes the public to know about him. In his preface to the section of his autobiography called *Reveries* (1914), he writes: 'I have changed nothing to my knowledge; and yet it must be that I have changed many things without my knowledge; for I am writing after many years and have consulted neither friend, nor letter, nor old newspaper and describe what comes oftenest into my memory.' The final clause, in particular, begs several questions. When he came to write the section *The Trembling of the Veil* (published in 1922), he was aware that some of his most crucial but private experiences, such as his affair with Olivia Shakespeare, could not be included, but still claimed in the preface, 'I have kept nothing back necessary to understanding.' Sometimes he held to the opinion that a poet's life becomes public property; sometimes he seemed intensely private and possessive of his privacy. In a lecture in 1910 he was adamant:

> I have no sympathy with the mid-Victorian thought to which Tennyson gave his support, that a poet's life concerns nobody but himself. A poet is by the very nature of things a man who lives with entire sincerity, or rather, the better his poetry the more

sincere his life. His life is an experiment in living and those that come after have a right to know it. Above all it is necessary that the lyric poet's life should be known, that we should understand that his poetry is no rootless flower but the speech of a man, [that it is no little thing] to achieve anything in any art, to stand alone perhaps for many years, to go a path no other man has gone, to accept one's own thoughts when the thought of others has the authority of the world behind it...to give one's life as well as one's words which are so much nearer to one's soul to the criticism of the world.[1]

In the opening paragraph of 'A General Introduction for my work' (1937) he takes a rather different view: 'A poet writes always of his personal life, in his finest work out of its tragedy, whatever it be, remorse, lost love, or mere loneliness; he never speaks directly as to someone at the breakfast table, there is always a phantasmagoria ... he is never the bundle of accident and incoherence that sits down to breakfast; he has been reborn as an idea, something intended, complete.' He went further in conversation with his wife when he said about the public, 'I don't want them to know all about everything.'[2]

His presentation of himself, Yeats the literary figure, in his mature work was carefully stage-managed and, when interpreted biographically, has caused misconceptions in many readers. He was not as rooted geographically as he repeatedly claims. Throughout his life he travelled a great deal, and seldom remained in any place for long. There was something deeply restless in him despite the favoured images of tradition and order. Also, for much of his life he had to struggle for money, not because he was extravagant but because he was relatively poor. According to his own account, he was almost 50 before his writing earned him two hundred pounds a year. He was lent money (mainly by Lady Gregory over twenty years), he took dull copying and journalistic jobs and bargained for writing fees in order to make ends meet. Only in his late fifties, with a Civil List pension (first awarded in 1910), lecture fees from tours of America, his Senatorial salary of £350, the Nobel Prize worth £7500 in 1923, and gifts from bodies such as the American Testimonial Committee, did he achieve financial comfort. The earlier struggle does not feature strongly in Yeats's projection of himself, but it must have lurked in him as a residual fear.

When we attempt to understand how a person develops, we have to balance various factors which are never entirely measurable: for example, genetic inheritance, early conditioning before the child has any choice, location and time, random happenings, and individual inclination. We are not reliable assessors of the proportions in our own development. Yeats sometimes gives an impression, as do other historians, that his career and even the events around him had a clear pattern. He declares in the introduction to his *Oxford Book of Modern Verse* (1936) that, 'in 1900 everybody got down off his stilts; henceforth nobody drank absinthe with his black coffee; nobody went mad; nobody committed suicide; nobody joined the Catholic church' and then adds as an afterthought, 'or if they did I have forgotten'. We all know, Yeats included, that social change does not take place in such a tidy pattern but we like patterns and formulae. Although Yeats delights in categories and pivotal points, his poetry is enriched by a constant subversion of such glib notions. He revalues his previous positions and his mind readjusts to new awareness of his previous blinkered notions. In one of his final poems, 'The Circus Animals' Desertion' he looks back to his early phase with a new awareness of what his poeticising then involved. The menagerie of his created characters was, in part, a disguise for his emotions, and he sees

> Those masterful images because complete
> Grew in pure mind, but out of what began?
> A mound of refuse or the sweeping of a street,
> Old kettles, old bottles, and a broken can,
> Old iron, old bones, old rags, that raving slut
> Who keeps the till. Now that my ladder's gone,
> I must lie down where all the ladders start,
> In the foul rag-and-bone shop of the heart.

If he so misunderstood his circus animals, his images, how can we trust his earlier accounts of what he thought he was creating? Or did he not misunderstand, and is his late reappraisal of himself merely the final act of the drama he has created for and out of himself?

As Yeats developed from an awkward youth into a man whose public performance in writing and action impressed his audience with its assurance, he did establish an authority which could look to some like affectation or arrogance. (By 1900 he was no longer Willie to any but his earliest friends and family; he had become W. B. Yeats or Yeats.) We often have to penetrate this carapace of self-confidence when we read his increasingly magisterial poetry. His stance, once adopted, had to be maintained. A generous view of him was offered by Sean O'Casey, a person who might be thought to have no good reason to be charitable to the poet. When the mystical George Russell (AE) died in 1935, and he had often been contrasted favourably with Yeats, O'Casey commented: 'He's the fairest and brightest humbug Ireland has. There's a genuine humility in Yeats's arrogance, but there's a deeper arrogance in AE's humility.'[3] The authority of his work remains a vital force with which we have to struggle. In a lecture in 1940, T. S. Eliot made an enormous claim for Yeats's position in the twentieth century; I return to this claim at the end of this book but, for the present, I leave Eliot's quotation uncommented upon:

There are some poets whose poetry can be considered more or less in isolation, for experience and delight. There are others whose poetry, though giving equally experience and delight, has a larger historical importance. Yeats was one of the latter: he was one of those few whose history is the history of their own time, who are a part of the consciousness of an age which cannot be understood without them. This is a very high position to assign to him: but I believe that it is one which is secure.[4]

1

Family and Place

'I wish Willie had Jack's tender gracious manner, and did not sometimes treat me as if I was a black beetle.'[1] So John Butler Yeats in a
letter to his daughter in 1904 describes his two sons; and the contrast to which he points had been remarked on by others when the
two were mere infants. Willie was a difficult child and his relationship with his father was to remain complicated and intense until his
father died in 1922.

John Butler Yeats was born in County Down in 1839, the eldest
son of a well-to-do and sociable Rector in the Church of Ireland
whose own father had been Rector at Drumcliffe near Sligo. The
Butler part of the name had entered the family through a marriage
in the eighteenth century to a Butler, a branch of the aristocratic
Ormondes, one of the oldest Anglo-Irish families in the country.
With the name came also several hundred acres of land in County
Kildare. John Butler Yeats's father in 1835 married Jane Corbet, a
member of a well-connected family with links back to one of
Marlborough's generals; her brother owned a large house on the
outskirts of Dublin called Sandymount Castle. In 1863 John Butler
Yeats married Susan Pollexfen; she belonged to a family of substantial traders and ship-owners from Sligo. Thus, in the course of
a few generations, the Yeatses increased their wealth and social
status.

The successive heads of the Yeats family in the nineteenth century
shared a reputation for intellectual ability, social adeptness, liberal
attitudes and liveliness. John Butler Yeats followed in the footsteps
of his father and grandfather in attending Trinity College, Dublin
and the expectation was that he would follow them into the Church;
this was not to be. He had been sent by his father to a private school
on the Isle of Man, run by a Calvinist Scotsman who believed that
each child was gifted by God with intelligence and it was the
teacher's responsibility to develop that intelligence in the child, if
necessary by some rather brutal methods and punishments.
Although the Irish boy came to have a grudging respect for the

headmaster and his stern idealism, and although he was a successful pupil, he discovered a sharp contrast between the amiable religious views of his father and the dourly obsessive ones of the
Scottish Calvinist. The actual details of his studies at Trinity College
appear to have survived only in a very vague way. He did not enjoy
the educational regime but used his time there (a considerable
amount, almost ten years in all) to read widely and discuss ideas
with student friends. Originally, he studied Classics, then decided
that he would take a degree in Law, and then gave up the idea in
order to train as a painter.

In 1862, between the Classics stage and the Law stage, he inherited on his father's death the family estates in County Kildare now
heavily mortgaged. He also became engaged and in 1863 he married
Susan Pollexfen. Susan was the sister of his best friend in the school
on the Isle of Man and he had come to Sligo to visit George
Pollexfen when he met her. He already knew Sligo well because his
father had been born there and considered it, not Ulster, as his real
home. George and his brother Charles Pollexfen had been enigmas
to most of their school companions and were poor learners,
unsociable and unpopular. To John Butler Yeats, however, they
appeared as mysteriously powerful, self-contained and magnetic.
George revealed, in the right company, a gift for story-telling:

> Night after night he would keep those boys awake and perfectly
> still while he told them stories, made impromptu as he went
> along.... He talked poetry though he did not know it.[2]

As a family, the Pollexfens were utterly unlike the Yeatses; for all
their commercial success, they were taciturn and superior with
other people and gloomy and untrusting with each other. John
Butler Yeats was attracted to something he saw as opposite to
himself and later summed up the marriage (and its offspring
poet) in the words: 'We [Yeatses] have ideas and no passions, but
by marriage with a Pollexfen we have given a tongue to the sea
cliffs.'

The marriage was to be a strange one. John Butler Yeats never ful-
filled the promise he showed to the Pollexfens in 1863. His decision
not to become a barrister, his lingering study at Heatherley's Art
School in London, his inability to earn a decent living as a painter,
his artistic, eccentric friends, all diminished him in the eyes of his
financially successful and ambitious in-laws. These same factors

made life difficult for Susan and it appears she had a tendency to find life difficult. Between 1865 and 1875 she gave birth to six children, two of whom died in infancy. William was the first-born and he was to bear a sense of familial responsibility throughout his life. The family or various parts of it moved about between different houses in Dublin, Sligo and London, never with any financial security or solid plan for the future. She was unaccustomed to such irregularities and had no reservoir of cheerfulness or circle of friends on which she could call. In 1887 she suffered two strokes and from then till her death in 1900, aged 59, she had a meagre existence as an increasingly senile invalid. What kind of person had she been? In appearance she was slightly built, pretty but rather glum, and with unmatching eyes, one blue and one brown. From the beginning of her marriage, she seemed to have no understanding of, or sympathy for, her husband's interests. Writing to a friend in 1917, John Butler Yeats reflects: 'I don't think she approved of a single one of my ideas or theories or opinions, to her only foolishness.'[3] Her son Willie, in his *Reveries over Childhood and Youth* in 1914 wrote of her love of Sligo and stories about the people there:

> I can see now that she had great depth of feeling, that she was her father's daughter. My memory of what she was like in those days has grown very dim, but I think her sense of personality, her desire of any life of her own, had disappeared in her care for us and in much anxiety about money. I always see her sewing or knitting in spectacles and wearing some plain dress…. My father was always praising her to my sisters and to me, because she pretended to nothing she did not feel. She would write him letters telling of her delight in the tumbling clouds, but she did not care for pictures, and never went to an exhibition even to see a picture of his, nor to his studio to see the day's work, neither now nor when they were first married. I remember all this very clearly and little after it until her mind had gone in a stroke of paralysis and she had found, liberated at last from financial worry, perfect happiness feeding the birds at a London window.

Her son, Jack, who spent most of his childhood living with his maternal grandparents in Sligo, had little to say about his mother in any of his writings. He did destroy many of his letters and personal papers but, according to his biographer, Hilary Pyle, on his mother's death 'he was characteristically silent'.[4]

In John Butler Yeats, who always applauded his own outgoing and extravagant qualities, there was a fear that his sons would be affected (or infected) by the morose and economical traits of the Pollexfens. Because Jack grew up away from his father, because his painting went in a different direction to that of his father, and because he showed a Pollexfenian dexterity in avoiding tussles with his father, the main concern centred on Willie. Before her strokes removed her from social situations, Mrs Yeats had revealed a chilling ability to switch her attention to people on or off, and his father saw the same characteristic in his son. Many years later he confided in his friend John Quinn that his son kept an unsympathetic gap between himself and others for much of the time:

> I used to tell her [his wife] that if I had been lost for years and then suddenly presented myself she would have merely asked 'Have you had your dinner?' All this is very like Willie.[5]

What some commentators saw as a 'snobbishness' or 'loftiness' or 'vanity' in Willie may have been developments of a Pollexfen manner.

The poet was 22 years old when his mother experienced her first stroke and he was 34 when she died; the scarcity of his comments on her in his writings, particularly in *Autobiographies*, is remarkable. One factor in this neglect (or evasion) was the very prominence of his father in his early life. John Butler Yeats was an extraordinary man but, despite all the pleasure he undoubtedly gave to those who met him, he posed a problem for anyone who was closely involved with him. From the time that he decided to become a painter he committed his family to financial insecurity and frequent moves from one house to another between Ireland and England. His career had brighter moments and he found admirers and supporters but some deep reticence or lack of confidence prevented him from producing regularly and even, often, from completing paintings. His son describes one such failure:

> My father was painting the first big pond you come to if you have driven from Slough through Farnham Royal. He began it in spring and painted all through the year, the picture changing with the seasons, and gave it up unfinished when he had painted the snow upon the heath-covered banks.

Switches from portraiture to landscapes to book illustration and back to portrait-painting did not provide him with a stable subject or give him the confidence to finalise the execution of a work. In 1911 he was commissioned to paint a self-portrait; when he died in 1922 the canvas, still unfinished, was sent by John Quinn, the New York lawyer and art collector, to his son. In his early period he was something of a Pre-Raphaelite and with three friends formed a group called the Brotherhood. Gradually he became influenced by Impressionist ideas and latterly he concentrated on portraits, some of them wonderfully perceptive and fresh although with a tendency to romanticism.

Both in Dublin and London he was friendly with many of the leading intellectual figures and his son grew up with easy access to writers and painters. For several spells between 1879 and the turn of the century he lived in Bedford Park, a hive of tasteful professional and artistic people. Bedford Park, in South West London, was designed and built as one of the early garden suburbs, very closely identified with the Aesthetic Movement, and engendering a sense of community with its own Clubhouse where the Dramatic, Music and Debating societies could meet. Such a situation suited the Irish painter very well socially and he delighted in the vigorous exchange of ideas on art without being any more commercially successful as a painter.

Two of his closest friends were particularly appreciated by his son Willie. John Todhunter had left Ireland in 1879 and was to remain in England for the rest of his life. Like John Butler Yeats, he had abandoned his profession – in his case, as a doctor – and had chosen to write poetry and plays. For Willie, he demonstrated a point evident also in his father: without ambition, talent does not develop:

> If he had liked anything strongly he might have been a famous man, for a few years later he was to write, under some casual patriotic impulse, certain excellent verses now in all Irish anthologies; but with him every book was a new planting, and not a new bud on an old bough.

Although in later years Willie Yeats revised his opinion downward, in the 1880s he admired some of Todhunter's verse plays, particularly *A Sicilian Idyll* which, when it was performed in Bedford Park in 1890, impressed the young poet with its unornate language and straightforward production. The other very good friend of John Butler Yeats, but also a flawed figure in the eyes of his son, was York Powell, a Professor of History at Oxford, and a man of easy self-confidence. In *Autobiographies* the poet looks back and compares his own response to York Powell with that of his father:

> I was too full of unfinished speculations and premature convictions to value rightly his conversation, informed by a vast erudition, which would give itself to every casual association of speech and company, precisely because he had neither cause nor design. My father, however, found Powell's concrete narrative manner in talk a necessary completion of his own, and when I asked him in a letter many years later where he got his philosophy replied, 'From York Powell', and thereon added, no doubt remembering that Powell was without ideas, 'by looking at him'.

The father enjoyed the very waywardness of Todhunter and Powell; his son, although he liked both of them, could not approve of them because they lacked direction.

The land in Kildare which John Butler Yeats had inherited had been sold off in 1886 under a government scheme which paid compensation to the seller. In 1900, after the death of his wife, he discovered that some money was still owed to him and with it he was able to clear his debts. An exhibition in Dublin in 1901 was showing some of his paintings and his visit there became prolonged and he never did return to Bedford Park. Over the next few years he painted many of the prominent figures in Irish public life and had a certain financial success; but in 1907 a visit to New York with his daughter, Lily, also became prolonged and he remained in America for the rest of his life. However, his contact with his family, particularly Willie, remained strong. He wrote frequent letters, sometimes two in one day, to his son and these letters offer a strikingly intimate insight into the man. A selection of his letters edited by Ezra Pound was published in 1917 and *Further Letters of John Butler Yeats*, edited by Lennox Robinson, followed in 1920; his *Early Memories* appeared the year after his death.

Up to the end, when he died with fourteen dollars in his account, he reasserted his claim to be his son's best critic and guide:

> When is your poetry at its best? I challenge all the critics if it is not when the wild spirit of your imagination is wedded to concrete

fact. Had you stayed with me and not left me for Lady Gregory, and her friends and associations, you would have loved and adored concrete life for which as I know you have a real affection.... Never are you happier and never more felicitous in words than when in your conversation you describe life and comment on it. But when you write poetry you as it were put on your dress coat and shut yourself in and forget what is vulgar to a man in a dress coat.[6]

The choice of subject matter in his letters is unpredictable but, in his correspondence with his son – and it must be remembered that Willie was over forty and already famous when his father left for America – he maintains a commentary on many of the issues in his son's poetry and writes as a very self-conscious educator. Ideas on beauty, taste, character, art and humour are probed and pronounced on with aphoristic authority. Often he seems to be thinking aloud and at random; often he seems to be instructing his son in his high calling as an artist:

The poet is not primarily a thinker, but incidentally he is a thinker and a stern thinker, since the source of his magic is his personal sincerity. What he says he believes, and from this it follows that he must have few beliefs and those of the *simplest*, for time will not allow him to be travelling over the whole world of thought – that is for the professional thinker. Yet the brilliant talker and rhetorician can do this. Macaulay, for instance, out of his facile habit of belief could proceed everywhere, except [to] poetry, Carlyle was such another, only with the difference Macaulay flattered his audience whereas Carlyle insulted it – yet neither had the real instinct for truth, the primal deep-lying sincerity, which is the poet's virtue.[7]

In the year (1916) following that letter to his son, an old concern surfaces when he writes to his daughter:

... 100 cities contended for the honour of being Homer's birthplace and the question was never solved, and now it may be debated whether Willie (whom the Pollexfens used to hate declaring over and over again that he was just like his father) is a Pollexfen or a Yeats. The fact is he is both, one side of him not a bit like the Pollexfens and the other side of him not a bit like Yeats.[8]

And at the end he fretted that the son he had made such an effort to shape had eluded him and that large areas of his son's mind were quite foreign to him. We, looking back at John Butler Yeats's letters and reading them alongside his son's work, are struck over and over by the consanguinity of thought. The very emphasis on blood and inheritance; the high claims of Irish nationalism; the notion of art as play and a drama of masks; the basis of art in the portrait; the essential solitariness of the artist; the dramatic climax and its appropriate gesture; the defiant pride in what you make out of yourself; the contempt for the mediocre, the cowardly and the popular; all these were worked out, or rubbed off, on father and son. Nonetheless, several crucial differences are apparent. There is a human warmth and sympathy in the father which is only periodic in his son. John Butler Yeats's letters are good-humoured, generous, alert to oddities, petty foibles, the absurd and whimsical even in himself; Willie's letters lack any casual abandon. Also, the poet saw his father, as an artist, largely as a negative example: the failure to fulfil promise and the acceptance of excuse. Time after time, the old man's letters are in conditional mood ... 'if' ... 'should' ... 'when' ... 'I hope' ... 'sometime soon' ... 'I may'; he remains unrealistically optimistic. Some time in his school days, John Butler Yeats discarded any belief in God, but his attempt to bring his son up as a materialist was eventually unsuccessful and he could never understand Willie's interest in the occult and his striving for a knowledge of some force beyond what could be explained by contemporary science.

'The father of all the Yeatssssss' (Ezra Pound's title for him), he was a remarkable father to a remarkable family. The four surviving children were born within six years of each other: Willie was the eldest, then Susan Mary (Lily), then Elizabeth Corbet (Lollie), and finally John Butler (Jack). None of the children received a straightforward school education; all of them, whatever drawbacks and disadvantages were evident, profited from their father's often passionate concern with their individual development. Lily did attend school for some time in London and received some training at the Metropolitan School of Art and later at the home of William and May Morris, Kelmscott House. After working for May Morris as an embroiderer, she went to France for a year as a governess. Lollie had a similar training but went on to qualify as a kindergarden teacher, following the Froebel method. She developed a particular method of painting which she taught to children. Both sisters had medical problems which interfered with any possible plans of a career but in 1902 they entered into a business partnership with a Miss Evelyn Gleeson to establish a crafts workshop near Dublin. They called it Dun Emer (Emer's Fort) after the wife of the legendary Irish warrior Cuchulain: she was famous for her skill in domestic crafts. Lollie had taken a course in painting in London and now, with a secondhand press, she was ready to produce books. Relations between Evelyn Gleeson and the two sisters were not helped by uncertainties about the financial arrangements and, by 1908, they were to go their separate ways with the changing of Dun Emer to Cuala Industries, including the Cuala Press.

Neither of the sisters married, although both at various times entertained hopes in that direction. The two were forced by circumstances into an onerous closeness. Because their mother had found domestic arrangements so difficult they must have been obliged to help and after she had her stroke and become progressively more helpless they had to share the burden of looking after her and organising the house. Jack, their younger brother, left home and got married in 1894; Willie left the family house in the following year. After their mother died in 1900 and they moved back to Ireland with their father and started their business, finance was a constant problem. When, in 1908, Lily returned from what had begun as a business trip to New York to promote products of Dun Emer, her father, who had, without planning, decided to join her on her journey, then declined to return home. The two sisters were now in business and apart from some financial help and advice, often undesired, from Willie, they were on their own, living together and working together.

Lollie was an unfortunate person. She had talent and she worked hard but was subject to chronic depressions, was moody, and felt suspicious of, or hostile to, many of the people with whom she came into contact. Despite her own unpleasantness to others, she required endless reassurance and support. Her brother Jack went his own way; her father tried through letters to comfort her and intervened with others on her behalf. With Willie she had an antagonistic and often bitter relationship. They were the two children who most manifested their mother's Pollexfen ungivingness and what they had in common made them quarrel. Much of the unpleasantness centred on their differences of opinion concerning the choice and production of books by Lollie's Cuala Press. Willie was unyielding in his standards and often abrasive in his criticisms of Lollie's. Without his prestige and financial subvention the Press could not have survived and Lollie probably conceded this fact (to herself) and resented it. Over the years of its existence into the 1940s, the Cuala Press published a fascinating list, including Yeats's own work and books by many of the leading writers in the Irish Renaissance such as Lady Gregory, Synge and Gogarty.

In the 1920s she experienced a relatively calm spell which her sister attributed to Lollie taking up knitting as a hobby. Earlier, Lily was barely able to cope with her awkwardness and paranoia and, in a letter in 1914, warned her father not to believe a word of what Lollie wrote to him: 'She is not normal on any subject and more than abnormal on a few.'[9]

It may not have helped Lollie that everyone was enchanted by Lily. It is (and, no doubt, was) very obvious that Lily was her father's favourite child; her light charm, brightness and openness were in marked contrast to the sour demeanour of her sister. Her father's absence in America was an enormous loss to her, not just of a father but of her greatest friend. Her letters to him answer in kind his own wit, sharp observation and amiability. In one she describes a party in Dublin:

> I sat between Moore and Gogarty, an almost overpowering posi-
> tion, Gogarty brilliant, Moore slow and fumbling for his words.
> The talk was more or less general. Moore is fat and white, not
> unlike an old sheep, his hands very fat and womanish… He sim-
> mered with pleasure whenever the talk touched a book of his.[10]

And in another letter to her father's friend John Quinn she offers a touching description of G. K. Chesterton, severely damaged by alcohol:

> He looks as if something was wrong from his birth – his great
> body abnormal in size and build. He cannot walk more than a few
> yards and then uses a stick. He pants, he perspires, he wheezes,
> he looks far older than Papa – nothing young about him but his
> hair and eyes and centre of his face. The rest is all double chins
> and hanging cheeks – and with it all and in spite of it all he is
> wonderful and so very likeable. He looks at one as if begging you
> not to see all that is wrong – just go on listening *but not looking*.[11]

Lily's potential remained partly unfulfilled because various family situations tied her down. For six years from 1888 she had worked as an embroiderer with May Morris, daughter of William Morris; she did develop her skills but the money she earned was necessary to help the Yeats family budget even if she did not enjoy the work. Later she had to remain with her sister because there was no one else available to care for Lollie.

She was closest in age to Willie and for certain periods in their lives they were very friendly. As children they shared their unhappiness at being in London and their nostalgia for Sligo. As an adult, Lily took a lively interest in her brother's writing and in the setting up of the theatre in Dublin. In the disputes about the Cuala Press, she tended to take her sister's side against Willie but she herself did not usually fall out with people and she often had to act as peacemaker. On William Morris, however, she certainly disagreed with her brother, who admired his style of life; she felt that the Morris household was gloomy and that his 'temper hung over all like a thundercloud.... Morris hated most things and many people and May [his daughter] hated everyone.'[12]

The remaining youngest member of the family, Jack, grew up somewhat apart from the other three children. From 1879, at the age of eight, he lived with his mother's parents in Sligo and rejoined the rest of the family only in 1887. He attended a number of art schools in London without taking their instruction very seriously. Despite being the youngest of the children, he was the first to leave home; in 1892–93 he had a job in Manchester as a black-and-white illustrator and in 1894 he married 'Cottie' White from Devon. After a stay of thirteen years in Devon, they crossed to Ireland in 1910 and lived in Greystones, County Wicklow. In 1917 they moved into Dublin.

Easy-going and unobtrusive, Jack took pleasure in his surroundings wherever he found himself and, like that of his sister Lily, his company was eagerly appreciated. Although so generally popular, he seemed to reserve a special friendship and intimacy for carefully selected people; he retained a privacy without being rude or unwelcoming. In Sligo, which provided such an inspiration for his art, he did not bother with his scholastic progress but spent his time watching people at work on boats and horses or telling stories and bargaining and fighting. He had begun to draw when he was able to hold a pencil and his father liked to relate how Jack had, as a small child, burst into tears of dismay at the poor drawing of a horse done for him by one of his sisters. What he developed an eye for was the drama of situation, what he later called 'the living ginger' and he delighted in the performances he found at a fair or a regatta or circus. He devised a toy theatre and would give performances for local children. In fact, although his own marriage was childless, he loved the immediacy of children and his early publications were his stories for young people. Later, he was to write books of reminiscences, novels and plays. *Sligo* was published in 1930, *The Charmed Life* in 1938, and probably his best play, *La La Noo*, in 1943. He took his writing very seriously and saw it as having the same genesis as his painting:

> In my writing, as in my painting, my inspiration has always been affection wide, devious, and, sometimes, handsome... in every book there is somewhere in it a memory of Sligo... to which lovely place the beak of my ship ever turns, as turns the beak of the rushing carrier pigeon of the skies to his old harbourage.[13]

There is something in the freedom and economy of his writing which anticipates the early work of Samuel Beckett.

Willie Yeats admired his brother's writing but loved his paintings. One favourite was a watercolour, *Memory Harbour*, painted in 1906. Of it he writes in *Reveries over Childhood and Youth* (1914):

> When I look at my brother's picture, 'Memory Harbour' – houses and anchored ship and distant lighthouse all set close together as in some old map – I recognise in the blue-coated man with the mass of white shirt the pilot I went fishing with, and I am full of disquiet and excitement, and I am melancholy because I have not made more and better verses. I have walked on Sinbad's yellow shore and never shall another's hit my fancy.

Apart from illustrative work for magazines, mainly done in his early period, Jack illustrated many books over the years and made a major contribution to some enterprises of the Cuala Press. Two of his most engaged series of illustrations were done for books by J. M. Synge, *The Aran Islands* (1907) and *In Wicklow, West Kerry, and Connemara* (1911). In 1905 he had spent part of the summer exploring the west of Ireland with Synge, who had been commissioned by the *Manchester Guardian* to write articles on the area. The two men travelled well together and had similar reactions to the scenery and the people. After 1915, when he suffered some kind of breakdown, Jack's paintings became more elaborate, more serious and more involved with myths and large perspectives.

The two brothers shared many interests, applauded the quality of each other's work, but also acknowledged their differences of temperament and maintained a distance from each other. In certain respects, Jack was courteous and easy with strangers where his brother could appear shy, mannered or rude; on the other hand, Willie had an appetite and a flair for organising people and events, whereas Jack protected his privacy and could appear to have no opinions on public situations. During the Civil War of 1922 and the subsequent developments in Ireland, the brothers stood on opposed political sides but they gradually became reconciled as events moved on. Jack was a different kind of Irish nationalist; and he was the only member of the family to make a serious attempt to learn Irish.

Father Yeats often reminds one of Coleridge in his vast memory, his garrulous eloquence, his endless ability to fabricate ambitious and unrealisable schemes, the resourcefulness of his evasive moves and procrastination, his charm and his eagerness to devise obligations for other people. His wife was a special case but, of his family, Willie, as the eldest and male offspring and the one on whom his father lavished his ideals, benefited most and suffered most from his oddities. The unsettled domestic arrangements retarded the boy, who was physically and mentally awkward, and he lacked any sense of permanence and security. *Reveries over Childhood and Youth* (written when he was 49) begins: 'My first memories are fragmentary and isolated.... It seems as if time has not yet been created, and all thoughts are connected with emotion and place without sequence.' This could stand as a truism about all our earliest memories but the lack of 'sequence' was acutely evident in Willie Yeats. The misery was still present when he wrote his account: 'Indeed I remember little of childhood but the pain. I have grown happier with every year of life as though gradually conquering something in myself, for certainly my miseries were not made by others but were a part of my own mind.' Attempts were made to teach the boy how to read but he failed to respond and when, at the age of seven or eight he still did not know all the letters of the alphabet, his father felt obliged to intervene; the resulting clash of personalities led John Butler Yeats to throw the reading-book at his son's head. If the ability to read did eventually come, spelling certainly did not, and throughout his career the poet spelt words in a completely idiosyncratic manner.

All the shifting about between Dublin and Sligo and London made formal education difficult but when he was 11 he was enrolled at the Godolphin School in London and remained there for four years. He felt foreign and frightened of the other boys and displayed no competence academically or in sport. In *Autobiographies* he claims that he mastered a trick of pretending not to be out of breath after a bout of exertion; the claim sounds symptomatic of the person deemed a failure but who maintains that he has a secret gift. He was bullied for his Irishness and, for most of the time, he hated the English attitudes of the school and he loathed London. (It is interesting to observe that, certainly before he was fifty, there is no significant reference to anything or anywhere specifically English in any of his poems. However, references to his childhood are also curiously absent.) In letters written in the 1880s he several times compares himself in London with Robinson Crusoe. An incident is recalled in which he is walking near Holland Park with his sister and they declare their feelings of homesickness for Ireland: 'I know we were both very close to tears and remember with wonder, for I had never known anyone that cared for such mementoes, that I longed for a sod of earth from some field I knew, something of Sligo to hold in my hand.'

What did Sligo represent in Yeats's mind? It is a small, busy seaport town on the west coast of Ireland between County Mayo and Donegal. The bay, with its harbour, is framed by the mountains Ben Bulben and Knocknarea and inland there is a cluster of freshwater loughs centred on Lough Gill. The whole area is rich in archaeological sites and is associated with some of the main legends in Irish culture; for example, the tragic climax of the love-affair between Grania and Diarmuid in stories is often located on Ben Bulben. Elements of an oral tradition in songs and stories survived into the twentieth century and Irish was still spoken by some as their mother tongue. The young boy usually travelled to Sligo by steamship because some of his mother's family were directors in the shipping company, and as the ship made its way round the north coast of Ireland, he moved into more familiar territory where his family was known and he was recognised. Despite his unpopularity with many of his relatives, he enjoyed a wonderful freedom to be on his own or to mix with all sorts and enter into the life of a small, stable community. In his solitary ramblings in the countryside, his establishment of hideouts and secluded islands, and his schemes for these private areas, possibly lie the seeds of a later fascination with secret societies and initiations. Certainly his early poetry is closely bound up with a special knowledge gained from a meditative intimacy with forces of nature. He was much taken with Thoreau's *Walden* and Yeats's most anthologised poem, 'The Lake Isle of Innisfree' (written 1888), is a compound of his unhappiness in London, the happiness he had experienced around Sligo and a Walden vision of self-sufficiency:

> I will arise and go now, and go to Innisfree,
> And a small cabin build there, of clay and
> > wattles made:
> Nine bean-rows will I have there, a hive for the
> > honey-bee,
> And live alone in the bee-loud glade.

As maker or finder of his mystery he becomes a special person, a shaman:

> I began to play at being a sage, a magician or a poet. I had many idols but as I climbed along the narrow ledge I was now Manfred [Byron's character] on his glacier, and now Prince Athanase with his solitary lamp, but I soon chose Alastor [characters in Shelley] for my chief of men and longed to share his melancholy, and maybe at last to disappear from everybody's sight as he disappeared drifting in a boat along some slow-moving river between great trees.

He dates this development as taking place when he was about 16 and the family had moved from London to live in Howth, a promontory to the north of Dublin Bay.

When he was 17 he fell in love. Laura Armstrong was a distant cousin who was about 20 and already engaged to be married. She flirted with Willie and treated him as her confidant, telling him of the vicissitudes in her engagement with her fiancé. Her wild beauty smote Willie but he could not bring himself to declare to her how smitten he was. They corresponded for a time and in 1884 she married the troublesome fiancé. Some of Yeats's early poems and attempts at plays were written for her or with her as the spur. In his *Autobiography* (unpublished till 1972), he describes how his personal awareness of sex began and how he suffered over the following few years:

I was tortured by sexual desire and had been for many years. I have often said to myself that some day I would put it all down in a book that some young man of talent might not think as I did that my shame was mine alone. It began when I was fifteen years old. I had been bathing, and lay down in the sun on the sand on the third Rosses [near Sligo] and covered my body with sand. Presently the weight of the sand began to affect the organ of sex, though at first I did not know what the strange, growing sensation was. It was only at the orgasm that I knew, remembering some boy's description or the description in my grandfather's encyclopedia. It was many days before I discovered how to renew that wonderful sensation. From then on it was a continual struggle against an experience that almost invariably left me with exhausted nerves. Normal sexual intercourse does not affect me more than other men, but that, though never frequent, was plain ruin. It filled me with loathing of myself; and yet at first pride and perhaps, a little, lack of obvious opportunity, and now love [after he met Maud Gonne in 1889] kept me in unctuous celibacy.[14]

For a couple of years he attended a school in Dublin but, as before, his father constantly interfered and would forbid him to do many of the exercises set by the teachers. Consequently he felt that he learned nothing with any confidence and was forced to 'face authority with the timidity born of excuse and evasion'. Each morning his father travelled with him into Dublin and they breakfasted in his studio before Willie went on to his school. The painter recited to his son huge stretches of poetry, always emphasising the dramatic element as central to the greatest poetry.

In *Reveries over Childhood and Youth* (and we must remember that the reveries were written in middle age) two images of his youth are presented in a section without introduction or comment. They represent a precarious ambivalence in the schoolboy in London, pulled and pushed, encouraged and discouraged, mainly by his father, told he was special but seeing around him omens of disaster:

Two pictures came into my memory. I have climbed to the top of a tree by the edge of the playing-field, and am looking at my school-fellows and am as proud of myself as a March cock when it crows to its first sunrise. I am saying to myself, 'If when I grow up I am as clever among grown-up men as I am among these boys, I shall be a famous man.' I remind myself how they think all the same things and cover the school walls at election time with the opinions their fathers find in the newspapers. I remind myself that I am an artist's son and must take some work as the whole end of life and not think as the others do of becoming well off and living pleasantly. The other picture is of a hotel sitting-room in the Strand, where a man is hunched up over the fire. He is a cousin who has speculated with another cousin's money and has fled from Ireland in danger of arrest. My father has brought us to spend the evening with him, to distract him from the remorse that he must be suffering.

A further two years were spent at the Metropolitan School of Art, although he appears to have devoted much more time to writing than to painting and, in 1885, when he was 19, he had his first poems published in the *Dublin University Review*. The fact that his father was a painter, and kept laying down various artistic laws, again inhibited his son from developing a style of his own in any straightforward way and helped to push him away from painting altogether. J. B. Yeats had expected his son to study at Trinity College in the Yeats family tradition but Willie would not go there and, although his father did not quite acknowledge the fact, could not, because his academic qualifications were inadequate. However, 1885 turned out to be a highly significant year for Willie Yeats in several ways. John O'Leary returned to Ireland and the young poet was introduced to him by his father. O'Leary had studied medicine but joined the Irish Revolutionary (later Republican) Brotherhood and edited its newspaper *Irish People*. He was arrested in 1865, charged with treason and sentenced to penal servitude for 20 years. In 1871 he was released from hard labour on condition that he remain outside Ireland till 1885. Although only 55, he had the appearance of an old man, 'the handsomest old man I had ever seen', according to young Yeats. He had a dignity and moral straightness which were deeply impressive. His sister Ellen, who acted as his housekeeper, also impressed Willie; both brother and sister scorned fanaticism and their political idealism was not based on bitterness. The impression one receives in reading *Autobiographies* is that Yeats was close to O'Leary for a period of only a few years but the influence on him lasted all his life. The older man introduced him to serious issues of nationalism and persuaded him, by the force of a personality developed in harsh experiences, of the value of standing by what he could work out for himself: no authority of country or party or Church could over-rule conscience. 'From these debates, from O'Leary's conversation, and from the Irish books he lent or gave me has come all I have set my hand to since.' O'Leary had an excellent library of Irish books and he urged his protégé to read back through Irish literature in order to understand the patterns of culture. He himself had a highly developed literary sense and always distinguished care-fully between books as worthwhile literature and books as some other thing.

The 'debates' referred to in the quotation were the meetings of the Contemporary Club founded by C. H. Oldham, later to be Professor of Political Economy in the new University College, Dublin, and who was also one of the people who set up the *Dublin University Review*, in which the poet was first published. Although the Club was not a nationalist organisation, many of the discussions con-cerned nationalist issues. On Yeats the debates had two crucial influ-ences. Some of the people taking part, particularly O'Leary, educated him to understand the cultural context and content of national identity. Second, he needed training in presenting and countering arguments or, as he put it, 'I wished to become self-possessed, to be able to play with hostile minds as Hamlet played, to look in the lion's face, as it were, with unquivering eyelash.' At this time, when he was about 20, he was painfully self-conscious and he now sought to cultivate a manner with which he could handle the world of people. He was looking for examples on whom he could model himself and he deliberately visited uncomfortable social situations so that he could learn to cope. His speech, his dress, even his walk, based on Henry Irving's Hamlet seen in 1879, were thought out. Although he did not meet Oscar Wilde till 1888, he had seen him lecture as early as 1883 and Wilde's cultivated pose made a considerable impression.

One effect of meeting O'Leary and reading the Irish books recom-mended by him, particularly Irish writers of the nineteenth century, was that Yeats could confront the ignorance of Irish literature dis-played by people such as Edward Dowden. Dowden had become Professor of English at Trinity when he was 24 and came to have a very high reputation as a critic and scholar for his books on Shakespeare, Shelley and others. A friend of J. B. Yeats, who rather distrusted his fastidious and ironic cast of mind, he was encouraging to the young Yeats but Dowden fell severely in Yeats's eyes on con-fessing that his *Life of Shelley* was completed (1886) as a duty, not as a pleasure. Also in 1886 Yeats castigated the Professor for having failed to support Irish literature, particularly the poetry of Sir Samuel Ferguson. This new confidence stemmed directly from Yeats's respect for O'Leary and his own new reading.

Towards the end of 1885 Yeats became acquainted with Douglas Hyde, later to be the driving force in the Gaelic League and the selector-translator of one of the classics in Irish literature, *The Love Songs of Connacht* (1893). He came from a similar background to that of Yeats but he had steeped himself in the Irish language and that side of Irish culture so often neglected by the Anglo-Irish. His enthusiasm seemed boundless and in his long life he achieved much, eventually becoming the President of Ireland. Like O'Leary's, his nationalist ideals were not narrowly political and in 1915 he resigned as President of the Gaelic League because it had become politicised. Yeats learned much from him but felt that Hyde had, to an extent, wasted his great talents on a cause, when they should have been used to create literature; however, despairing of achieving anything in the theatre (1911), he appealed to Hyde (see 'At the Abbey Theatre') to divulge his secret gift for popularity. Hyde's pen-name, An Craoibhinn Aoibhinn (The Pleasant Little Branch) was indicative of his wish to be adopted into the tribe of the Irish language, and Yeats valued the insights into folklore gained from the man who was to become in the 1930s the Chairman of the Folklore Institute.

However, if any one person could take the credit for creating in Yeats an interest in the mythical and spiritual history of Ireland it would have to be Standish James O'Grady. In 1880 he had published the second volume of his *History of Ireland*, dealing with the ancient myths and legends of the country, and he wrote several romances using the same material. For Yeats and many others, he succeeded in bringing the old stories out of a scholarly limbo and making them come alive. As a person he was irascible and fiercely reactionary and he argued with a passionate eloquence which made him majestic in the poet's eyes. As was the case with many of these powerful people, Yeats wished to employ O'Grady or his writings as part of his strategy for realigning Irish consciousness: 'I do think that if... we had got all his histories and imaginative works into the hands of our young men, he might have brought the imagination of Ireland nearer the Image and the honeycomb.' Certainly Yeats's own imagination was, according to himself, turned by O'Grady's writings from foreign themes to Irish mythology and especially the legends associated with the hero Cuchulain. O'Grady's own vision of a new Ireland was dogmatically based on the idea of society led by enlightened landlords; when Ireland took a totally different direction he did not wish to be part of it, and went into exile in England, where he lived till his death in 1928.

A very different figure, but one of Yeats's closest associates for a number of years, was George Russell, usually known as AE, two years younger than Yeats. His family had moved to Dublin from County Armagh when he was 11 and he went on to attend the Metropolitan School of Art. What amazed Yeats when he first encountered him at the School was that Russell made no attempt to paint the model posing for the students but presented the visions appearing in his mind; and 'he saw visions continually, perhaps more than any modern man since Swedenborg'. His career was odd. After his time at the Art School he was clerk to a draper for seven years before becoming an organiser of rural banks and cooperative groups with the Irish Agricultural Organisation. Between 1905 and 1930 he edited *Irish Homestead*, the weekly journal of the Irish cooperative movement and, after its demise, went on lecture tours of America to talk about redeveloping depressed rural communities. In disillusionment with the political, religious and materialist tendencies in Ireland in the 1930s, he left Ireland and spent his final two years in England. His career seems odd because, through the years, he was also a painter, poet and writer of a most spiritual sort. When Yeats knew him best he shared a house in Ely Place with an assortment of Theosophists:

> At the top of the house lived a medical student who read Plato and took hashish, and a young Scotsman who owned a vegetarian restaurant, and had just returned from America, where he had gone as a disciple of the Prophet Harris…. When one asked what set him on his wanderings, he told of a young Highlander, his friend in boyhood, whose cap was always plucked off at a certain twist in the road, till the fathers of the village fastened it upon his head by recommending drink and women. When he had gone, his room was inherited by an American hypnotist, who had lived among the Zuni Indians…. On a lower floor lived a strange red-haired girl, all whose thoughts were set upon painting and poetry, conceived as abstract images like Love and Penury in the *Symposium*; and …. had lived for many weeks upon bread and shell-cocoa….

For the same person to be considered as one of the agricultural experts of his time, be consulted several times by the British government and be called on to advise President Roosevelt's Secretary for Agriculture, and to proclaim in Bray the return of the gods to Ireland and believe (1897) that the genius of the Irish Renaissance was living in a cottage (as yet undetected but seen in dreams) in Donegal or Sligo – this combination is extraordinary. For twenty years he and Yeats were partners in a multitude of enterprises but, in the early years of the new century, they fell out with considerable bitterness and were never very close again. However, in 1925, Russell could still state that to reread Yeats's *Early Poems and Stories* 'is to recall my first love in literature…. Who under the spell can be critical of the enchanter? I was not then, and hardly now can I do anything but surrender myself anew to the music.'[15] Yeats's appreciation of Russell in the late 1880s and through the 1890s was profound; and the example of a man who often 'seemed incapable of coherent thought' in speech but who became holy in his art encouraged him in a development towards symbolism:

> He, more than any other, has a subtle rhythm, precision of phrase, an emotional relation to form and colour, and a perfect understanding that the business of poetry is not to enforce an opinion or expound an action, but to bring us into communion with the moods and passions which are the creative powers behind the universe; that though the poet may need to master many opinions, they are but the body and symbols for his art, the formula of evocation for making the invisible visible.[16]

In later life Yeats conceded that he had wanted Russell to become something that was impossible for the kind of person he was, but Yeats proposes a general lesson: 'We are never satisfied with the maturity of those whom we have admired in boyhood; and because we have seen their whole circle – even the most successful life is but a segment – we remain to the end their harshest critics.' Even in the 1890s he considered Russell's otherworldly focus as vapid and it was he who recommended that Russell be given the job with the Agricultural Society, partly because he thought that handling practicalities would help to ballast Russell's visions. It would be seriously incorrect to say that Russell was not prepared to commit himself politically – he did so many times – but his aim was always beyond the practical and towards the spiritual. His tolerance of good intentions in art, whether in the theatre or in poetry, was offensive to Yeats, who believed that progress in Irish intellectual life was needed and it could come about only when people's standards and expectations were raised.

A major interest shared by Russell and Yeats was the occult. On this, as on so many other shared interests, they disagreed. Russell experienced innumerable visions and he was content to accept them as revelations but did not wish to analyse or explain them and, initially, he was opposed to any attempt to organise such knowledge. Yeats, less visited by visions himself, was eager to discover whence visions came and what their symbolism could tell. In 1885, partly as a result of reading A. P. Sinnett's *Esoteric Buddhism* (gifted to him by his aunt Isabella Pollexfen), with some friends, including Russell, he became one of the founding members of the Dublin Hermetic Society. In Yeats's mind, this development was of the utmost importance: 'It was only when I began to study psychical research and mystical philosophy that I broke away from my father's influence.'

In the same month, June, that saw the first meeting of the Hermetic Society, Yeats was introduced to Katharine Tynan, already widely published in journals and with her first collection appearing that year, 1885. Older than him by six years, she was the first female, apart from Laura Armstrong, with whom he had a close association and, indeed, he was often uncertain as to the nature of their association:

> I had much trouble with my senses, for I am not naturally chaste and I was young. Other young men that I know lived the life Edwin Ellis told me of [sexually promiscuity], but I had gathered from the Romantic poets an ideal of perfect love. Perhaps I should never marry in church, but I would love one woman all my life. I wrote many letters to Katharine Tynan, a very plain woman, and one day I overheard somebody say that she was the kind of woman who might make herself very unhappy about a man. I began to wonder if she was in love with me and if it was my duty to marry her. Sometimes when she was in London, I in Ireland would think it possible that I should, but if she came to stay, or I saw her in Ireland, it became impossible again. Yet we were always very great friends and I have no reason to think she ever thought of me otherwise.[17]

Although written in 1916 (as part of his private *Autobiography*), this seems to reflect accurately Yeats's emotional gaucheness in his relationship with Katharine Tynan. There was no physical side to the relationship. In 1888 she formed an attachment with a Henry Hinkson and they were eventually married in 1893. Yeats and she remained friendly although, from 1892, their correspondence, which had been brisk, became more sporadic. In the second half of the 1880s they had tried out new ideas on each other, given encouragement, criticism and promotion to each other's work. She, looking back in 1913, remembered him, 'beautiful to look at, his dark face, its touch of vivid colouring, the night black hair, the eager dark eyes … all dreams and gentleness…. He lived, breathed, ate, drank and slept poetry.'[18] In 1886 they attended a seance together. She was a Catholic and at the climax of the seance she withdrew from the table and intoned the Lord's Prayer. The manifestations touched something fearful in Yeats, he was violently agitated and felt himself in the presence of something evil. Having been brought up without religion, he had no prayer to use and resorted to uttering the opening lines of *Paradise Lost*. He did not return to a seance for many years but the experience posed a question which recurs throughout his life: '[I] would often ask myself what was that violent impulse that had run through my nerves. Was it a part of myself – something always to be a danger perhaps; or had it come from without, as it seemed?'

With Katharine Tynan, he hammered out his thoughts on using Irish material in his writing and it was she who prompted him towards writing *The Wanderings of Oisin*, which was eventually to appear in 1889. It was also through her and her connections in the Catholic Church that in 1886 Yeats met Gerard Manley Hopkins. Hopkins, who had arrived in Ireland in 1884 to teach classics at University College, was given copies of the Irish poet's 'The Two Titans' and *Mosada*, both published in 1886. In a letter to Coventry Patmore he comments:

> Now this *Mosada* I cannot think highly of, but I was happily not required then to praise what presumably I had not then read, and I had read and could praise another piece. It was a strained and unworkable allegory about a young man and a sphinx on a rock in the sea (how did they get there? what did they eat? and so on); people think such criticisms very prosaic, but commonsense is never out of place anywhere.[19]

Yeats, fifty years on, confessed that he remembered 'almost nothing' about the meeting and explained, 'A boy of seventeen, Walt Whitman in his pocket, had little interest in a querulous, sensitive scholar.' He had been, in fact, 21.

In the main, this chapter has concentrated on Yeats before he was 21, and many of the central concerns of his writing life are already introduced: a fascination with eccentric characters, cultural Irish nationalism, the occult, a sense of place, self-examination, women, exclusive societies, and poetry. Often his own written memories of episodes are used and, of course, these have to be regarded with some caution. However, he is a vivid, perceptive and humorous commentator on his development and observers could often vouch for the substantial accuracy of his account. 'Substantial' is the operative word and certainly there are other versions of the events and people concerned. And questions do arise. For example, if Yeats is often described as digesting his friends in his poetic stomach and if George Russell (AE) and Katherine Tynan were such substantial friends, why do they not appear in his poems? Why, indeed, are they given so little attention in *Autobiographies*? The beginning of an answer must be that Yeats, from early on as a writer, is highly selective and it is as if he knew from early on who the *dramatis personae* of his poetry had to be. His worries about his beginnings and what he can develop into remain throughout the poems. In 1914, after enumerating the boldnesses of some forebears, he concludes with an apology:

> Pardon that for a barren passion's sake,
> Although I have come close on forty-nine,
> I have no child, I have nothing but a book,
> Nothing but that to prove your blood and mine.

The question, the self-scrutiny returns with fresh urgency in the late poems, for example, 'Are You Content?', 'The Circus Animals' Desertion', 'Politics', but most passionately in 'What Then?':

> His chosen comrades thought at school
> He must grow a famous man;
> He thought the same and lived by rule,
> All his twenties crammed with toil;
> *'What then?' sang Plato's ghost, 'what then?'*

Everything he wrote was read,
After certain years he won
Sufficient money for his need,
Friends that have been friends indeed;
'What then?' sang Plato's ghost, 'what then?'

All his happier dreams came true –
A small old house, wife, daughter, son,
Grounds where plum and cabbage grew,
Poets and Wits about him drew;
'What then?' sang Plato's ghost, 'what then?'

'The work is done,' grown old he thought,
'According to my boyish plan;
Let the fools rage, I swerved in nought,
Something to perfection brought;'
But louder sang that ghost, 'What then?'

2

Yeats and the 1890s: Celtic Twilight and Golden Dawn

After six years in Dublin, the Yeats family in 1887 moved back to London, where Mrs Yeats had the first of her strokes and the members of the family had to be distributed among relatives. In the following year they settled again in Bedford Park. Only John Butler Yeats enjoyed the idea of the move; as usual, he thought that his prospects would be better elsewhere. The Dublin they were leaving was, despite James Joyce's analysis of it as a centre of paralysis, a place of considerable intellectual activity, where eccentricity in behaviour and language was tolerated or even encouraged and where a new talent could make itself known. Granted that Joyce's first story found publication in the farmers' journal, *The Irish Homestead*, and that his shame at appearing in what he called the 'pig's paper' necessitated a pseudonym ('Stephen Daedalus'), his major work went on to use and rework innumerable elements of Dublin as he had known it around the turn of the century.

By the time of the family move, Willie Yeats had established something of a place and name in Dublin and had begun to develop a confidence in public which he could exploit in London. Initially, he was desperately awkward but his experience of talking at meetings, defending himself against verbal onslaughts, organising other people and being recognised in Dublin, allowed him to move forward. In the following years, he moved ceaselessly between Ireland and England and, in these years, his enterprises in the two countries were intermeshed and mutually supportive. He came to be a remarkable nurturer of contacts and manipulator of groups.

He first met William Morris in Dublin in 1886, when Morris had been invited to give a lecture, and in the following year he met Morris's daughter and became a regular guest at 'Sunday Nights' in Morris's Kelmscott House. Like John O'Leary, Morris was of Yeats's father's generation and sometimes the admiration of Yeats for both seemed tinged with a wish to find an acceptable substitute for his exciting but disappointing father. Certainly both, in his eyes, appeared to possess the calmness of a life worked out, an aura of achievement; curiously, when he met O'Leary he saw the 50-year old as very old and he describes Morris at 53 as 'an ageing man content at last to gather beautiful things rather than to arrange a beautiful house'. He recounts in *Autobiographies* how he 'soon discovered his [Morris's] spontaneity and joy and made him my chief of men. Today [1921] I do not set his poetry very high, but for an odd altogether wonderful line, or thought; and yet, if some angel offered me the choice, I would choose to live his life, poetry and all, rather than my own or any other man's.' As a boy he had read the early poetry of Morris and, because he liked it, had clashed with his father; although he came to prefer later writings by Morris, an influence on his own early poetry may be discerned. The self-absorbedness of the singing dreamer can be traced in the Apology to Morris's *The Earthly Paradise* (1868):

> Dreamer of dreams, born out of my due time,
> Why should I strive to set the crooked straight?
> Let it suffice me that my murmuring rhyme
> Beats with light wing against the ivory gate,
> Telling a tale not too importunate
> To those who in the sleepy region stay,
> Lulled by the singer of an empty day.

The cadence here is heard in Yeats's 'The Song of the Happy Shepherd':

> Then nowise worship dusty deeds,
> Nor seek, for this is also sooth,
> To hunger fiercely after truth,
> Lest all thy toiling only breeds
> New dreams, new dreams; there is no truth
> Saving in thine own heart.

It was, however, the later prose romances, particularly *The Wood Beyond the World* (1894) and *The Well at the World's End* (1896), that so enchanted Yeats that he slowed down his reading in order to prolong his pleasure. With hindsight, he recognised that Morris 'had little self-knowledge' and 'knew nothing of suffering', but in his own development of a Celtic literary ambience he found a parallel model in Morris's mediaevalist and Spenserian saga-fictions.

Through Morris, rather than through his father, Yeats was introduced to the aesthetic theories and controversies which had dominated artistic circles in the previous generation. The Pre-Raphaelites from around 1850, Ruskin and Whistler, Tennyson, Pater – all in some measure fed into Morris and he was a culminating point of notions about social values and art. His socialism, his emphasis on hand-crafts and opposition to machines, the diction of his writing, even his utopianism, hark back towards an unhistorical view of mediaeval Europe. Some of his theories rubbed off on the younger Yeats, and we can look forward, beyond the artificial heroic Celtic dimension devised in the early poetry, to his concept of courtesy, decorum and a regulated social order in the later work. Perhaps Yeats came to concede that there was something too easy in Morris's fecundity in so many directions, and a more arduous passion was to be his own direction. He acclaimed the resounding doctrine of Pater:[1] 'To burn always with this hard, gemlike flame, to maintain this ecstasy, is success in life.' In his poetic career he was to swing about between an espousal of hermetic poetry, seemingly related to a notion of 'Art for art's sake', and a deployment of poetry as an instrument for ideological or attitudinal change and promotion. In the 1890s it appears that the former concept predominates but the actuality is more complicated.

In the English tradition, two poets who appealed to Yeats lay behind some of Morris's own thinking: Blake and Shelley. For four years from 1889 Yeats worked with Edwin Ellis on an edition of Blake's poetry. He had first met Edwin Ellis, a friend of his father, when he was four years old. (The child asked Ellis if he was related to Cinder Ellis in the story.) The poet and painter, very eccentric, made a considerable impact on his younger colleague, who acknowledged his help in his own writing and in spiritual awareness. Together they copied out manuscripts and, indeed, discovered and were possibly the first people to read Blake's *The Four Zoas* (or *Vala*) since it was written in 1797. Part of Blake's appeal for Yeats was that he had formulated a total system which could accommodate and account for all human behaviour. The two editors worried away at this system and succeeded in providing one of the earliest and boldest elucidations of its symbolism. By the time he came to work on Blake, Yeats had already embarked on explorations in the mystical tradition and he discovered connections between Blake and such mystical writers as Swedenborg (whose life overlapped that of Blake) and Jacob Boehme, who died in 1624. Blake, it emerged, was very well-versed in these authors and shared with them the idea that the material world is a manifestation of the forces of the spiritual world and that we can learn to read these manifestations and so understand the true nature of our existence. Blake shared with Boehme a view that a dialectic of contrary forces operates and gives a dynamic quality to our lives. Yeats accepted a version of this dialectic and the interaction of contraries comes to be a central feature of his thinking. Furthermore, Blake anticipated in his poetry many of the theories advanced a century later by Jung, and some of these theories are integral to Yeats's own system to be ordered in *A Vision* (1926).

Just as in his meeting with people, the young Yeats seemed to be looking for figures of authority, figures whom he could revere as gurus, so in his reading he searched for what he called sacred books. In Shelley's *Prometheus Unbound* he discovered one. In 1900 he published 'The Philosophy of Shelley's Poetry', one of the essential essays on the symbolic patterns in the poetry, and in 1932 he wrote *'Prometheus Unbound'*, a retrospective glance at what he still saw as one of the main influences on his own thinking:

> When I was in my early twenties... the orthodox religion, as our mothers had taught it, was no longer credible; those who could not substitute connoisseurship, or some humanitarian or scientific pursuit, found a substitute in Shelley. He had shared our curiosities, our political problems, our conviction, that despite all experience to the contrary, love is enough; and unlike Blake, isolated by an arbitrary symbolism, he seemed to sum up all that was metaphysical in English poetry. When in middle life I looked back I found that he and not Blake, whom I had studied more and with more approval, had shaped my life, and when I thought of the tumultuous and often tragic lives of friends or acquaintance, I attributed to his direct or indirect influence their Jacobin frenzies, their brown demons.

Many readers of Yeats would probably see a greater influence of Blake than of Shelley in his poetry. Blake's elaborate system and his concern with emotion against reason seems closer to Yeats than Shelley's political idealism and his deep scepticism. Blake, the mystic, is a poet primarily of metaphor; Shelley, the visionary, perceives the world in terms of similes. Yeats is more inclined to metaphor than to simile. However, when one recalls Shelley's *Adonais, The Triumph of Life* and some of the late lyrics addressed to Jane Williams, there are certain strains of thought and emotion which are very much present in Yeats. A further consideration is that Shelley who, admittedly, died at the early age of 29, had not resolved his existential and spiritual questions, just as Yeats was not to do in poetry, whereas Blake appeared to have concocted a scheme which gave the impression that he could accommodate all the factors of life. Yeats certainly found something abstract and schematic in Blake while Shelley was still vulnerable and enquiring and painfully subject to the circumstances of his life. Shelley's symbols, according to Yeats, and I think he is correct, were adaptations of symbols which can be traced back through European poetry; Blake, although he was centrally involved in a mystical tradition known to Yeats, devised a curiously arbitrary and inaccessible symbology for his psychic drama. The life of Shelley, also, with his nympholeptic drives and his failures in attaining his dreams with women, his involvement in political issues and his disillusionment with these issues made him a more sympathetic figure with whom Yeats could identify. The very impossibility of realisation in Shelley's high vision, symptomatised for Yeats by the figure of Demogorgon in the sacred book *Prometheus Unbound*, appealed to him and, in his contradictory way, Yeats found more to admire, more to resist in Shelley than he found in Blake.

In the quotation above, Yeats attributes to Shelley's baneful influence the 'Jacobin frenzies' and 'brown demons' of his friends in the 1890s, what he calls 'The Tragic Generation'. By 1890, he tells us in *Autobiographies*, he has met most of the poets who were well-known and in 1890 he and a Welsh publisher and poet, Ernest Rhys, who knew even more writers because of his work as a publisher, founded the Rhymers' Club. The Club met each night over several years in an upstairs room of the Cheshire Cheese, an eating-house in Fleet Street. The venue was there and members and their guests attended when they chose; Yeats names some of those who attended regularly: Lionel Johnson, Ernest Dowson, Victor Plarr, Ernest Radford, John Davidson, Richard le Gallienne, T. W. Rolleston, Edwin Ellis, John Todhunter, Arthur Symons. Oscar Wilde attended only when they occasionally met in someone's house. They read and discussed each other's poems but, according to Yeats, there was an embarrassment about taking the discussion into wider areas and theories. He felt that some of them, including himself, were very provincial in their attitudes and only a rough readiness on the part of some of the Irish members allowed the Club to survive.

Although he had heard a lecture by Oscar Wilde in Dublin as early as 1883, he did not meet Wilde properly till 1888 in London. Their first meeting is described as 'an astonishment. I never before heard a man talking with perfect sentences, as if he had written them all overnight with labour and yet spontaneous.' Oscar Fingal O'Flahertie Wills Wilde was the son of Sir William Wilde, an eye-surgeon famous throughout Europe (and notorious throughout Ireland), and Jane Francesca Elgee, large in body and with a considerable reputation as a writer under her pen-name 'Speranza'. Both parents were interested in Irish folklore and nationalism but Oscar adopted a pose or series of poses apparently unconnected with Ireland. One of the aspects of him which so intrigued Yeats, younger by eleven years, was the very rejection by him of sincerity, consistency and truth. His writings play with these conventional virtues and turn the handed-down maxims on their heads: 'In matters of grave importance, style, not sincerity, is the vital thing' (*The Importance of Being Earnest*) and 'It is only shallow people who do not judge by appearances' (*The Portrait of Dorian Gray*). His conversation, although it emerged perfectly enunciated, as if it had been rehearsed, could be extraordinarily varied and, according to Yeats, 'could pass without incongruity from some unforeseen, swift stroke of wit to elaborate reverie'. Yeats was also captivated by the 'slow, carefully modulated cadence [which] sounded natural to my ears'. When Wilde's collapse happened with his trial and imprisonment in 1895 for homosexual offences, and his subsequent bankruptcy and exile in France on his release in 1897, Yeats gave him his support throughout. Although he never claimed to admire Wilde as a writer, he did remember his kindness to a gauche fellow-Irishman and he learned much about style in life and social masks from Wilde's example. A savage irony – or is it bitterness? – underlies much of Wilde's work and his paradoxes are often reductive rather than enlarging. Yeats found 'a terrible beauty' (the phrase made famous by the refrain of 'Easter 1916') in a story related by Wilde in conversation but later spoiled with the 'verbal decoration of his epoch'. The original is given in *Autobiographies*:

Christ came from a white plain to a purple city, and as He passed through the first street He heard voices overhead, and saw a young man lying drunk upon a window-sill. 'Why do you waste your soul in drunkenness?' He said, 'Lord I was a leper and You

healed me, what else can I do?' A little further through the town
He saw a young man following a harlot, and said, 'Why do you
dissolve your soul in debauchery?' and the young man
answered, 'Lord, I was blind, and You healed me, what else can I
do?' At last in the middle of the city He saw an old man crouch-
ing, weeping upon the ground, and when He asked him why he
wept, the old man answered, 'Lord, I was dead, and You raised
me into life, what else can I do but weep?'

Wilde further claimed to murmur this story to himself at intervals
through the day as others might murmur the Lord's Prayer or say
Grace.

It was precisely this mixture of iconoclasm and ostentation that
outraged Yeats's friend Lionel Johnson. If Wilde celebrated his
paradoxicality, Johnson, whose life was a mesh of paradoxes, tried
to disguise his. Two years younger than Yeats, he is described in
Autobiographies as if he were considerably older, vastly better-read
and more experienced. They first met in 1889 when Johnson was
already an admirer of Yeats for *The Wanderings of Oisin*, which had
been published earlier in that year. They saw a great deal of each
other, and Johnson, from an upper-class family in Kent and with a
brilliant student career behind him, claimed, with Yeats's encouragement, Irish descent and became deeply involved in various
schemes, mainly controlled by his friend, to foster Irish cultural
awareness. In 1891 he had joined the Roman Catholic Church and
his religion was to be a central concern of his remaining years, satisfying his taste for elaborate ritual and tradition and providing
some framework for the guilt he felt concerning his homosexual
tendencies and his alcoholism. He was to die pathetically at the
age of 35 by falling off a bar stool and fracturing his skull. Despite
the mess in Johnson's life, Yeats always saw a purity and true
devoutness in his mind, not so much towards religion as towards
learning and taste. When he discovered the extent of Johnson's
drinking and his untruths, he was reluctant to concede such blem-
ishes in one of his model persons. Later he came to a more
balanced acceptance of him and he was certainly aware that,
although he had been taught much by Johnson's discussions of
poetry, Johnson's own poetry was, with a few exceptions, strained
and desiccated. In 1918 in his elegy 'In Memory of Major Robert
Gregory', he summons up his old friend as a special guest:

Lionel Johnson comes the first to mind,
That loved his learning better than mankind,
Though courteous to the worst; much falling he
Brooded upon sanctity
Till all his Greek and Latin learning seemed
A long blast upon the horn that brought
A little nearer to his thought
A measureless consummation that he dreamed.

Another of the Rhymers, Ernest Dowson, who died when he was only 33, carried many of the symptoms of this Decadent condition. Yeats was not friendly with him in the way that he was with Johnson, but he compares the two and their tortured careers. According to his account, Johnson's body remained undeveloped beyond adolescence and only his brain matured; Dowson was sexually gluttonous but very inhibited when without alcohol: 'Sober, he would look at no other woman, it was said, but drunk, desired whatever woman chance brought, clean or dirty.' Also a convert to Roman Catholicism, his poetry, more sustained and passionate than that of Johnson, was often praised by Yeats. Often, however, the impression given in *Autobiographies* is that Yeats learned from his contemporaries more how not to live and write than to follow them. For example, John Davidson, a bristling, fiercely independent Scot, fascinated him as a figure responding to a situation but his poetry, later much admired by T. S. Eliot, had little effect on Yeats. Davidson's anarchic passion was, for Yeats, his undoing (he eventually took his own life by drowning) and his example causes Yeats to sum up what he gained from mixing with such desperate people:

They had taught me that violent energy, which is like a fire of straw, consumes in a few minutes the nervous vitality and is useless in the arts. Our fire must burn slowly, and we must constantly turn away to think, constantly analyze what we have done, be content even to have little life outside our work, to show, perhaps, to other men, as little as the watch-mender shows, his magnifying-glass caught in his screwed-up eye. Only then do we learn to conserve our vitality, to keep our mind enough under control and to make our technique sufficiently flexible for expression of the emotions of life as they arise.

It was at the house of William Henley, not one of the Rhymers, that Yeats met Wilde in 1888, and Henley became one of the young poet's main encouragers. The story of his life is colourful and his energetic straightforwardness and editorial acumen won Yeats's respect. He was one of Dr Joseph Lister's early patients and the use by Lister of antiseptic saved Henley from having to have his second leg amputated. While in Edinburgh for this treatment he became friendly with Robert Louis Stevenson and he was almost certainly part of Stevenson's inspiration for the figure of Long John Silver. Yeats describes a memorable lithograph of him by Sir William Rothenstein and adds his own assessment: 'He was most human – human, I used to say, like one of Shakespeare's characters – and yet pressed and pummelled, as it were, into a single attitude, almost into a gesture and a speech as by some overwhelming situation. I disagreed with him about everything, but I admired him beyond words.' This remarkable editor gathered round him a strange assortment of writers, some of whom, like Kipling, supported Henley's increasingly Imperialist views. Many of Yeats's early poems and prose pieces were published by Henley in the *Scots Observer*, renamed the *National Observer* in 1890, and Yeats accepted the often severe revisions of his work made by the editor. In his career, Henley did not find the right outlet or backing for his considerable talents; as Yeats put it, he was 'like a great actor with a bad part'.

A contrary figure to Henley, and one that fascinated Yeats, was the artist Aubrey Beardsley, who died of consumption when only 26. In a letter Yeats concluded that Beardsley was 'not lovable, only astounding and intrepid'. He wrote this in 1913 when Beardsley's sister Mabel was dying of cancer, and his mind had been much exercised about his dead companions from the 1890s; in 'The Grey Rock' he writes:

> Since, tavern comrades, you have died,
> Maybe your images have stood,
> Mere bone and muscle thrown aside,
> Before that roomful or as good. [in the afterlife]
> You had to face your ends when young –
> 'Twas wine or women, or some curse –
> But never made a poorer song
> That you might have a heavier purse,
> Nor gave loud service to a cause

That you might have a troop of friends.
You kept the Muse's sterner laws,
And unrepenting faced your ends,
And therefore earned the right – and yet
Dowson and Johnson most I praise –
To troop with those the world's forgot,
And copy their proud steady gaze.

Yeats was intrigued by people who were absolute, who had an intensity of vision; his approval of their goals was irrelevant. For him, Beardsley, notwithstanding his adopted Catholicism, saw through what defends most of us from despair or disillusion and touched an irredeemable horror at the base of life. He provided Yeats with a inkling of something very like evil and also an insight into the nature of art:

Does not all art come when a nature, that never ceases to judge itself, exhausts personal emotion in action or desire so completely that something impersonal, something that has nothing to do with action or desire, suddenly starts into its place, something which is as unforeseen, as completely organized, even as unique, as the images that pass before the mind between sleeping and waking?

Beardsley is often connected now in people's minds with Wilde, but the two were not friends and Beardsley certainly disapproved of Wilde and caricatured him often. Nonetheless, his illustrations for Wilde's *Salomé* are among his best work. He was the art editor of *The Yellow Book* but the scandal around Wilde in 1895 led to his dismissal. His term as art editor of *The Savoy* was equally short-lived.

The editor of *The Savoy* was Arthur Symons. In 1895 when Yeats decided to live away from his parents' house in Bedford Park, he chose to live alongside Symons in rooms in the Middle Temple. He found Symons an admirable companion, straightforward and sympathetic to others, a relief to Yeats after his friendship with Johnson, which had become strained. Before Symons edited the eight issues of *The Savoy* in 1896, he was already well-known as a poet and his poems remain as symptomatic of the Decadent fashion for sordid, morbid situations but also contain elements reminiscent of some of the Impressionist painters. He was a firm proponent of the ideas on art of Pater, and Symons's knowledge of French enabled him to read developments in French poetry comparable with certain tastes in Britain. Yeats found him a helpful companion in two quite different ways: 'Arthur Symons, more than any man I have ever known, could slip as it were into the mind of another, and my thoughts gained in richness and in clearness from his sympathy, nor shall I ever know how much my practice and my theory owe to the passages that he read me from Catullus and from Verlaine and Mallarmé.' Symons's literary interests were wide-ranging and he wrote essays and books on a variety of authors, past and present. His most significant book, certainly as far as Yeats, to whom the work is dedicated, was concerned, is *The Symbolist Movement in Literature*, published in 1899. Not that it was the book itself that enlightened Yeats; rather, it was the endless discussions he enjoyed with Symons and the translations of such poets as Baudelaire, Verlaine and particularly Mallarmé made for him by his friend. In *Autobiographies* he suggests that the influence of Mallarmé and Villiers de l'Isle-Adam acted on some of the poems in *The Wind Among the Reeds* (1899) as did that of Walter Pater. In presenting *Les Symbolistes* to English readers, Symons introduced an area of confusion over terms and it is difficult to keep our feet in such slippery territory.

In this context, it seems advisable to keep to Yeats's understanding of the term Symbolism. In the year following Symons's book, Yeats published an essay called 'The Symbolism of Poetry', a companion-piece to, and development of, a previous essay called 'Symbolism in Painting'. In the previous essay he quotes the declaration on the Emerald Tablet of Hermes Trismegistus (supposed to be the Egyptian God of Knowledge, Thoth), 'The things below are as the things above.' And he quotes Blake: 'If the spectator could enter into one of these images of his imagination, approaching them on the fiery chariot of his contemplative thought, if ... he could make a friend and companion of one of these images of wonder, which always entreat him to leave mortal things (as he must know), then would he arise from the grave, then would he meet the Lord in the air, and then he would be happy.' He cites Blake, Wagner, Keats, Rossetti, Villiers de l'Isle-Adam, Whistler, Beardsley, Maeterlinck and Verlaine as artists who utilise an eclectic symbolism. In the later essay he is more analytical, even if the diction sounds rather rhetorical to our ears. He locates the Symbolist movement in the post-Darwin period:

The scientific movement brought with it a literature which was always tending to lose itself in externalities of all kinds, in opinion, in declamation, in picturesque writing, in word-painting, or in what Mr Symons has called an attempt 'to build in brick and mortar inside the covers of a book'; and now writers have begun to dwell upon the element of evocation, of suggestion, upon what we call the symbolism, in great writers.

In 1894 he had met Paul Verlaine in Paris and, with Maud Gonne, attended a performance of *Axel* by Villiers de l'Isle-Adam. *Axel* is an extraordinary play and Yeats's poor French required that Maud Gonne provide him with a running commentary. In it, Axel, a young aristocrat, renounces his material life and the family obsession with their lost treasure, and goes down into the vaults of his castle where he discovers Sara, a runaway novice who has been led by Rosicrucian knowledge to the vaults where the treasure is concealed. After a struggle they realise the beauty of each other, pledge their love and take a fatal poison together: death, not sex, is the supreme consummation of their high love. As their famous word of farewell and renunciation puts it, 'Live? Our servants will do that for us.' For Yeats, *Axel* was another sacred book. It seemed to operate in a different, more spiritual dimension from that of other contemporary plays.

Through Symons and his own stumbling reading, he knew something of the theories of the French Symbolist poets. He would have known Baudelaire's formulation of a theory of inbuilt analogies between the world of nature and the spiritual world, between the inner world of the mind and the outside world: 'Everything, form, movement, number, colour, perfume, in the spiritual as in the natural world, is significative, matching, converse, correspondent.' Yeats, in his essay, offers his formulation:

All sounds, all colours, all forms, either because of their preordained energies or because of long association, evoke indefinable and yet precise emotions, or, as I prefer to think, call down among us certain disembodied powers, whose footsteps over us we call emotions; and when sound, and colour, and form are in a musical relation to one another, they become, as it were, one sound, one colour, one form, and evoke an emotion that is made of their distinct evocations and yet is one emotion.

He connects poetry with this notion of simultaneous significances and justifies his own incantatory style of writing and reading:

> The purpose of rhythm, it has always seemed to me, is to prolong the moment of contemplation, the moment when we are both asleep and awake, which is the one moment of creation, by hushing us with an alluring monotony, while it holds us waking by variety, to keep us in that state of perhaps real trance, in which the mind liberated from the pressure of the will is unfolded in symbols.

Where did Yeats's theory of symbolism originate? Certainly he did not discover it for the first time when he was reading the French poets: his reading of them confirmed something he already knew but about which he sometimes felt doubts. When his long narrative poem *The Wanderings of Oisin* was being published in 1889, he first says (in a letter to Katharine Tynan) that the symbolism of the poem is a disguise under which he can say things to which he alone has the key. 'The romance is for my readers. They must not even know there is a symbol anywhere. They will not find out. If they did it would spoil the art, yet the whole poem is full of symbols – if it be full of aught but clouds.' The final comment reveals not so much modesty as a lack of confidence in his poetic methods; indeed, the poem seemed very obscure to many readers, and Yeats came to worry that it might require an interpreter. He was never very interested in pictorial or narrative or witty poetry but rather in poetry which aspired to move through words, beyond words, towards an awareness of some more ultimate condition; it would operate through suggestion, not declaration. Because he did not have a formal academic training, his knowledge of the English tradition in poetry was very patchy but he did know what he was looking for: sacred books. Blake and Shelley were probably his most trusted exemplars and from Shelley, in particular, he gleaned patterns of symbols: caves, sages, rivers, journeys, shells, towers, winds, and the eagle and the serpent. He did not use all these symbols himself but he learned how a symbol can be introduced to the reader, then developed, repeated and echoed in a way comparable with Wagner's deployment of *Leitmotivs*. Another recurring feature of many Romantic poems which has clear connections with Symbolist practice is synaesthesia, where a sensation derived through one sense is described in terms of one of the other senses. Shelley's poetry is rich in synaesthesia; for example, in lines from 'The Sensitive Plant':

And the hyacinth purple, and white, and blue,
Which flung from its bells a sweet peal anew
Of music so delicate, soft and intense,
It was felt like an odour within the sense.

In Yeats's early prose, synaesthesia is common but, curiously, it is not frequent in the poems.

Often in his autobiographical writings and in letters there are discussions of a major clash with his father on the subject of religion. His father was persuaded by the new scientists, Darwin, Huxley and Tyndall, who had called into question a fundamentalist reading of the Bible, its claims concerning the physical laws of the universe, and hence the authority of traditional Christianity. Yeats felt thwarted and deprived by the strength of the atheistic or agnostic (Huxley's coinage) fashion around him and, as a result,

I had made a new religion, almost an infallible Church of poetic tradition, of a fardel of stories, and of personages, and of emotions, inseparable from their first expression, passed on from generation to generation by poets and painters with some help from philosophers and theologians. I wished for a world where I could discover this tradition perpetually.

Certainly by the age of 20 he was well on his way to constructing a religious alternative to what he saw as the emptiness and bleakness of atheism in religion and Realism in art. By the age of 20 he had helped to establish the Dublin Hermetic Society. His father was upset by his son's involvement in magical practices and, in 1892, persuaded John O'Leary, so deeply respected by Yeats, to write to him to see sense. Yeats replied forcefully:

As to Magic. It is surely absurd to hold me 'weak' or otherwise because I chose to persist in a study which I decided deliberately four or five years ago to make, next to my poetry, the most important pursuit of my life. Whether it be, or be not, bad for my health can only be decided by one who knows what magic is and not at all by any amateur. The probable explanation however for your somewhat testy postcard is that you were at Bedford Park and heard my father discoursing about my magical pursuits out of the immense depths of his ignorance as to everything that I am doing or thinking. If I had not made magic my constant study I could not have written a single word of my Blake book, nor would *The Countess Kathleen* have ever come to exist. The mystical life is the centre of all that I do and all that I think and all that I write.

Many critics, in assessing Yeats's work, have either tried to ignore the esoteric side or have given it a patronising pat on the head, as if to say, 'Poets will have their eccentricities – and we must remember that he was Irish – but they do not really interfere with the poetry.' Neither of these positions is tenable in a serious consideration of Yeats. He may well have held some views and engaged in activities that most readers would find daft, but his involvement in what he called Magic was as he stated in the letter, integral to his life and work. What did he take 'Magic' to mean? In an essay in 1901 entitled 'Magic' he tries to explain:

> I believe in the practice and philosophy of what we have agreed to call magic, in what I must call the evocation of spirits, though I do not know what they are, in the power of creating magical illusions, in the visions of truth in the depths of the mind when the eyes are closed; and I believe in three doctrines, which have, as I think, been handed down from early times, and been the foundations of nearly all magical practices. These doctrines are:–
>
> (1) That the borders of our mind are ever shifting, and that many minds can flow into one another, as it were, and create or reveal a single mind, a single energy.
> (2) That the borders of our memories are as shifting, and that our memories are a part of one great memory, the memory of Nature herself.
> (3) That this great mind and great memory can be evoked by symbols.

Here we have a statement not just about magic but also about symbolism; the two were inseparable for Yeats.

What did his involvement in magic entail? For the moment, the question will be answered by charting the figures, societies and activities with which he was associated. A second answer will be offered later. In his late teens Yeats began to discuss with friends various sources of knowledge alternative to the teachings of Christianity and modern science. He learned much from a visit to

Dublin in late 1885 of the Brahmin Mohini Chatterjee. Although Yeats was not then enticed into the Upanishads, he did help to translate them in the 1930s. About the age of 20 he, with his friends, came on two books by A. P. Sinnett, *The Occult World* and *Esoteric Buddhism*. These books explain the basis of, and evidence for, theosophical views, particularly those of Madame Blavatsky, whom Sinnett had met in India. Extraordinary powers are available to human beings, if a process of self-development is followed, and such powers are used by the Tibetan Brotherhood, the Masters who had instructed Blavatsky. Helena Petrovna Blavatsky, the founder of the Theosophical Society in 1875, was in her mid-fifties when Yeats met her first in 1887. Born in southern Russia, she had travelled in India and Tibet. In 1877 she published *Isis Unveiled* and in 1888 *The Secret Doctrine*. Although some of her sayings and exploits sound totally ridiculous, and accusations, probably well-founded, of fraud were levelled against her by the Society of Psychic Research, she was widely read in the occult tradition and Yeats was impressed by the total scheme of life proposed in her books and by her own personality. Her system is based on the idea of a constant clashing of polarities and the development of each soul through a series of reincarnations. In *Autobiographies* he describes his impressions of her: 'a sort of old Irish peasant woman with an air of humour and audacious power... . A great passionate nature, a sort of female Dr Johnson, impressive, I think, to every man and woman who had themselves any richness, she seemed impatient of the formalism and the shrill abstract idealism of those about her, and this impatience broke out in railing and many nicknames.' She weighed almost 17 stone and her features were, according to herself, Kalmneko-Buddhisto-Tartaric. His descriptions of attending theosophical sessions at her house suggest that he enjoyed a spectacle, a show, sometimes preposterous or comic, sometimes uncanny; he seems unpersuaded about her Masters and the total enterprise but certainly respectful of her readings of people and her spiritual genius, whether it was intuitive or given by Tibetan Masters. He had joined the Esoteric Section of the Theosophical Society when she established it in 1888 but he was expelled two years later for conducting psychic experiments without the Section's approval. Madame Blavatsky, described by Yeats as a chain-smoker with a huge, shapeless body, died in 1891.

It would be extremely difficult to attribute particular aspects of Yeats's writings to the specific influence of Madame Blavatsky: her

Theosophical theories overlap and interact with his reading in other mystical writers and with his other occult involvements. Some months before his expulsion from the Esoteric Section of the Theosophical Society, he had been initiated into the Hermetic Order of the Golden Dawn. The Golden Dawn was more concerned with ritual, demonstrations of psychic power and a hierarchy of secrets than was the Theosophical Society, part of whose function was to preach a new gospel and attract converts. It was also more firmly based on a European or quasi-Judaic–Christian tradition with additional rites and ceremonies derived from Egyptian sources: the London branch was called the Isis-Urania Temple. Some of the prominent members were, or had been, Freemasons and a connection was claimed with the Rosicrucian Movement. This latter has been traced back to the mysterious or invented figure of Christian Rosenkreuz, possibly in the fifteenth century, when various people – Paracelsus, Bacon, Dürer, Henry Cornelius Agrippa, Edmund Spenser, John Dee – have been linked, particularly in the fascinating studies by Frances A. Yates, with its body of secret knowledge. The mystical writings of mediaeval Jewish scholars known as the Cabbala, alchemical notions of transmutation, devices for summoning spirits and with their help transcending the usual human constraints – all these fed into the Golden Dawn. Although there is strong speculation that the name Rosenkreuz is really *ros crux*, dew being deemed the strongest solvent of gold in alchemy and the cross being the symbol of light, Yeats appears to have accepted the name as a mingling of rose and cross and he uses the tension between these two forces in his collection *The Rose* (1893). The opening poem is entitled 'To the Rose upon the Rood [cross] of Time'. He remained a member of the Order through many rows, scandals and schisms till the early 1920s, shortly before it finally collapsed. There were three main stages of initiation, with various sub-divisions, and each one had its examinations for which the member had to prepare; Yeats eventually reached high up the second stage. He spent an enormous amount of his energies in the practices and organisation of the Order and many of his most regular correspondents were people exchanging information on such matters.

One of the leading members of the Order was Samuel Liddell Mathers, who adopted the name MacGregor Mathers, 'Comte de Glenstrae'. (He claimed that a Scottish ancestor had been given the title by Louis XV. With the title he took to wearing extravagant

Highland dress.) In many ways he epitomises the seriousness and the silliness of the Order. Many of the rituals, symbols and ceremonies were devised by him from an extensive knowledge of the religious lore of the Ancient Egyptians, Freemasonry (he was a mason) and the esoteric tradition through Madame Blavatsky. He was also interested in psychic experiments and Yeats cooperated with him on many occasions. In 1892 he and his French wife, Moina (the sister of the philosopher Henri Bergson) settled in Paris but remained active in the London temple, till he was eventually expelled in 1900. Expulsion is a corollary of secret societies, and a repeated feature of such grandiose ventures is the extraordinary pettiness of many of the participants. His follower Aleister Crowley had been sent to London to take possession of the Order's inner vault but, despite Crowley (who called himself 'The Beast') wearing a mask and Highland dress, Yeats (with the help of the police) succeeded in evicting him. MacGregor Mathers fell into poverty, drink and obscurity. His death in 1914 was rumoured to have been caused by a psychic duel with Crowley. Looking back on their relationship, Yeats, as he had with Madame Blavatsky, experienced very ambivalent feelings. He had respect for the erudition of Mathers' book, *The Kabbala Unveiled* (1887) and he saw a dignity and integrity in him under all the nonsense. He also credited Mathers with giving him an insight into the greater mind, what he called *anima mundi*, which features so prominently in his poetry: 'It was through him mainly that I began certain studies and experiences, that were to convince me that images well up before the mind's eye from a deeper source than conscious or sub-conscious memory.'

There is one further element to his development as a symbolist poet. A mutual acquaintance of Mathers and Yeats was William Sharp. Sharp was a journalistic writer from Lowland Scotland who, as a result of holidays spent in the Gaelic-speaking Highlands, came to develop a Celtic *alter ego* called Fiona Macleod. He wrote quite differently in his two personae, even to the extent of having different handwriting and separate entries in *Who's Who*. Although Sharp did give a hint of the actual situation in a letter, Yeats firmly believed until after Sharp's death in 1905 that there were two distinct personalities. Under the name Fiona Macleod, adopted in 1894, Sharp wrote a series of romantic-Celtic spiritual novels, plays and essays, beginning with *Pharais, a Romance of the Isles*. This novel appeared a year after Yeats's *The Celtic Twilight* (1893) and Fiona Macleod's output is very much part of an attempt at a Celtic cultural revival, not just in Ireland but also in Wales and Scotland. One of the essays by Fiona Macleod collected in *Studies in the Spiritual History of the Gael* was originally a review of Yeats's *The Shadowy Waters*, and in it he writes:

> Mr Yeats is assuredly of that small band of poets and dreamers who write from no other impulse than because they see and dream in a reality so vivid that it is called imagination. With him the imagination is in truth the second-sight of the mind. Thus it is that he lives with symbols, as unimaginative natures live with facts.[2]

Sharp collected folk-tales in Scotland and he was deeply engaged in psychic phenomena. When they first met in 1887, Yeats disliked the look of Sharp but ten years later wrote: 'I feel that I never properly used or valued this man, through whom the fluidic world seemed to flow, disturbing all; I allowed the sense of comedy, taken by contagion from others, to hide from me my own knowledge. To look at his big body, his high colour, his handsome head with the great crop of bristly hair, no one could have divined the ceaseless presence of that fluidic life.'[3] In *Autobiographies*, Yeats recounts a bizarre story related to him by Sharp one day in Paris and comments: 'I did not believe him, and not because I thought the story impossible, for I knew he had a susceptibility beyond that of any one I had ever known, to symbolic or telepathic influences, but because he never told me anything that was true; the facts of life disturbed him and were forgotten.' Liar or not about what occurred to him, Sharp confirmed from a Scottish Celtic angle what Yeats believed was there to be found in Ireland.

When considering Yeats's interest in esoteric matters and in folklore it is important to remember that he was very much part of a fashion in both areas. The end of the nineteenth century saw a huge curiosity in paranormal phenomena and many people, who in every other part of their lives seemed conventional and staid, joined societies, engaged in mild experiments or consulted occultists. Even Queen Victoria and Gladstone were rumoured to consult mediums or astrologers. Parallel to that fashion, and for most people unconnected, there was a sudden acceleration in the collection of lore – music, customs, vocabulary, stories – particularly from groups of people still in contact with an oral culture. For Yeats and Sharp and some likeminded people there was an intimate link between the possibilities of alternative knowledge and power (alternative to conventional Christianity and rationalist science) and the different cosmologies to be discovered in societies or parts of society outside the main line of nineteenth-century development. After the Ossianic fashion, which persisted much longer in Continental Europe than in Britain and Ireland, the main nomination of the Celts as a desirable alternative to the main direction of modern Europe came in Ernest Renan's 'The Poetry of the Celtic Races' in 1859. Renan, who wrote lavishly on very large historical and intellectual subjects, achieved massive notoriety for *The Life of Jesus* (1863), the first of seven volumes re-examining the Christian story. His influential essay on the Celts identifies certain characteristics:

> The Celtic race has worn itself out in resistance to its time, and in the defiance of desperate causes. It does not seem as though in any epoch it has had any aptitude for political life .... To them life appears as a fixed condition, which man has no power to alter .... Thence ensues its sadness ... . Its songs of joy and as elegies ... . Sentimental – always ready to react against the despotism of fact.

Renan was himself a Breton but his romantic view of the Celts was taken up and developed by Matthew Arnold in his essay 'On the Study of Celtic Literature' in 1866:

> The Celts, with their vehement reaction against the despotism of fact, with their sensuous nature, their manifold striving, their adverse destiny, their immense calamities, the Celts are the prime authors of this vein of piercing regret and passion.

Arnold writes of the 'magical charm of nature' in Celtic poetry and traces the heart of Romantic poetry back to Celtic sources, as if the Celts had a unique access to the underlying laws of life itself. The first volume of Sir James G. Frazer's huge compilation *The Golden Bough* appeared in 1890. Alexander Carmichael spent the last forty years of the century in collecting orally transmitted lore in Gaelic Scotland and the first volumes of his *Carmina Gadelica* were published in 1900. In Ireland, attempts had been under way for some time to record what were sometimes the last rendering of a song or story before the oral tradition succumbed to social change and education in English.

Between 1888 and 1894 Yeats went out to collect folklore and over the following years he continued this practice, either around Sligo or in Connaught, in cooperation with Lady Gregory. However, from his earliest childhood holiday in Sligo he took a delight in the stories related around him by the country people, harbour pilots and itinerants. He deduced that he had derived this interest from the Middletons, on his mother's side of the family, and he recalled how they always accepted 'the nearest for friends and were always in and out of the cottages of pilots and of tenants'. It was among these people that he heard his first fairy-stories; his appetite for such was thereafter insatiable. In 1888, Ernest Rhys, who was later to be the originator of Dent's Everyman's Library, commissioned Yeats to edit a book of Irish folklore. He worked hard on the project and within the year *Fairy and Folk Tales of the Irish Peasantry* was published. Various related publications took place over the following years, the most famous of which is *The Celtic Twilight* in 1893. One of the stories in the volume appears to be based on an experience related in a letter to Richard Le Gallienne in 1892:

> Last night I had a rather interesting magical adventure. I went to a great fairy locality – a cave by the Rosses sands [near Sligo] – with an uncle and a cousin who is believed by the neighbours and herself to have narrowly escaped capture by that dim kingdom once. I made a magical circle and invoked the fairies. My uncle – a hard headed man of about 47 – heard presently voices like those of boys shouting and distant music but saw nothing. My cousin however saw a bright light and multitudes of little forms clad in crimson as well as hearing the music and the far voices. Once there was a great sound as of little people cheering and stamping with their feet away in the heart of the rock. The queen of the troop came then – I could see her – and held a long conversation with us and finally wrote in the sand 'be careful and do not seek to know too much about us'. She told us before she wrote this however a great deal about the economy of the dim kingdom. One troop of the creatures carried quicken berries in their hands.

(It is odd that they carry quicken berries (rowan or mountain ash) because quicken is a traditional guard against the power of the fairies.) How do we read such an account? Do we believe that Yeats

actually saw or thought he saw, with his uncle and cousin, a gathering of fairies? If we do, what do we understand fairies to be? And
can they communicate with humans? No acquaintance of the poet
has claimed that he lied about mundane events and it seems that we
have to accept that Yeats 'saw' what he described to Le Gallienne.
Furthermore, he had witnesses. His uncle, George Pollexfen, was a
fit but hypochondriacal bachelor with very routine habits who
became interested in magic and astrology because of his nephew.
They conducted experiments together. Uncle George's housekeeper,
Mary Battle, was a source for Yeats of amazing stories: 'She could
neither read nor write and her mind, which answered his gloom
with its merriment, was rammed with every sort of old history and
strange belief. Much of my *Celtic Twilight* is but her daily speech.'
She was gifted with second sight. Yeats was convinced that 'there
must be a tradition of belief older than any European Church, and
founded upon the experience of the world before the modern bias ....
It was this search for a tradition that urged George Pollexfen and
myself to study the visions and thoughts of the country-people ....
These visions, we soon discovered, were very like those we called
up by symbol.' And he records how for Mary Battle, unblinkered
with the modern bias, the ancient myths and legends were still alive
and being re-enacted in the landscape around her.

This habitation in the landscape by mythical figures was crucial
for Yeats, not merely because of his belief in the evocative power of
symbols, but as part of his cultural nationalism and his ambition for
Irish literature. In 'The Celtic Element in Literature' (1902) he
proclaims:

> Literature dwindles to a mere chronicle of circumstance, or pas-
> sionless fantasies, and passionless meditations, unless it is con-
> stantly flooded with the passions and beliefs of ancient times, and
> that of all the fountains of the passions and beliefs of ancient
> times in Europe, the Slavonic, the Finnish, the Scandinavian, and
> the Celtic, the Celtic alone has been for centuries close to the main
> river of European culture.

In 'Ireland and the Arts' (1901) he urges a programme on his fellow-
artists in Ireland:

> The Greeks looked within their borders, and we, like them, have a
> history fuller than any modern history of imaginative events; and

legends which surpass, as I think, all legends but theirs in wild beauty, and in our land, as in theirs, there is no river or mountain that is not associated in the memory with some event or legend; while political reasons have made love of country, as I think, even greater among us than among them. I would have our writers and craftsmen of many kinds master this history and these legends, and fix upon their memory the appearance of mountains and rivers and make it all visible again in their arts, so that Irishmen, even though they had gone thousands of miles away, would still be in their own country.

His own attempt to master Ireland's history and legends did not rely on any power of recall that a magical use of symbols might effect; he embarked in the 1880s on a massive reading programme in available literature and when he found gaps in the literature he persuaded scholars and writers to fill them. Although he was often deeply involved in the immediate political issues of the day, his perspective on Ireland was based on a larger vision, a longer view of what we mean by history. The myths and legends of ancient Ireland, the stories of Cuchulain, Deirdre, Diarmuid and Grania, operate, according to Yeats, like Jungian archetypes and they demonstrate patterns of conduct and imagination which lie behind our individual lives and minds. In the essay 'By the Roadside' in *The Celtic Twilight*, there is a radiant description of the power of traditional song, where he claims that folk-art is 'the oldest of the aristocracies of thought'; the essay also demonstrates how emotionally moved Yeats was by hearing such songs. Sir Samuel Ferguson, who died in 1886, will be considered more fully in Chapter 4, but it is only fair at this stage to point out how crucial he was to Yeats at the very beginning of his literary career. The earliest published essays by Yeats are on Ferguson just after his death. He is given the credit for initiating the attempt to restore Ireland's myths to their proper centrality in the country's modern cultural awareness. His translations, adaptations and poems based on mythic material encouraged the young poet to see a way forward by repossessing the past.

Throughout the 1890s Yeats entertained various schemes by which Ireland could be revitalised spiritually. His mind kept returning to the idea of an elite missionary corps who would operate as a collective receiver for the wisdom of the ages and would also propagate this wisdom. In 1896 he decided that the uninhabited castle on the little island in Lough Key would make an ideal centre for his planned group. With Maud Gonne, George Russell, William Sharp (and Fiona Macleod) and MacGregor Mathers he tried to devise the magic rituals and procedures for his Castle of Heroes, and worked hard on the project without much success till about 1902 when he abandoned the venture. With himself and Maud Gonne as the priest-leaders, it sounds like the training camp run by Laon and Cythna in Shelley's *The Revolt of Islam*. Maud Gonne later described their thinking behind the plan:

> The land of Ireland, we both felt, was powerfully alive and invisibly peopled, and whenever we grew despondent over the weakness of the national movement, we went to it for comfort. If only we could make contact with the hidden forces of the land it would give us strength for the freeing of Ireland.[4]

She imparts a characteristically political slant to the project but the intimate link between the land and the spirit is made abundantly clear.

Parallel to, or continuous with, his plan for a mystical order, Yeats threw himself into schemes intended to raise the consciousness of Irish people, in London as well as in Ireland. His own collections of verse, prose and plays appeared at the rate of more than one a year throughout the 1890s. He also brought out anthologies and editions of other writers' works, older and contemporary folklore and issued a deluge of essays to journals, articles and letters to newspapers, and lectures. One of the first writers whose work he made more readily available was William Carleton (1794–1869), who had complained, 'For nearly a century we were at the mercy of our British neighbours, who probably amused themselves at our expense with the greater license, and a more assured sense of impunity, inasmuch as they knew that we were utterly destitute of a national literature.' Yeats dug out and, it might be claimed, devised a 'national literature'; at this stage in his life he gave little prominence to the Anglo-Irish writers such as Swift, Burke, Goldsmith and Berkeley, whom he would elevate later on, but brought into prominence a writer such as Carleton, of peasant, Irish-speaking people and the traditional oral compositions of the Irishry. He argued and lobbied and fought in innumerable committees, societies and clubs. No one who encountered Yeats in these organising situations complained of vagueness or Celtic Twilit behaviour; he shocked people with his singlemindedness, energy and amazing tenacity.

How can we reconcile this practical and highly-organised committee person with the person seeing miraculous happenings, talking to fairies, in touch with long-dead masters? Some pages back I queried the validity of Yeats's paranormal experiences or, rather, I wondered how his account should be assessed. There was nothing superficial or glibly curious about Yeats's interest in the occult: he would not have remained in an esoteric society for over thirty years merely to indulge a whim. I have tried to indicate that he was deeply serious about the activities of the Order of the Golden Dawn and the area called the Celtic Twilight, and that the two were aspects of one concern: a belief in a dimension beyond the material and historical, and the access available to that dimension through symbols. In his poetry up to, and including *The Wind Among the Reeds*, we can see the interplay of these two areas. He came to be aware that something in the poetry, although it might be consistent and might make perfectly reasonable sense in itself, if read with the appropriate knowledge (of a hermetic tradition), did not quite square with where he actually was in his life. As early as 1888, in a letter to Katharine Tynan, he confided: 'I have noticed some things about my poetry I did not know before ... it is almost all a flight into fairyland from the real world, and a summons to that flight .... It is not the poetry of insight and knowledge, but of longing and complaint – the cry of the heart against necessity.' He cites his poem 'The Stolen Child' as an example. However, underlying Yeats's fascination with the possibilities or actualities of a kind of being apart from the corporeal life, is a trepidation and a caution. Time and time again, in stories in *The Celtic Twilight*, for example, and in other pieces in what is collected in *Mythologies*, if a commitment to the other realm is demanded, he pulls back and a sinister side to that dimension is indicated. Similarly, in the poem 'The Stolen Child', the fairies appear to be leading the child away from human cares and it is only in the final stanza that we realise what the child is losing and that in human terms it is 'solemn eyed' because it is dead. In *The Wanderings of Oisin* all the gaiety, battles and repose of the other world prove an inadequate substitute for life with the Fenians.

Just as Yeats's interest in the esoteric can be seen as an extension of a fashion of the period, equally his delight in a Celtic heritage was partly shaped by a European vogue. This consideration does not dismiss, or belittle Yeats's own seriousness of study and the eagerness of his quest; to give him his due, however, he often conceded that this impulse of his life had to be balanced by other pressures.

3
Yeats and Politics

'W. B. Yeats is known as a literary enthusiast, more or less of a revolutionary, and an associate of Dr Mark Ryan.' So reads a police report in Dublin Castle dated October 1899.[1] (Dr Ryan was the main organiser of the Irish Republican Brotherhood, which could be seen as a continuation of the Fenians of the 1850s and Clan na Gael of the 1880s, and something of a precursor of Sinn Fein, set up in 1905, and the later Irish Republican Army.) In 1936, in a letter to Dorothy Wellesley, Yeats writes: 'Besides, why should I trouble about communism, fascism, liberalism, radicalism, when all, though some bow first and some stern first but all at the same pace, all are going down stream with the artificial unity which ends every civilization? Only dead sticks can be tied into convenient bundles.' Is there any consistency in his political stance over the years? Was the police report accurate? Was Yeats in 1936 reliable? After all, most affectionate letters are written with the sentiments of the addressee in mind.

In Ireland, more than in most other places, a declaration of a political stance is deemed insufficient as a guarantee of correctness. Credentials must be displayed in the form of proper responses to historical events and personages, not simply in the current generation or even century, but going back to the fated love of Dermot MacMurrough and Dervorgilla through which the Normans under Strongbow became masters of eastern Ireland around 1170. Yeats's poignant play, *The Dreaming of the Bones*, written in 1917, handles this stain of memory in Irish history. His own credentials were hardly impeccable in relation to his vision of a new Ireland and the role he saw for himself in its creation. His ancestors, on both sides of the family, were of English extraction and continued to see themselves as Irish of a particular sort, Anglo-Irish in fact. Although the term 'The Ascendancy' is often taken to refer only to the aristocratic ruling class of Ireland, from the seventeenth to the late nineteenth century its currency was wider than that, as Roy Foster has shown in the excellent chapter, 'The Ascendancy Mind', in *Modern Ireland 1600–1972*. The term 'Ascendancy' or 'Protestant Ascendancy' emerged in the late eighteenth century and, according to Foster, was centred most firmly on membership of the Church of Ireland, Anglicanism. It admired material success, the display of cultivated taste, had a bastion of training for its young gentlemen in Trinity College, and considered English as its natural language. The relationship with England was always problematic: dependent, resentful, competitive, distrustful; the English in London were deemed, rightly, to be ignorant of Ireland's situation and had to be reminded that the Anglo-Irish were 'no petty people'. The phrase was used by Yeats in 1925 in his speech to the Senate on divorce, a speech in which he insisted to Catholic Ireland that the Anglo-Irish tradition had made a vital contribution to the culture of modern Ireland. To people brought up in this tradition, there were difficulties of identification and loyalty. Louis MacNeice was later to dismiss its distinctiveness as merely 'an insidious bonhomie, an obsolete bravado, and a way with horses'. George Russell (AE) felt a helplessness; in a letter to Yeats he complained: 'The Anglo-Irish were the best Irish but I can see very little future for them as the present belongs to that half-crazy Gaeldom which is growing dominant about us.'

Could it be that towards the end of the nineteenth century a momentum of change had become apparent to observant people in Ireland and that the so-called Irish Renaissance, so dominated by offspring of the Ascendancy, was a final desperate manoeuvre for power on the part of the Ascendancy, to rescue what influence it could in the new Ireland? I shall return to this question shortly. Certainly there was a very considerable backlash against the Renaissance and this may, in part, explain the fierceness of the protests against Synge's *The Playboy of the Western World*. How else can we interpret the bitterness in such comments as, '[It] is not a truthful or a just picture of the Irish peasants, but simply the outpouring of a morbid, unhealthy mind ever seeking on the dunghill of life for the nastiness that lies concealed there.'?[2] Daniel Corkery, author of *The Hidden Ireland* (1925) and *Synge and Anglo-Irish Literature* (1931), launched a ferocious and sustained assault on what he saw as the monopolist and blinkered claims of the Anglo-Irish to represent Irish culture and went so far as to declare: 'the ingrained prejudices of the Ascendancy mind are so hard, so self-centred, so alien to the genius of Ireland, that no Ascendancy writer has ever succeeded in handling in literature the raw material of Irish life'. Some Ascendancy writers conceded a defeat and gave up their struggle or even left Ireland. Standish O'Grady lambasted the spine-lessness of his own Protestant landed class:

> Aristocracies come and go like the waves of the sea; and some fall nobly and others ignobly. As I write, this Protestant Anglo-Irish aristocracy, which once owned all Ireland from the centre to the sea, is rotting from the land in the most dismal farce-tragedy of all time, without one brave deed, without one brave word.[3]

Some subsumed their concern with Irish issues into an internation-alist or non-nationalist position. George Bernard Shaw, from early on in his career, moved out of Ireland physically and psychologi-cally and, by 1923 when the new state of Ireland had just come into existence with much pain, he could write:

> Now Ireland is at the moment a regular rag and bottle shop of superseded ideas or superstitions …. There are formidable vested interests in our huge national stock of junk and bilge, glowing with the phosphorescence of romance. Heroes and heroines have risked their lives to force England to drop Ireland like a hot potato. England, after a final paroxysm of doing her worst, has dropped Ireland accordingly. But in doing so she has destroyed the whole stock-in-trade of the heroes and heroines… .
>
> Nationalism must now be added to the refuse pile of supersti-tions. We are now citizens of the world; and the man who divides the race into elect Irishmen and reprobate foreign devils (espe-cially Englishmen) had better live on the Blaskets, where he can admire himself without much disturbance. Perhaps, after all, our late troubles were not so purposeless as they seemed. They were probably ordained to prove to us that we are no better than other people; and when Ireland is once forced to accept this stupendous new idea, good-bye to the old patriotism.[4]

Fortunately or unfortunately, patriotism is not so easily dismissed, whatever it means and whoever chooses to ride it. In 1913 the *Catholic Bulletin* offered its view on the blessing conferred on Ireland by the Renaissance:

> For the past twenty years the Gael has been crying … for help to beat back the Anglicisation he saw dragging its slimy length along – the immoral literature, the smutty postcards, the lewd plays and

the suggestive songs were bad, yet they were merely puffs from the foul breath of a paganized society. The full sewerage from the *cloaca maxima* of Anglicisation is now discharged upon us. The black devil of Socialism, hoof and horns, is amongst us.[5]

Could the *Catholic Bulletin* and Shaw conduct a discussion? And this was before O'Casey wrote his plays. In 1900 D. P. Moran set up the weekly *The Leader* and in its columns attacked every person, institution and event in which any English influence was evident. He even looked back to Daniel O'Connell and Thomas Davis, and accused them of national corruption for using the English language.

As a young man, Yeats was aware of different attitudes in different groups of Irish society, different readings of the past, different linguistic frameworks. In *Autobiographies* he writes of what he felt when he was about 20:

I had noticed that Irish Catholics among whom had been born so many political martyrs had not the good taste, the household courtesy and decency of the Protestant Ireland I had known, yet Protestant Ireland seemed to think of nothing but getting on in the world. I thought we might bring the halves together if we had a national literature that made Ireland beautiful in the memory, and yet had been freed from provincialism by an exacting criticism, a European pose.

What an odd phrase: 'made Ireland beautiful in the memory'. What about the atrocities and suffering in its history? What about the savage depletion of its population through starvation, disease and emigration? What about the repressions and divisions fostered by the Penal laws and the inequality of opportunity in favour of the minority Protestants maintained by every instrument of government power? When Yeats had his vision of a harmonious Ireland he was very responsive to the guidance of his mentor, John O'Leary, and it was he who introduced him to the poems of Davis, Mangan and Ferguson. O'Leary himself had become a nationalist when he read Davis's poems, although he made no claim for their literary merit. In 1842, Thomas Davis (1814–45) had founded *The Nation*, an organ for nationalist ideas, and was a leading figure in the Young Ireland Movement which, although shortlived as an organised group, was influential in Ireland and America. Davis's rousing verses, with titles such as 'A Nation Once Again', 'We Must not Fail' and 'A Song for the Irish Militia', did not particularly impress Yeats but he was moved by Davis's plea for cooperation, even if the words were trite:

> Landlords fooled us;
> England ruled us,
> Hounding our passions to make us their prey;
>> But in their spite,
>> The Irish UNITE,
> And Orange and Green will carry the day!

His strenuous efforts, and he lived only to the age of 31, to bring the religious groups and the languages together inspired many people to a new awareness of Irish history and, more especially, of the part songs could play in a national movement.

James Clarence Mangan (1803–49) was a very eccentric figure, with an undeniable but inconstant poetic genius. Educated by a priest and competent in several languages (but not Irish), he worked in the library of Trinity College. Poems, translations and adaptations appeared in *The Nation* and *Dublin University Magazine* but it appears that his life was blighted by illness, alcoholism and opium addiction. Some of his own poems have a macabre power and in such pieces as 'The Nameless One' and 'Siberia' there is a chilly blankness. He was interesting to Yeats, however, more for what he made of poems and songs originally in Irish and often anonymously composed. The original Irish on which he based his most famous poem, 'Dark Rosaleen', had been straightforwardly translated by Ferguson but Mangan developed an aspect of the original and produced a poem which is much more in the *Aisling* tradition than Ferguson's version. Briefly, the *Aisling* is a vision poem in which Ireland is a lover who waits to be freed from a cruel oppressor. Ferguson saw the original as an ordinary love poem; in Mangan, Rosaleen takes on a political burden and his poem concludes on an apocalyptic, even a resurrectionist note:

> O! the Erne shall run red
>> With redundance of blood,
> The earth shall rock beneath our tread,
>> And flames wrap hill and wood,
> And gun-peal, and slogan cry,
>> Wake many a glen serene,

> Ere you shall fade, ere you shall die,
>   My Dark Rosaleen!
>   My own Rosaleen!
> The Judgement Hour must first be nigh,
> Ere you can fade, ere you can die,
>   My Dark Rosaleen!

Although Yeats, in a note on the symbolism of the rose in his collection *The Rose*, specifically separates his symbolism from that of Mangan, there is, for me, an element of the *Aisling* tradition and Mangan in some of the *Rose* poems. The figure of Maud Gonne, the beloved, is very much part of the Rose, and she is often taken by the poet to represent Ireland.

Of the poets recommended by O'Leary, it was to Sir Samuel Ferguson (1810–86) that Yeats owed his biggest debt. Ferguson was born to a Protestant Scottish-Irish family in Belfast but he was educated at Trinity College and lived in Dublin as a lawyer. In 1867 he was appointed Deputy Keeper of the Irish Records and in 1878 was knighted for his archaeological/archivist work. Over a long career he produced a considerable body of poetry, translations and essays both scholarly and contentious, though very little of the work of this central figure in Irish culture is readily available to the ordinary reader today. Under a staid exterior he was a man with a complicated psychology. He put his Irishness before his Protestantism, and part of his impact was made by his redrawing of the tribal lines. His appeal was to his own class, the Anglo-Irish, and we must remember that he developed his views in the 1830s before the Famine and before legislation designed to equalise the opportunities of all people in Ireland:

> We address in these pages the Protestant wealth and intelligence of the country, an interest acknowledged on all hands to be the depository of Ireland's fate for good or evil. The Protestants of Ireland are wealthy and intelligent beyond most classes, of their numbers, in the world: but their wealth has hitherto been insecure, because their intelligence has not embraced a thorough knowledge of the genius and disposition of their Catholic fellow-citizens. The genius of a people at large is not to be learned by the notes of Sunday tourists. The history of centuries must be gathered, published, studied and digested, before the Irish people can be known to the world, and to each other, as they ought to be. We hail, with daily-increasing pleasure, the spirit of research and

liberality which is manifesting itself in all the branches of our national literature, but chiefly in our earlier history and antiquities – subjects of paramount importance to every people who respect, or even desire to respect themselves.

This quotation comes from a series of articles on Irish poetry contributed to the *Dublin University Magazine* in 1834, eight years before Davis started *The Nation*. He was writing with the Protestant Ascendancy still very much the dominant 'partner' in Irish affairs; what is revolutionary about his proposal is that he asks, or perhaps demands, that in the interests of harmony and security for all, the dominant group must come to a proper understanding of a despised majority and that, to do so, they must learn the language, literature and culture of that majority. Ferguson himself learned Irish and sought to make the ancient literature of Gaelic Ireland available through translation to the widest possible audience. Listening, however, would not be enough: the process would need to go further and deeper. There had been translations from the Irish before, but they are often effete and prettified: the aim of previous translators seemed to be to make old, rough, uncivilised writing into something decent and acceptable to the taste of a modern reader. Although, by our standards, many of Ferguson's translations and versions are tame and modest compared with the original, he did make an effort to present the poetry as the expression of a different culture and he did try to catch some of the rhythms natural in Irish, unusual in English poetry. His translations persuaded Yeats that the old Irish poets wrote in a very explicit way, not in the vague, rather abstract manner of MacPherson's Ossian. Something of Ferguson's rebuke to the narrowness of his own Ascendancy class rubbed off on Yeats and the richness and drama of the old epics put the pretensions and barriers of modern Ireland in perspective. In the final poem of *The Rose* collection, 'To Ireland in the Coming Times', the young writer locates himself:

Know that I would accounted be
True brother of a company
That sang, to sweeten Ireland's wrong,
Ballad and story, rann and song
...
Nor may I less be counted one
With Davis, Mangan, Ferguson, ...

In the literary and cultural chain there appears to be a gap between the 1840s and the 1880s. Although Ferguson continued to write his heroic verse tales into the 1880s the excitement of the earlier period and the Young Ireland enthusiasm seemed to wane or take a different direction. In fact, events overwhelmed ideas. The Famine, from 1845 when the blight in potatoes was noticed, led to horrifying suffering and to desperate political actions. During the following generation, major disturbances broke out, new militant groups were formed, legislation was introduced to enlarge the electorate, facilitate the purchase and holding of land by Catholics, fix rents and disestablish the Church of Ireland. Murders took place, the Land League was organised, the Boycott campaign ostracised unscrupulous landlords, and the general divisiveness created the opportunity for Parnell's spectacular rise to dominance. Conditions in the period after the Famine were shockingly described by visitors to the island. Carlyle saw the workhouse at Westport as 'the acme of human swinery'. Charles Kingsley offers a picture of rural degradation in 1860 which is as revealing about his own attitudes as it is descriptive of the unfortunate people:

I am haunted by the human chimpanzees I saw along that hundred miles of horrible country. I don't believe they are our fault. I believe there are not only more of them than of old, but that they are happier, better, more comfortably fed and lodged under our rule than they ever were. But to see white chimpanzees is dreadful; if they were black, one would not feel so much, but their skins, except where tanned by exposure, are as white as ours.[6]

The degree of compassion in these comments is difficult to gauge and in many cartoons of the time, for example, by John Tenniel (the illustrator of *Alice's Adventures in Wonderland* and *Through the Looking Glass*) the Irish were often portrayed as apes or animals. In his poems and plays, Yeats makes very few references to the events and conditions of the nineteenth century. However, two of his most celebrated plays can be related to the period and certainly they were considered extremely topical when they were produced. *The Countess Cathleen* [originally 'Kathleen'] was written in 1889, published in 1892 but produced on stage only in 1899. The play was written with Maud Gonne in mind shortly after she met Yeats although the story of the play was based on a traditional tale, 'The Countess Kathleen O'Shea', anthologised by him in 1888. (The odd coincidence of the heroine's name being virtually the same as that of Parnell's mistress, paraded through the divorce court in 1890, cannot have been missed by audiences in Ireland.) In structure and subject it is a morality play and, although 'the scene is laid in Ireland in old times', connections with recent and, indeed, current events were obvious. The saintly Countess gives up her wealth and finally sells her soul to the Devil in exchange for the lives of the peasants, beset with famine. Maud Gonne who, Yeats hoped, would play the Countess, had already sacrificed much of herself, possibly her soul, according to Yeats, to help peasants faced with starvation and eviction in Donegal and Mayo. Her autobiography opens with the ringing affirmation:

> I was returning from Mayo triumphant. I had stopped a famine and saved many lives by making the people share my own belief that courage and will are unconquerable, and where allied to the mysterious forces of the land, can accomplish anything. Had I not seen death and despair recede![7]

The production opened amid fierce controversy. Various nationalist and religious groups resented the play's content and a pamphlet, *Souls for Gold*, claimed that the 'pseudo-Celtic drama' was blasphemous and degraded, a moral danger to any Irishman, and that it was written for an English market. Threats of disruption and riot were made and Yeats organised police protection for the opening.

In 1902 his *Cathleen Ni Houlihan* was first performed, with Maud Gonne in the title role. The play had a mesmeric effect on audiences. Some critics complained that Maud Gonne made no attempt to act but addressed the audience as a political agitator; others felt that her statuesque beauty was the very embodiment of Ireland, and to the Dublin crowds she became Cathleen Ni Houlihan. Cathleen is the female figure of Ireland in the *Aisling* poems, otherwise known as Shan Van Voght (Sean Bhean Bhochd: the wretched old woman). In the play she has lost her fields to the foreigner and needs help to regain them. When the young man in the play agrees to sacrifice himself in fighting for her she is transformed from being a poor old woman to being a beautiful young queen:

Peter: Did you see an old woman going down the path?
Patrick: I did not, but I saw a young girl, and she had the walk of a queen.

Stephen Gwynn, a friend of Yeats, was disturbed by the play
when he saw the first performance and wondered, 'if such plays
should be produced unless one was prepared for people to go out
to shoot and be shot. Yeats was not alone responsible ... above all
Miss Gonne's impersonation had stirred the audience as I have
never seen another audience stirred'[8]. Others spoke of the play
as like a religious sacrament and saw the occasion as a major
turning-point in Irish political consciousness. Yeats himself in the
poem of self-examination, 'The Man and the Echo', written in
1938, asks:

> Did that play of mine send out
> Certain men the English shot? [in 1916]

How did the poet of the Celtic Twilight, of the escapist
Innisfree, of hermetic symbolist poems, come to be at the very
heart of the political struggle in Ireland? In his lecture in
Stockholm in 1923 while receiving the Nobel Prize, he offered
some explanation:

> The modern literature of Ireland, and indeed all that stir of
> thought which prepared for the Anglo-Irish war, began when
> Parnell fell from power in 1891. A disillusioned and embittered
> Ireland turned from parliamentary politics; an event was
> conceived; and the race began, as I think, to be troubled by that
> event's long gestation. Dr Hyde founded the Gaelic League,
> which was for many years to substitute for political argument a
> Gaelic grammar, and for political meetings village gatherings,
> where songs were sung and stories told in the Gaelic language.
> Meanwhile I had begun a movement in English, in the language
> in which modern Ireland thinks and does its business: founded
> certain societies where clerks, working men, men of all classes,
> could study the Irish poets, novelists and historians who had
> written in English, and as much of Gaelic literature as had been
> translated into English. But the great mass of our people, accus-
> tomed to interminable political speeches, read little, and so from
> the very start we felt that we must have a theatre of our own.

This is an interesting piece of history-writing and has some truth in
it although not as much as has been accepted by many followers of
Yeats, including Conor Cruise O'Brien. Certainly the demise of

Parnell and his early death represented a watershed in Irish affairs and he became a shibboleth according to which a person's Irishness could be gauged and categorised (a recurring motif in James Joyce's fiction). Virtually no evidence survives of any interest in Parnell by Yeats before the divorce case in 1890 but immediately after Parnell's death in the following October, Yeats had an obituary poem, 'Mourn – And Then Onward', published in the Parnellite *United Ireland*. The poem concludes:

> Mourn – and then onward, there is no returning,
> > He guides ye from the tomb;
> His memory now is a tall pillar, burning
> > Before us in the gloom.

(The bizarre image of the memory of Parnell as a burning pillar alludes to the pillar of fire at night by which God in the Bible led the Israelites out of Egypt and across the wilderness to the Promised Land.) It is true that the Gaelic League came into being in 1893 but, after four years, only 43 branches had been established; by 1904 there were 600 branches. And other developments took place before Parnell's period of dominance: the Gaelic Athletic Association, for example, was founded in 1884 and Standish O'Grady's seminal work, *History of Ireland: Heroic Period* was published in 1878–80. Furthermore, Yeats's own involvement in practical politics intensified in the 1890s. Apart from his frenetic activity in the various literary societies, which all had contained political aspects and had political repercussions, he was tirelessly engaged in protest and celebratory meetings about political issues and he collected money, organised events and lectured on behalf of such causes as opposition to British action in the Boer War, the centenary of the 1798 Rising, the protests against Queen Victoria's Jubilee and visit to Dublin. Furthermore, he was friendly with many of the activists in the Nationalist struggle and in the attempts to organise trade unions (very late in Ireland) and provide help for people threatened with eviction. He took seriously for several years, from 1896 to 1900, his membership of the Irish Republican Brotherhood. He led his militant friend Maud Gonne into organisations as much as she led him. Increasingly he deplored her incitements to violence and, although his father criticised his dedication to agitation and proselytising, Yeats at this stage of his life remained close to the politics of John O'Leary and even his father.

John O'Leary had once said to him, 'In this country a man must have upon his side the Church or the Fenians, and you will never have the Church.' Yeats certainly courted the Fenian groups and even made some effort not to alienate Catholic opinion. Behind all his wheelings and dealings, however, in the political arena he maintained a programme of reform in Ireland which was primarily cultural. In a speech given in New York in 1904 he offers a vision:

> And then Ireland too, as we think, will be a country where not only will the wealth be well distributed but where there will be an imaginative culture and power to understand imaginative and spiritual things distributed among the people. We wish to preserve an ancient ideal of life. Wherever its customs prevail, there you will find the folk song, the folk tale, the proverb and the charming manners that come from ancient culture. In England you will find a few thousands of perfectly cultivated people, but you will find the mass of the people singing songs of the music hall .... In Ireland alone among the nations that I know you will find, away on the Western sea-board, under broken roofs, a race of gentlemen keep alive the ideals of a great time when men sang the heroic life with drawn swords in their hands.

The key terms in this quotation recur through all of his thinking on politics: 'imaginative and spiritual', 'ancient culture', 'gentlemen', 'heroic life'. Near the beginning of this chapter I asked a question about the Ascendancy's role in the Irish Literary Revival. When one thinks again of Samuel Ferguson and Yeats as Protestants trying to devise a harmonious ideal for Ireland, one realises that they, and others, jump back beyond the ordinarily recorded history of the island to an ancient, heroic time. This jump allows them to ignore the Roman Catholic emphasis in the life of the huge majority of the Irish people for a thousand years. Their vision of Ireland does not include the actual history. It is difficult to conclude that this skirting manoeuvre was not, in part, a desperate ploy by a beleaguered class. And it failed. John O'Leary died in 1907, and in the essay 'Poetry and Tradition', written in that year, Yeats discusses the ideals he and O'Leary had shared. In the essay he makes an assertion which has often been read also as his hope for Irish society:

Three types of men have made all beautiful things. Aristocracies have made beautiful manners, because their place in the world puts them above the fear of life, and the countrymen have made beautiful stories and beliefs, because they have nothing to lose and so do not fear, and the artists have made all the rest, because Providence has filled them with recklessness. All these look backward to a long tradition, for, being without fear, they have held to whatever pleased them.

However simplistic this sounds, he tried to hold on to it but in the new century he accepted that 'power passed to small shopkeepers, to clerks... to men who had risen above the traditions of the countrymen, without learning those of cultivated life or even educating themselves, and who because of their poverty, their ignorance, their superstitious piety, are much subject to all kinds of fear'. This utilitarian ethos of the new Ireland was abhorred by Yeats and in 'September 1913' he snarls sarcastically:

What need you, being come to sense,
But fumble in a greasy till
And add the halfpence to the pence
And prayer to shivering prayer, until
You have dried the marrow from the bone;
For men were born to pray and save:
Romantic Ireland's dead and gone,
It's with O'Leary in the grave.

His disillusionment was not peculiar to him but was shared by many of the Anglo-Irish who had worked alongside him in the Literary Revival in the 1890s: George Russell, O'Leary himself, Standish O'Grady, and Douglas Hyde who seemed so rooted in the rural Ireland of his time, even Hyde who had delivered his inspirational address, 'The Necessity of De-Anglicising Ireland', in 1892, had founded the Gaelic League in the following year, and worked tirelessly for the Irish language, even Hyde became exasperated and in 1915 resigned from the presidency of the Gaelic League because the cause of Irish had, he felt, been commandeered by political and uncultured opportunists.

Throughout his life Yeats felt the pull of opposing ideas of the heroic: the hero as representative of a people; or the hero as solitary, often in opposition to his own people. Writing, late in life, of

Thomas Davis and the poets of *The Nation* in the 1840s, he says: 'They had one quality I admired and admire: they were not separated individual men; they spoke or tried to speak out of a people; behind them stretched the generations.' In the Introduction to his play *Fighting the Waves* (prose version of *The Only Jealousy of Emer*), in 1934, he challenges this view:

> Here in Ireland we have come to think of self-sacrifice, when worthy of public honour, as the act of some man at the moment when he is least himself, most completely the crowd. The heroic act, as it descends through tradition, is an act done because a man is himself, because being himself, he can ask nothing of other men but room amid remembered tragedies, a sacrifice of himself to himself, almost, so little may he bargain, of the moment to the moment.

Although in the first case he is considering authors and in the second he has men of action in mind, he does not always distinguish these when he is thinking of a heroic stance. He was very impressed when O'Leary said, 'There are things that a man must not do to save a nation' and, when Yeats asked what he meant, replied, 'Cry in public'. He appreciated the immediate power of someone who could play a crowd, exploit that collective energy, but his respect was towards the figure daring all without obvious support. His hope for Ireland, soon to be disappointed, was expressed in *Autobiographies* when he talks of the country turning away from 'the bragging rhetoric and gregarious humour of [Daniel] O'Connell's generation and school... to the solitary and proud Parnell'. And his militant friend Maud Gonne, often deplored by him as a rabble-rouser, is heroicised in 'No Second Troy' as 'high and solitary and most stern'. In the decade before the Rising of 1916, events and attitudes seemed to lurch away from his direction and a twistedly Catholic sentimentality came to be associated with violence and suffering. In 1913 Patrick Pearse pronounced: 'The people itself will perhaps be its own Messiah, the people labouring, scourged, crowned with thorns, agonizing and dying, to rise again immortal and impassable.' The same Pearse says: 'We may make mistakes in the beginning and shoot the wrong people; but bloodshed is a cleansing and a satisfying thing, and the nation which regards it as the final horror has lost its manhood.' Yeats's sense of isolation and disappointment re-emerges in 1915 in the rather awkwardly assembled poem, 'The Leaders of the Crowd':

They must to keep their certainty accuse
All that are different of a base intent;
Pull down established honour; hawk for news
Whatever their loose phantasy invent
And murmur it with bated breath, as though
The abounding gutter had been Helicon
Or calumny a song. How can they know
Truth flourishes where the student's lamp has shone,
And there alone, that have no solitude?
So the crowd come they care not what may come.
They have loud music, hope every day renewed
And heartier loves; that lamp is from the tomb.

His query about the heroic, and whether it is primarily solitary or communal, is a worry about his own role in public affairs. While the bloody and dramatic events of the Civil War happened next to his carefully chosen vantage-point, Thoor Ballylee in County Galway, he wondered,

> how many times I could have proved my worth.
> In something that all others understand or share.

He recognised, however, that his 'ambitious heart' would not have been satisfied in such a commitment to the public.

Yeats was very experienced in dealing with the public and with public bodies. After his apprenticeship as instigator and committee member of numerous groupings in the 1890s, he emerged as a prime mover in several major enterprises and a protagonist in several public struggles. His most committing public role was in the theatre. A fuller account of his involvement will be given in Chapter 4 but in the context of this chapter it is necessary to be aware of his activity in helping to create and run an innovative and controversial company. The Abbey Theatre was developed from the Irish National Theatre Society and, before that, the Irish Literary Theatre. There were difficulties to be surmounted of financial backing, a patent for the actual theatre, recruiting of suitable actors and producers, clashes of strong personalities and ideas of what the Company should be aiming for, the choice of dramatists and plays, and the day-by-day management of the Company. At every stage of difficulty, Yeats was totally involved, from checking the night's receipts to confronting the officialdom of the British government. The latter occurrence took place in 1909 when Dublin Castle in the person of His Excellency, the Lord-Lieutenant, attempted to ban the premiere of Shaw's play *The Shewing-up of Blanco Posnet*, on the grounds that it had been banned by the English Censor for performance in England. Claiming that jurisdiction of the English Censor did not extend to Ireland, Yeats, Shaw and Lady Gregory dared the Castle to cancel the Abbey's patent and close the theatre, and they won. The more publicised uproar at the performances of Synge's *The Playboy of the Western World* will be attended to later, but the situation revealed all the skills, guile and ideals that Yeats possessed. When the play opened on 26 January 1907, he was in Scotland on a lecture tour but he returned to Dublin in time for the third night, announced that the play would continue, and that there would be a public discussion on the issues in a week's time. The central issue, as he saw it, was censorship and the necessity not to be bullied into silence. In his speech he denounced some of the very Irish societies he had helped to initiate:

> The generation of young men and girls who are now leaving schools and colleges are weary of the tyranny of clubs and leagues. They wish again for individual sincerity, the eternal quest for truth, all that has been given up for so long that all might crouch upon the one roost and quack or cry in the one flock. We are beginning once again to ask what a man is, and to be content to wait a little before we go on to that further question: What is a good Irishman?

One of the audience later commented, 'I never witnessed a human being fight as Yeats fought that night, nor knew another with so many weapons in his armoury.'[9]

By 1907 he was used to dominating a platform and used to manipulating different kinds of audiences. In 1903–4 he had made his first tour of the United States and Canada. Over a period of several months he delivered lectures in dozens of venues, including many colleges, and had lunch with President Roosevelt. (Some of the money he earned was desperately needed by the Dun Emer Press, which he ran with his sisters and by his impecunious father.) In 1907 he accompanied Lady Gregory and her son Robert on a tour of Northern Italy. Ravenna (later to influence his Byzantium poems), Milan, Ferrara, Florence and Urbino were visited. He had an introduction to Urbino through his reading of *The Courtier* (1528) by

Baldassare Castiglione who set his dialogues, on the subject of the perfect gentleman, in the court of Urbino. The discussions lead to a conclusion that what is required is a blend of artistic, athletic, military, intellectual and moral qualities, carried with modesty and tact. The first Duke of Urbino, Federico da Montefeltro, towards the end of the fifteenth century, and his son Guidobaldo who succeeded him, could have provided models for Castiglione's debate about the balanced Renaissance man. Federico was an excellent military strategist who was able to defend his independence but he had a distinctive intellect and taste with which he created the beautiful Ducal Palace and the surrounding buildings. At his court, scholars and artists were treated with respect. The example of Urbino and its enlightened rulers consolidated in Yeats a notion of leadership, of the taste of a powerful few being able to devise something magnificent and original without concession to cost or public consensus.

From 1905, Yeats was to be exasperatingly enmeshed in a problem which constantly recalled Urbino to his mind but only as a contrast to what happened in Dublin. Lady Gregory's nephew, Hugh Lane, exhibited his strong collection of French paintings, including work by Puvis de Chavannes, Ingres, Pissarro, Renoir, Manet and Vuillard; and made it known that he would like the collection to be housed by Dublin Corporation in a gallery, designed by the English architect (with Irish mother) Lutyens, which would span the River Liffey rather as the Ponte Vecchio does the Arno in Florence. The bridge gallery would cost £22000 to build. His proposal was greeted with waves of denunciation and vituperation, beginning in the clerical newspaper *Irish Catholic* and taken up with vigour in *The Evening Herald* and *The Irish Independent*, two popular daily papers owned by a certain William Murphy. Who wants these foreign paintings? Who says they're better than our Irish pictures? Why should Dublin pay for a monument for picture-dealer Lane? A bridge across the Liffey? By an English architect? Shouldn't all that money go to the poor of the city? And so the campaign continued to thwart Lane's offer to Dublin. In January 1913, Yeats published in the *Irish Times* a fiercely satirical poem with the prosaic title, 'To a Wealthy Man [Lord Ardilaun] who promised a second Subscription to the Dublin Municipal Gallery if it were proved the People wanted Pictures'. Dublin, 'the blind and ignorant town', is contrasted with the Italian cities of the Renaissance and their rulers; they had aimed for the best without kowtowing to the taste of the populace:

And Guidobaldo, when he made
That grammar school of courtesies
Where wit and beauty learned their trade
Upon Urbino's windy hill,
Had sent no runners to and fro
That he might learn the shepherds' will.

He looked back from Lane's offer to the fate of Parnell and noted a connecting villain in the person of William Murphy, the newspaper proprietor and an anti-Parnellite. In 'To a Shade' he addresses the ghost of Parnell and relates to him the new rejection of Lane,

                             A man
Of your own passionate serving kind who had brought
In his full hands what, had they only known,
Had given their children's children loftier thought,
Sweeter emotion, working in their veins
Like gentle blood, has been driven from the place,
And insult heaped upon him for his pains,
And for his open-handedness, disgrace;
Your enemy, an old foul mouth, had set
The pack upon him.

The 'old foul mouth', Murphy, also led in 1913–14 a lock-out of 20 000 workers by 400 employers in a successful attempt to break the power of the recently-formed Irish Transport and General Workers' Union under Jim Larkin and James Connolly. Yeats supported the workers.

Hugh Lane withdrew his offer and lent the paintings to the National Gallery in London. Shortly before he drowned in the sinking of the *Lusitania* in 1915 he wrote a codicil to his will by which he bequeathed the collection to Dublin on condition that a gallery be found for it within five years of his death. This codicil was not witnessed and the struggle for ownership of the paintings continued with strenuous efforts by Yeats and, even more so, by Lady Gregory to regain them for Ireland. It was only in 1979, long after their deaths, that a solution was found by which the paintings are on show alternately in London and Dublin. The Municipal Gallery in Dublin held a room empty until the paintings were returned and the building is now called The Hugh Lane Gallery of Modern Art.

The demise of Parnell, the attacks on the Abbey and Synge's *The Playboy of the Western World*, and the hostility to Lane's gift of his paintings had a cumulative effect in souring Yeats's attitude to the Ireland emerging into the twentieth century. He understood that there could be differences of opinions, taste, priority, expediency; he was aware that sensitive choices have to be made between material benefit to poor people and the gratification of taste and style. What enraged him in the three instances was the hypocrisy, pettiness and vindictiveness of urban Ireland and the crushing power of what we would now call the media when its owners pick on a victim. In a note to *Responsibilities: poems and a play* (1914) he writes:

Religious Ireland – and the pious Protestants of my childhood were signal examples – thinks of divine things as a round of duties separated from life and not as an element that may be discovered in all circumstance and emotion, while political Ireland sees the good citizen but as a man who holds to certain opinions and not as a man of good will. Against all this we have but a few educated men and the remnants of an old traditional culture among the poor. Both were stronger forty years ago, before the rise of our new middle class which made its first display during the nine years of the Parnellite split, showing how base at moments of excitement are minds without culture.

What were Yeats's political attitudes beyond Ireland? In the first place, what was his attitude to England? As a child and schoolboy he had detested London when his family lived there and yet in adult life he spent a considerable proportion of time in England. It is common for colonial powers to see colonies only in relation to the mother country; and for colonised countries to define their identity in terms set by the colonial power. Yeats found the prevailing English view of the Irish parochial and condescending; he was determined from early on to change Ireland's view of itself. Part of the motivation for his expertise in committees, his care in dealing with money, his shift from a Celtic Twilight phase to 'theatre business, management of men', stems from his determination to elude English stereotypes of the Irish. He swung against his own Anglo-Irish background and often identified himself with the 'Irishry' (the other part of Irish culture) as if to defeat glib attempts to categorise him. He was embarrassed at knowing so little Irish but defended his upbringing by saying 'Gaelic is my national language, but it is not my mother tongue.' In the same essay, 'A General Introduction for my Work', written in 1937, he reminds his readers of Lecky's *Ireland in the Eighteenth Century* (1892) in which the historian claims that no people endured greater persecution (from the English) than the Irish and, as a result, Yeats concludes:

> No people hate as we do in whom the past is always alive, there are moments when hatred poisons my life and I accuse myself of effeminacy because I have not given it adequate expression ... then I remind myself that though mine is the first English marriage I know of in the direct line; all my family names are English, and that I owe my soul to Shakespeare, to Spenser and to Blake, perhaps to William Morris, and to the English language in which I think, speak and write, that everything I love has come to me through English; my hatred tortures me with love, my love with hate.

His ambivalent attitude to England and English authority must have struck many observers in 1910 when Yeats and the Abbey Theatre defied official protocol and the total disapproval of their sponsor, Miss Horniman, in keeping the theatre open on the day of Edward VII's death and when, later in the year, he accepted a Civil List pension (given from the Crown). Although he has often been mocked for pretensions to aristocracy and for courting influential members of the English establishment, he refused the offer of a knighthood in 1915 and repeatedly denounced English policies in Ireland; most tellingly at the Oxford Union in 1921, when feelings were running high about the activities of Sinn Fein and the British Black and Tans. In 1914 the Irish Home Rule Bill had, at long last, been passed by the British Parliament, but its implementation had been suspended because of the European situation which shortly led to the First World War. This was why Yeats, after the Easter Rising of 1916, could ask:

> Was it needless death after all?
> For England may keep faith
> For all that is done and said.

In fact, he was in England when the Rising took place and, apparently felt slightly peeved that he had not been consulted or informed in advance. The story of the rather uncoordinated Rising is well-known and its futility in military terms was widely accepted, even by some of those taking part in it. Tension had been mounting for some years, arms and military training pointed to an insurrection and, with Britain engaged in the war in Europe, the old adage, 'England's weakness, Ireland's opportunity', came into play. The Rising and its immediate aftermath shocked Yeats in two main ways. First, his disillusionment with the new Ireland, expressed in such poems as 'September 1913', 'Paudeen' and 'To a Shade', was severely jolted by the preparedness of people he knew (and had come to take for granted) to sacrifice themselves for an ideal. As he had listed the heroes of 1798, Edward Fitzgerald, Robert Emmet and Wolfe Tone, so he now had to revise his view of his contemporaries and list them as something special:

> I write it out in a verse –
> MacDonagh and MacBride
> And Connolly and Pearse
> Now and in time to be,
> Wherever green is worn,
> Are changed, changed utterly:
> A terrible beauty is born.

Second, he was disgusted at the brutal manner of the executions of the arrested leaders but realised that this very brutality had translated the leaders into martyrs whose authority in death was quite beyond any power they had exerted in life. Perhaps Pearse had been right: the Rose Tree of Irish independence could bloom only with the fertilising help of a blood sacrifice. Yeats did not support violence as a political weapon but he had to concede that the Rising had achieved something. In 'Easter 1916' he wrestles with the paradox: only a stone (the fanatic heart) can alter the flow of the stream but to be a stone is to lose humaneness. The poem plays off against one another different senses of 'change', active and passive. In the subsequent years of retribution and civil war the same dilemma haunted him and the question recurred as to whether or not the new, independent Ireland could be achieved without corrosive hatred. In 'Meditations in Time of Civil War' he muses as he thinks of the killings:

> We had fed the heart on fantasies,
> The heart's grown brutal with the fare;

> More substance in our enmities
> Than in our love;

And earlier in 'Nineteen Hundred and Nineteen' he confesses:

> We, who seven years ago
> Talked of honour and of truth,
> Shriek with pleasure if we show
> The weasel's twist, the weasel's tooth.

With the inauguration in 1922 of the Free State and the effective acceptance of partition from Northern Ireland, the violence did not come to a halt and the repercussions of these times rumble on seventy years later. Yeats could not resolve his question about hatred and in his old age sometimes saw hatred as necessary, as a corollary of love:

> When I stand upon O'Connell Bridge [Dublin] in the half-light and notice the discordant architecture, all those electric signs, where modern heterogeneity has taken physical form, a vague hatred comes up out of my own dark and I am certain that wherever in Europe there are minds strong enough to lead others the same vague hatred arises; in four or five or in less generations this hatred will have issued in violence and imposed some kind of rule of kindred. I cannot know the nature of that rule, for its opposite fills the light; all I can do to bring it nearer is to intensify my hatred. I am no Nationalist, except in Ireland for passing reasons; State and Nation are the work of intellect, and when you consider what comes before and after them they are, as Victor Hugo said of something or other, not worth the blade of grass God gives for the nest of the linnet.

This large generalising tendency is typical of his last phase and why, for him, 'The Second Coming' was an explicitly political poem. There are few references in the poems after *The Tower* (1928) to contemporary events and he subsumes particular incidents and reaction to them into his scheme of cyclical development. A note of cynical disdain for puny political aspirations is now heard in the poetry as if he feels obliged to counter the glib optimism uttered by political leaders of the 1930s. The pendulum of historical change offers little consolation to the ordinary man. The title of a short piece, 'The Great Day', is heavily ironic:

Hurrah for revolution and more cannon shot;
A beggar upon horseback lashes a beggar upon foot;
Hurrah for revolution and cannon come again,
The beggars have changed places but the lash goes on.

For many readers, Yeats's detachment from local disasters seems cold or even cruel and, in reading 'Lapis Lazuli' (written 1936), they find themselves sharing the anxiety of the 'hysterical women' who are frightened that 'Aeroplane and Zeppelin will come out,/ Pitch like King Billy bomb-balls in/Until the town lie beaten flat'. Against the common hysteria, Yeats presents the gaiety of the artist and the contemplative mind, 'Gaiety transfiguring all that dread'. By 'gaiety', probably derived from Nietzsche, he means a heroic acceptance of, and nonchalance towards, whatever comes. In the 1930s and, remembering his often expressed dislike of democratic consensus and his brief association with O'Duffy's Fascist Blueshirts in 1933, it has been easy to brand Yeats as a fascist. The label is accurate enough if it means a believer in rule of the many by the enlightened few; it is not accurate if the brutalities and racial discriminations of Nazism are made synonymous with fascism. In common with other intellectuals he felt obliged to choose between Communism and Fascism and in common with many such as Lawrence, Eliot, Pound and even MacDiarmid, he found much to admire in the early stages of Mussolini's rule in Italy. His flirtation with the Blueshirts lasted only a few months and he quickly became disillusioned with the insignificant General O'Duffy. He was opposed to the materialism and appeal to the masses of Communism, and in his own intellectual explorations, provocatively expressed in *On the Boiler* (1937–39), he fumbled with ideas on genetic planning and social engineering. Also in some of the *Broadsides* he published songs which contain a violent ranting. However, if one looks back to his participation as a Senator in the Free State between 1922 and 1928, he stood firmly against censorship in any form and opposed discrimination by the state against any individual's freedom, irrespective of ethnic or class origin.

It was while he was a Senator and vexed by a precarious balance between government order and repression in an unruly, violent situation, that Yeats discovered a part of Ireland's literary and political tradition which he had bypassed earlier. He came to see Swift, Berkeley, Goldsmith and Burke as foundations to a spirit of free enquiry, figures who had shaped a notion of Ireland's separateness from England but without parochialness. They were, according to him, the intellects on whom a commendable Anglo-Irish tradition was based, a tradition of good order and spacious thinking, exemplified for him in some of the Georgian mansions set in landscaped estates. It was this side of Ireland that he wished to splice more firmly on to the Gaelic tradition and this wish forms part of his poetic testimony, 'Under Ben Bulben', written some months before his death:

> Irish poets learn your trade
> Sing whatever is well made,
> Scorn the sort now growing up
> All out of shape from toe to top,
> Their unremembered hearts and heads
> Base-born products of base beds.
> Sing the peasantry, and then
> Hard-riding country gentlemen,
> The holiness of monks, and after
> Porter-drinkers' randy laughter;
> Sing the lords and ladies gay
> That were beaten into the clay
> Through seven heroic centuries;
> Cast your mind on other days
> That we in coming days may be
> Still the indomitable Irishry.

4

Yeats and the Theatre: 'Baptism of the Gutter'

In the period from the late seventeenth century to the twentieth century, writers of Irish origin provided a contribution to the English theatre totally out of proportion to the population in Ireland and unexpected in that there was no indigenous Irish theatre in all that period. Congreve, Farquhar, Goldsmith, Sheridan, Wilde and Shaw each had an Irish beginning. Not that London in the eighteenth and nineteenth centuries was a hotbed of serious plays. New plays tended to be farces and melodramas and Shakespeare's plays were presented in very curious guises; however, by the middle of the nineteenth century it would have been possible to see less adulterated productions of Shakespeare, and *Macbeth* was actually produced without song and dance routines. New plays attempting to examine difficult subjects were not so lucky; for example, Shelley's *The Cenci*, which analyses the connection between power and morality in the Church, the family and sex, was written in 1820 but remained under the ban of the censor for a century. (A 'private' performance was given by the Shelley Society to an invited audience of 2400 in Islington in 1886.) Yeats located a shift in the English theatre in the works of T. W. Robertson performed in the 1860s. Plays with titles such as *Society, Caste, School* and *M.P.* were contrived comedies, but Robertson tried to use a more natural, contemporary dialogue. It was not, however, to England that Yeats looked for inspiration or instruction when he became interested in writing plays.

Many of the most significant developments in European theatre were taking place in locations usually considered as culturally peripheral: Norway, Sweden, Russia. In 1857, Henrik Ibsen was appointed Director of the Norwegian Theatre, established to promote specifically Norwegian drama. Although he had little success in that venture, he was to revolutionise drama in such a way that his work had to be translated into all the major European languages immediately. His first success in Sweden came with the companion verse plays *Brand* and *Peer Gynt* in the 1860s; these remain astonishing works, theatrically innovative, linguistically rich and profound examinations of the puritan and the hedonist mentality. *Peer Gynt* operates through a juxtaposition of folk motifs, psychological speculation and social satire which anticipates the most experimental cinematographic techniques. Wagner's *Ring*, produced during the years immediately following *Peer Gynt*, seems, for all its extraordinary virtuosity, curiously wooden and mechanical beside Ibsen's play. Ibsen's international impact, however, was not made by his verse plays but by his prose plays set in contemporary, middle-class Norway. *Ghosts* and *Hedda Gabler* were first performed in London in 1891 to wild accusations of immorality and filth. His exposure of social and moral hypocrisy affronted some, delighted others and passionate defences were advanced for him by Shaw, Edmund Gosse, William Archer (his main translator) and the young James Joyce. In his late plays he made more central an interest in the development of individual personality, the psychological and social conditioning which shape attitudes, the interplay of conscious and unconscious forces. This fascination with how the past and hidden elements emerge in gestures and linguistic mannerisms and his deployment of symbols mark him as an antecedent of Freud.

Yeats's feelings towards Ibsen were decidedly mixed. In a review of a translation of *Brand* in 1894, he commends the two verse plays, although he is suspicious of the dramatist's use of individual characters as 'the expression of broad generalisations and classifications'. In many places he recommends a study of Ibsen to young Irish dramatists seeking to learn about the construction of plays. He supported the social morality in the plays but detested what he saw as Ibsen's metaphysics of environmental determinism in line with the heretical Huxley, Darwin and Tyndall. His reading of Ibsen was strangely partial in that he did not fully appreciate the poetic vision of the early plays and he failed to read the late plays or, if he did, he failed to see the way in which symbolism deepens the social situation and makes the characters timeless and emblematic, just what Yeats wanted to achieve in his own plays. Surely he did not read *The Lady from the Sea* and *When We Dead Awaken*. In 1889 he saw the first production in England of *A Doll's House* and hated the play and its naturalistic dialogue. In *Autobiographies* he writes:

As time passed Ibsen became in my eyes the chosen author of very clever young journalists, who, condemned to their treadmill of abstraction, hated music and style; and yet neither I nor my generation could escape him because, though we and he had not the same friends, we had the same enemies. I bought his collected works in Mr Archer's translations out of my thirty shillings a week and carried them to and fro upon my journeys to Ireland and Sligo.

He describes *Rosmersholm* as having 'symbolism and a stale odour of spilt poetry'. He seemed to resent the direction Ibsen had taken and saw it as a waste of his talent. In 1906, the year of Ibsen's death, Yeats rejects the dominant drama of the new generation:

> Of all artistic forms that have had a large share of the world's attention, the worst is the play about the modern educated people. Except where it is superficial or deliberately argumentative it fills one's soul with a sense of commonness as with dust. It has one mortal ailment. It cannot become impassioned, that is to say, vital, without making somebody gushing and sentimental. Educated and well-bred people do not wear their hearts upon their sleeves, and they have no artistic and charming language except light persiflage and no powerful language at all, and when they are deeply moved they look silently into the fireplace.

Persiflage, of course, is the very stuff of Oscar Wilde's plays but is uttered by characters who take themselves seriously; characters in Wilde seldom laugh.

For Shaw, Ibsen's most vociferous British champion and follower, Yeats had a grudging respect; the grudge far outweighed the respect. In *Autobiographies* he recalls listening to Shaw's *Arms and the Man* in 1894 'with admiration and hatred. It seemed to me inorganic, logical straightness and not the crooked road of life, yet I stood aghast before its energy.' One of the earliest members of the Fabian Society (he wrote their *Manifesto* in 1884), Shaw seized on Ibsen's plays on social issues and rushed to his defence in *The Quintessence of Ibsenism* (1891). Shaw's first play *Widowers' Houses*, very Ibsenite, was produced without much success in 1892. Largely self-educated, an émigré from Dublin, he was vastly prolific in a variety of writing areas, including five novels, art and music criticism, book and theatre reviewing, lectures and essays. Something about his frenzied activity bothered Yeats deeply and he reveals his feelings in a recounted dream:

I had a nightmare that I was haunted by a sewing-machine, that clicked and shone, but the incredible thing was that the machine smiled, smiled perpetually. Yet I delighted in Shaw, the formidable man. He could hit my enemies and the enemies of all that I loved, as I could never hit, as no living author that was dear to me could ever hit.

In 1900 Yeats discussed with Shaw the possibility of the latter writing a play on the differences between the English and Irish mentalities. When in 1904 *John Bull's Other Ireland* was finished, it was staged in London, not in Dublin, because, according to Shaw, Yeats 'got rather more than he bargained for'. According to Yeats, the scale of the play put it beyond the resources of the Irish Literary Theatre. Shaw, who was a master of having the last word in any argument, also felt that his play was too dangerous for the careful ideological programme of the neo-Gaelic movement. His Preface of 1906, subsequently added to on several occasions, is as provocative and amusing as the play itself. Like his émigré compatriot, Wilde, he delighted in standing received wisdom on its head, particularly the received wisdom of half-educated English people: 'England cannot do without its Irish and its Scots today, because it cannot do without at least a little sanity.' In the play the see-saw of his wit comes close to overbalancing into a more directly political question and the jocularity takes a darker shade when the 'efficient' Englishman, Broadbent, cannot hear his rudeness and bigotry: 'It will be quite delightful to drive with a pig in the car: I shall feel quite like an Irishman.' Broadbent's faith in Ireland is the commercial faith of an exploiter to which the realist Irish Keegan has no viable parallel:

And we have none [i.e. no faith in Ireland]: only empty enthusiasms and patriotisms, and emptier memories and regrets. Ah yes: you have some excuse for believing that if there be any future, it will be yours; for our faith seems dead, and our hearts cold and cowed. An island of dreamers who wake up in your jails, of critics and cowards whom you buy and tame for your own service, of bold rogues who help you to plunder us that they may plunder you afterwards.[1]

When *John Bull's Other Island* was eventually performed at the Abbey Theatre in 1916, it proved immediately successful and has remained extremely popular in Ireland ever since. Whether or not

George Bernard Shaw became something of the very stereotype of an Irish entertainer to the English he so deplored is an open question. For all his wit, inventiveness, dexterity and good sense, there is a disconcerting grain of justice in Yeats's dream of him as a sewing-machine. Where was his emotional centre? Nonetheless, he was the dominant figure in the theatre in London for thirty years and it was his ability to dramatise social ideas that allowed writers such as John Galsworthy in *Strife* (1909) and *Justice* (1910) to examine current political issues on the stage. With his Prefaces and elaborate stage directions, Shaw wrote his plays not just to be seen but also to be read by people who lived far away from theatres.

Shaw presented himself as a propagandist for Ibsen but he also gave his encouragement to Ibsen's eccentric Swedish rival, August Strindberg, and made strenuous efforts, backed by some of his Nobel Prize money in 1925, to have the Swede's work translated into English. Who else but Strindberg could have written: 'My spirit has received in its uterus a tremendous outpouring of seed from Friedrich Nietzsche, so that I feel as full as a pregnant bitch. He was my husband', and 'See how my seed has fallen in Ibsen's brain-pan – and germinated. Now he carries my semen and is my uterus. This is *Wille zur Macht* [will to power] and my desire to set others' brains in molecular motion'? In 1908, Shaw met him in Stockholm and the Swede arranged for a performance of his *Miss Julie* seen only by the two dramatists and Mrs Shaw. Yeats had met him in Paris in 1896 and, years later, wrote:

> I have always felt a sympathy for that tortured, self-torturing man who offered himself to his own soul as Buddha offered himself to the famished tiger. He and his circle were preoccupied with the deepest problems of mankind. He himself, at the time I speak of, was seeking with furnace and athanor for the philosophers' stone.

As the quotations from him indicate, Strindberg had a most bizarre personality, sometimes fanatically religious, sometimes paranoid, always obsessive, but Yeats shared his interest in alchemy, spiritualism, oriental religions, and, of course, theatre. What he knew of his plays is not clear but Strindberg wrote or rewrote several of his works in French and a considerable number of his plays were performed in Paris; *The Father* was first produced (in Yiddish) in London in 1911 and *Miss Julie* was performed in 1912, the year of his death. If the huge range of the fertile Strindberg's work had been available, some of it, particularly the symbolist plays, *The Ghost Sonata*, *A Dream Play* and *To Damascus*, would certainly have excited Yeats. In an introductory note to *A Dream Play* in 1902 (twenty years before the publication of Eliot's *The Waste Land* and Joyce's *Ulysses*), Strindberg writes:

> The author has sought to reproduce the disconnected but apparently logical form of a dream. Anything can happen: everything is possible and probable. Time and space do not exist. On a slight groundwork of reality, imagination spins and weaves new patterns composed of memories, experiences, unbound fancies, absurdities and improvisations. The characters are divided, double and multiply; they evaporate, crystallize, scatter and converge. But a single consciousness holds control over them all – that of the dreamer. For him there are no secrets, no incongruities, no scruples and no law.

This tormented man, who often sounds like a parody of sensationalist Freudianism, comprehended in the gamut of his fecundity every experiment and -ism of twentieth-century literature. Yeats would probably have been particularly interested in Strindberg's attempt to develop an Intimate Theatre in Stockholm where what he called his Chamber Plays were performed.

Various parallel efforts were happening in theatres across Europe in an attempt to free drama from the constraints of the Romantic, ornate, operatic fashion which had dominated for much of the nineteenth century. In the late 1880s, Antoine's Théâtre Libre in Paris was followed by Otto Brahm's Freie Bühne in Berlin and, ten years later in Russia, the Moscow Arts Theatre was established with the help of Stanislavsky. Much of the impetus for this movement went back to the Realist spokesman, Zola and, behind him, the critic and literary historian Hippolyte Taine, famous for his determinist assertion that a literary work is a product of 'la race, le milieu, le moment'. In the 1860s Taine argued:

> The research into causes must come after the collection of facts. It does not matter whether the facts are physical or moral; they will still have causes. There are causes for ambition, courage and truthfulness as there are for digestion, muscular movement and animal warmth. Vice and virtue are products like vitriol and sugar, and every complex element has its origins in the combination of other simpler elements on which it depends.

Zola, in his novels and his bombardment of the literary public with his views, argued the case for a totally different kind of literature grounded in the miserable lives of the majority of working people and in the forces which shape their situations. He saw the theatre, the most public of the arts, as having a crucial role to play in the new dedication to truth. But:

> It would take a powerful personality, an innovator's mind, to overthrow the accepted conventions and finally install the real human drama in place of the ridiculous untruths that are on display today. I picture this creator scorning the tricks of the clever hack, smashing the imposed patterns, remaking the stage until it is continuous with the auditorium, giving a shiver of life to the painted trees, letting in through the backcloth the great, free air of reality.

Although Yeats often declared his admiration for Balzac's vast, minutely detailed and interconnected *Comédie Humaine* and felt that its solidity, its 'realism', was a necessary corrective to flighty, speculative theories, he reacted violently to the Realist and Naturalist writers of his generation. Equally, although he was excited by theatrical happenings, mockeries of conventional dramas and stock expectations in audiences, he had no artistic sympathy with some of the wilder performances, forerunners of what was to develop later as surrealism and the Theatre of the Absurd. In 1896 he attended in Paris the first performance of *Ubu Roi* by Alfred Jarry and in *Autobiographies* he describes what he saw: 'The players are supposed to be dolls, toys, marionettes, and now they are all hopping like wooden frogs, and ... the chief personage, who is some kind of King, carries for sceptre a brush of the kind that we use to clean a [water] closet.' In the row in the theatre caused by Jarry's iconoclasm and vulgarity, Yeats shouted in support of the play but felt dismay at its brutality: 'After Stéphane Mallarmé, after Paul Verlaine, after Gustave Moreau, after Puvis de Chavannes, after our own verse, after all our subtle colour and nervous rhythm ... what more is possible? After us the Savage God.'

His own commitment was to a poetic kind of drama. It is not known what his response was to Chekhov or even if he was acquainted with the plays; Chekhov's plays were available in translation soon after they appeared in Russia but the first production in English took place in Glasgow in 1909. It may be that even the unbusy and more spiritual naturalism of Chekhov would have proved too involved with 'modern educated people', so detested by Yeats. In his earlier phase as a dramatist, the Irishman sought models of a more definitely spiritual drama – plays, as he says in his essay 'The Autumn of the Body' (1898), concerned with 'essences of things, and not with things'. Villiers de l'Isle Adam's *Axel* stood against the Naturalists and the tired comedies of the conservative theatre; it represented for Yeats 'the first great dramatic invention of the new [romanticism]'. His experience of the play was described in Chapter 2 but it needs to be mentioned here because of the encouragement it provided for his developing idea of what he wished to achieve in drama. He felt around him in the 1890s 'an ever more arduous search for an almost disembodied ecstasy', and he saw *Axel* as an expression of this search, a search continued in the ethereal, melancholy plays of the Belgian Maurice Maeterlinck (1862–1949). In Maeterlinck's symbolist dramas the curiously passive characters are figures in a larger, enigmatic struggle of spiritual forces. In Yeats's early plays, *The Countess Cathleen*, *The Land of Heart's Desire*, *The Shadowy Waters* and even *Cathleen ni Houlihan*, this same pattern is evident, and it became clear to him, about the turn of the century, that drama in the theatre requires something much more positive in plot, language and characterisation.

In fact, by 1900, the various strands in his mind – political, literary, Celtic, symbolist – were coming together in his interest in theatre, and a new toughness is signalled in a letter to Lady Gregory in that year: 'In a battle like Ireland's which is one of poverty against wealth, one must prove one's sincerity by making oneself unpopular to wealth. One must accept the baptism of the gutter. Have not all teachers done the like?' (Lady Gregory genteelly replied that she preferred baptism in clean water.) In the context, he was talking of defying the conventional code of decent behaviour identified with their Ascendancy background, and he was also announcing his preparedness to do unseemly things in the theatre if such were demanded by artistic considerations. In this attitude there was an acceptance of the interrelatedness of art and the socio-political situation but, for Yeats, this did not entail an espousal of the Realists' naturalistic theatre. For him, art was central to life at its best but was not a mere reflection of day-to-day existence; he was fond of quoting a maxim from Goethe, 'Art is art because it is not life.'

Theatre is only half a literary art. It cannot exist solely on the genius of a single writer but relies on a cooperation of various skills, financial backing and a physical location. For all his talk of being stern and solitary, the main developments in Yeats's career emerged through his ability to form and work with groups of associates. In 1896, on a tour of the west of Ireland with Arthur Symons, he visited Edward Martyn and Lady Augusta Gregory. Later in the same year he first met John Millington Synge in Paris. These three were to form with Yeats the nucleus of a theatrical movement in Ireland.

Martyn, a friend of George Moore, was a very contradictory person whose life was fraught with problems of taste and conscience. A devout Catholic and a keen Ibsenite, his delight in the theatre was definite but dangerous (to himself). Almost as soon as the Irish Literary Theatre was founded in 1899, he was worried by the religious content of Yeats's *The Countess Cathleen*, threatening to withdraw his financial support from the venture, and was mollified only after priests cleared the play of accusations of blasphemy. Martyn's own plays, *The Heather Field* and *Maeve*, both probably written with substantial advice from George Moore, were considerable successes in the first years of the new theatre but, when Yeats and Lady Gregory were critical of his third play, he backed away from the developing enterprise.

Lady Gregory was made of very different mettle. One of the deftest portraits of her is by Sean O'Casey, although she was 70 years old when he met her:

> There she was, a sturdy, stout little figure soberly clad in solemn black, made gay with a touch of something white under a long, soft, black silk veil that covered her grey hair and flowed gracefully behind half-way down her back. A simple brooch shyly glistened under her throat, like a bejewelled lady making her first retreat, feeling a little ashamed of it. Her face was a rugged one, hardy as that of a peasant, curiously lit with an odd dignity, and softened with a careless touch of humour in the bright eyes and the curving wrinkles crowding around the corners of the firm little mouth. She looked like an old elegant nun of a new order, a blend of the Lord Jesus Christ and of Puck, an order that Ireland had never known before, and wasn't likely to know again for a long time to come.[2]

For all its extravagance and Catholic images, this description does indicate a vitality, strength and daring under the rather staid, matronly exterior. She has often been presented as a frump, a dull literary groupie or a late Ascendancy manipulator, but she was described by Shaw as 'the greatest living Irishwoman' and, on her death in 1932, Yeats lamented that he had lost someone who 'has been to me for nearly forty years my strength and my conscience'. Her proper place in Irish letters has not yet been fully charted and in a recent, much-praised but narrowly Republican survey, *A Short History of Irish Literature* (1986) by Seamus Deane, she receives what amounts to a token mention. Born in 1852 to landed parents at Roxborough, County Galway in 1880 she married Sir William Gregory, many years older than her, who owned the neighbouring estate at Coole Park. He had travelled the world, had been Governor of Ceylon and was scholarly in his interests. Her first publication was a pamphlet written in 1882, arguing the case of an Egyptian nationalist. When her husband died ten years later, she inherited Coole Park and slowly developed as a writer by compiling collections of family papers and her husband's autobiography. When she first met Yeats, in 1895, he encouraged a pleasure she already took in copying out tales and lore from the tenantry on her estate and in the area of Galway called Kiltartan; this material would later be published in several books leading up to the two volumes of *Visions and Beliefs in the West of Ireland* in 1920. Her nationalist sympathies and an excitement in the notion of a cultural revival prompted her to learn Irish and, again encouraged by Yeats, she brought out *Cuchulain of Muirthemne* (1902) and *Gods and Fighting Men* (1904), which provided highly accessible versions of the ancient epic material. In drama, she began by helping the poet with the dialogue in his plays but she discovered a talent in herself for writing plays, particularly one-acters, and went on to produce over the next twenty years about forty plays, some of them translations from Molière, Sudermann and Goldoni, displaying a range of subject and emotion. Her use of songs is often very telling, her construction is tight and, most of all, she had an acute ear for comic dialogue and how, for her characters, inventiveness in speech is more exciting than factual recounting but also how the fiction can take control; in this latter quality she has an obvious affinity with Synge and O'Casey.

Yeats was particularly impressed by a form of English she devised, based on her hearing of the peasant speech in her area of Kiltartan and holding on to something in its patterns of the structure and idiomatic idiosyncrasy of Irish. English in the west of Ireland had developed parallel with the native Irish language over a period of two centuries and often forms of English in modern Ireland seem to retain something of an English that in England would be considered as of the seventeenth century. The language of Synge's plays has many similarities with Lady Gregory's Kiltartan dialect and despite, or partly because of, Yeats's admiration, an accusation was made against both writers that, in their patronising Ascendancy way, they had created Irish characters who sounded quaint or fossilised. The district of Kiltartan came to be well-known to Yeats because, from the time of his first stay in 1897, he spent much of the summers at Coole Park and in 1917 bought the tower at Ballylee, five miles from Coole. Through her generosity and her wish to be centrally involved in the new movement in Irish literature, Lady Gregory made her home a meeting place and a retreat for most of the leading writers of her time:

> They came like swallows and like swallows went,
> And yet a woman's powerful character
> Could keep a swallow to its first intent;
> And half a dozen in formation there,
> That seemed to whirl upon a compass-point,
> Found certainty upon the dreaming air,
> The intellectual sweetness of those lines
> That cut through time or cross it widdershins.

This poem, 'Coole Park, 1929', 'Coole Park and Ballylee, 1931', 'Upon a House Shaken by the Land Agitation', 'In the Seven Woods' and 'The Wild Swans at Coole' all celebrate aspects of what Coole represented for Yeats, and Lady Gregory's son, killed in the War in Italy in 1918, is commemorated in 'In Memory of Major Robert Gregory', 'An Irish Airman foresees his Death' and 'Shepherd and Goatherd'.

Lady Augusta Gregory, often likened to a dumpy Queen Victoria, was not as straitlaced as her appearance suggested and she enjoyed at least two passionate affairs, one with the writer Wilfred Scawen Blunt and another with the American lawyer John Quinn. She exerted her exceptional energy, organisational powers and obstinacy to promote the vision of an Irish Theatre. It was at Coole Park in 1897 that, on a new Remington typewriter, she copied out a statement formulated by Yeats, Martyn and herself:

> We propose to have performed in Dublin in the spring of every
> year certain Celtic and Irish plays, which whatever be their

degree of excellence will be written with a high ambition, and so to build up a Celtic and Irish school of dramatic literature. We hope to find in Ireland an uncorrupted and imaginative audience trained to listen by its passion for oratory, and believe that our desire to bring upon the stage the deeper thoughts and emotions of Ireland will ensure for us a tolerant welcome, and that freedom to experiment which is not found in theatres of England, and without which no new movement in art or literature can succeed. We will show that Ireland is not the home of buffoonery and of easy sentiment, as it has been represented, but the home of an ancient idealism. We are confident of the support of all Irish people, who are weary of misrepresentation, in carrying out a work that is outside all the political questions that divide us.

Looking back at that statement in 1913, she suggests that it 'seems now a little pompous', but, sent as a letter to possible patrons, it elicited financial and artistic support. A clause had to be inserted in an Act of Parliament to allow the group to put on a play in a building they could afford, and actors had to be engaged and rehearsed in London, but on 8 May 1899 the first production took place: Yeats's *The Countess Cathleen*. Martyn's *The Heather Field* was performed on the following night. In the controversy surrounding *The Countess Cathleen*, it is not clear whether a police guard for the actors was necessary or that Yeats opportunistically welcomed the publicity.

Over the following five years, over two dozen new plays were performed, several of them in Irish, including Douglas Hyde's *Casadh an t Sugáin* (The Twisting of the Rope), the first play in Irish ever produced in a theatre. In 1901 Yeats saw William and Frank Fay acting in an amateur production of an historical play and was persuaded by their acting to negotiate with them to train a group of Irish actors to perform the Irish plays of what in 1902 became the Irish National Theatre Society. In 1902, AE's *Deirdre* and Yeats's *Cathleen ni Houlihan* were played to packed, enthusiastic audiences. In the following year the new company took some of the plays to London and their success there and the attraction Yeats exerted on a wealthy theatregoer led to a crucial development in the efforts to establish a permanent Irish Theatre in Dublin. Miss Annie Horniman, five years older than the poet, was a spinster from Manchester who had met him in London in the early 1890s in the Order of the Golden Dawn. Her passionate interest in drama (she was later to establish the Manchester Repertory Theatre) and her, probably passionate, admiration of Yeats overcame her antipathy to Irish matters and, when she saw the Fay actors in London, she agreed to help Yeats find a theatre for the company. The Irish Theatre Society was actually deeply divided among the contending interests of at least three distinct groups. One section saw the Society as a meeting-place for people involved in amateur dramatics; they were centred on George Russell and did not want the Society to become professional or too serious. The second group, centred on Maud Gonne and Arthur Griffith, wished the theatre and its choice of plays to be nationalistically political. The third group, with Yeats as their leader, wanted a professional company with high artistic standards to mount productions of Irish plays; the Fay brothers, Synge and Lady Gregory supported Yeats. By a series of manoeuvres worthy of Bismarck, Yeats and his faction gained control of the newly-issued patent (in the name of Lady Gregory), of the artistic policy and of the theatre bought and subsidised by Miss Horniman for the Company. The Abbey Theatre, reconstituted from the Mechanics' Institute and the old Morgue, opened its doors on 27 December 1904 with a performance of Yeats's *On Baile's Strand* and *Cathleen ni Houlihan* and Lady Gregory's *Spreading the News*.

In the shaping of his ideas for the new theatre, Yeats was influenced by two people: Florence Farr and Gordon Craig. He first met Florence Farr in 1890, and in 1894 she acted in the first public performance of one of his plays, *The Land of Heart's Desire*. He considered that she had a theatrical power, but she was wayward and her dedication was not to the stage but to experiments in the occult. Nonetheless, he chose her to be the manager of the Irish Literary Theatre in its first season and, from 1901, he and she gave talks with demonstrations on speaking verse to an accompaniment on the psaltery. His relationship with her (there was a brief sexual liaison in 1904) is described as 'an enduring friendship that was an enduring exasperation'. Baffled, and intrigued, by her lack of self-esteem, he still felt that she was a unique performer with 'a tranquil beauty... an incomparable sense of rhythm and a beautiful voice, the seeming natural expression of the image'. Despite these gifts, she was, he decided, untrainable. In 1912, she took her eccentricity to a further extreme by emigrating to Ceylon and steeping herself in the local culture; she died of cancer five years later. Her good performances persuaded Yeats that 'in the performance of all drama that depends for its effect upon beauty of language, poetical culture may be more important than professional experience'.

What he learned about language and voice from the example of Florence Farr was extended to stage sets, costume and gesture by the productions of Gordon Craig. Craig, who died in 1966 at the age of 94, was the illegitimate son of an architect and stage designer, E. W. Godwin, and the actress Ellen Terry. He grew up to follow the professions of his parents. In the early years of the century he achieved fame and notoriety for his direction of plays in a non-realist manner. Yeats was immediately excited by the use of colour, abstract or symbolic sets, lighting and the appeal of the whole production to the audience's imagination. The actors, in his scheme, are part of the design and he writes about production in terms of 'pattern', 'emotional design' and the coordination of 'action, scene and voice'. Yeats's attempts to employ Craig in the new Irish Theatre met with little support and Craig adopted a nomadic and sensational style of living across Europe (including a flamboyant affair with the dancer Isadora Duncan). His short book *The Art of the Theatre* (1905) is a central text of the anti-realist drama. In 1934, along with Maeterlinck and Luigi Pirandello, he attended a lecture given in Rome by the Irish poet.

Yeats's own views on the state of the contemporary theatre in Ireland in 1903 are stated at the opening of his essay 'The Reform of the Theatre': 'I think the theatre must be reformed in its plays, its speaking, its acting, and its scenery. That is to say, I think there is nothing good about it at present.' He goes on to make stipulations on the four aspects he has named:

> We have to write or find plays that will make the theatre a place of intellectual excitement – a place where the mind goes to be liberated as it was liberated by the theatres of Greece and England and France at certain great moments of their history, and as it is liberated in Scandinavia to-day. If we are to do this we must learn that beauty and truth are always justified of themselves, and that their creation is a greater service to our country than writing that compromises either in the seeming service of a cause.

> If we are to restore words to their sovereignty we must make speech even more important than gesture upon the stage.... . An actor should understand cadence from cadence, and so to cherish the musical lineaments of verse or prose that he delights the ear with a continually varied music.

We must simplify acting.... . We must get rid of everything that is restless, everything that draws attention away from the sound of the voice, or from the few moments of intense expression, whether that expression is through the voice or through the hands.

It is necessary to simplify both the form and colour of scenery and costume.... . Even when one has to represent trees or hills... they should be little more than an unobtrusive pattern.

In pursuit of such simplicity and emphasis on the words, he even considered conducting rehearsals with the actors standing in barrels on castors so that he could push them with a pole into new positions as the action required and they could concentrate entirely on speaking the words. (Did this suggestion give Samuel Beckett an idea?)

His own emphasis was very definitely on tragedy and he conscientiously studied Greek and Shakespearian plays in an attempt to identify the qualities which make a work tragic. He concludes his essay 'The Tragic Theatre' (1910) with this proclamation:

Tragic art, passionate art, the drowner of dykes, the confounder of understanding, moves us by setting us to reverie, by alluring us almost to the intensity of trance. The persons on the stage, let us say, greaten till they are humanity itself. We feel our minds expand convulsively or spread out slowly like some moon-brightened, image-crowded sea. That which is before our eyes perpetually vanishes and returns again in the midst of the excitement it creates, and the more enthralling it is, the more do we forget it.

His concern is not with character in Ibsen's sense or even with Shakespearian character, nor is he interested in intricacy of plot. In 1904 he explained what drew him to write plays:

What attracts me to drama is that it is... a moment of intense life. An action is taken out of all other actions; it is reduced to its simplest form, or at any rate to as simple a form as it can be brought to without our losing the sense of its place in the world. The characters that are involved in it are freed from everything that is not a part of that action.... . The subject of all art is passion, and a passion can only be contemplated when separated by itself, purified of all but itself, and aroused into a perfect intensity by opposition with some other passion, or it may be with the law, that is the expression of the whole whether of Church or Nation or external nature.

Shakespeare's Coriolanus and Cleopatra are cited as examples of such an absoluteness. In Yeats's *Deirdre*, performed in 1906, he funnels the story into that moment when Deirdre, in her love for Naoise, killed by the king, asserts her love and even a joy by killing herself.

However, in the two dozen plays he wrote in his whole career there is a considerable variety of subject and treatment, of verse and prose, of naturalism and symbolism. Even in the cycle of five plays based on the life and death of the legendary hero Cuchulain – *On Baile's Strand*, *The Green Helmet*, *At the Hawk's Well*, *The Only Jealousy of Emer* and *The Death of Cuchulain* – there is considerable room for experiment and a varying of dramatic stimulus. The choice of the intemperate warrior Cuchulain as a unifying hero or anti-hero challenges the reader's glib images of Yeats. The tensions in Cuchulain's story allowed the dramatist to explore aspects not only of himself but of political debate, authority, loyalty and the compulsion of obsession. The attachment to Cuchulain began in nationalist feelings and a wish to use mythical patterns to show certain continuities to an Irish audience and beyond, to touch a nerve in our lives:

> The greatest art symbolises not those things that we have observed so much as those things that we have experienced, and when the imaginary saint or lover or hero moves us most deeply, it is the moment when he awakens within us for an instant our own heroism, our own sanctity, our own desire.

In 1896 Yeats had met in Paris a man for whom he came to have enormous respect and who was to be crucial to the development of the Abbey Theatre and to Yeats's idea of drama. John Millington Synge was born in 1871 in a staid, Protestant and comfortably-off family; after Trinity College where he studied Hebrew and Irish, he wandered round Europe playing the violin and learning languages. Yeats, according to his own account, advised the younger man to give up translating French poetry, leave Paris and go to the Aran Islands off the Galway coast 'to find a life that had never been expressed in literature'. Four summers were spent on the Islands (where, some years earlier, one of his clergyman relatives had lived and worked) and his experience of the islanders' lives entered into all of his writings, irrespective of where they are set. He found the Aran Islands an odd mixture of acceptance, sometimes stoical, sometimes glum, of harsh conditions and death, and a free, defiant, inventive humour: the mixture was most evident to him in the islanders' delight in storytelling and fanciful language. Such a mixture could be found among country people elsewhere but the extremity at which the Aran Islanders lived gave a more marked quality to their mixture. What he heard in the speech of people in the Wicklow hills and on Aran fed into the dialogue of his plays. In acknowledging that 'all art is a collaboration' he emphasises his own good fortune:

> In a good play every speech should be as fully flavoured as a nut or apple, and such speeches cannot be written by any one who works among those who have shut their lips on poetry. In Ireland, for a few years more, we have a popular imagination that is fiery, and magnificent, and tender; so that those of us who wish to write start with a chance that is not given to writers in places where the springtime of the local life has been forgotten, and the harvest is a memory only, and the straw has been turned into bricks.

This commendation of Ireland ironically occurs in his Preface to *The Playboy of the Western World* in 1907, the play which incensed so many Irish people who saw the play as a scurrilous attack on Irish decencies.

However, with his very first play, *The Shadow of the Glen*, Synge had antagonised Maud Gonne, who considered in 1903 that the National Theatre Company was no longer sufficiently nationalist and, hence, resigned as Vice-President. She and others also considered that Synge's play presented Irish womanhood in an unfavourable way. Possibly his only play to cause no offence was *Riders to the Sea*, his concentrated one-act lament on the inevitability of death in an exposed fishing community. According to Yeats,

> He was the man that we [Ireland] needed, because he was the only man I have ever known incapable of a political thought or of a humanitarian purpose. He could walk the roadside all day with some poor man without any desire to do him good or for any

reason except that he liked him. He was to do for Ireland, though more by his influence on other dramatists than by his direct influence, what Robert Burns did for Scotland. When Scotland thought herself gloomy and religious, Providence restored her imaginative spontaneity by raising up Robert Burns to commend drink and the Devil.

One would need to add that substantial factions in Ireland were extremely reluctant to be liberated from their pieties. In 1907, with the production of *The Playboy of the Western World*, the opposition to Synge's 'imaginative spontaneity' erupted in riotous scenes and bitter attacks on all those associated with him. Some of the factions had been gathering stones to throw for several years and the Abbey Theatre and the Celtic movement had become an obvious target for certain reactionary forces. *The Stage Irishman of the Pseudo-Celtic Drama* by Frank Hugh O'Donnell was published in 1903, and D. P. Moran's *The Philosophy of Irish Ireland* in the same year accused Yeats's group of inventing a Celtic melancholia in which they could evade the need for political militancy. Synge posed a problem for his opposition because his irony and humour destabilised all orthodox values. As with O'Casey's *The Plough and the Stars* and *Juno and the Paycock* some years later, the audience of *The Playboy* laughed their way into an ambush and when serious questions confronted them they felt trapped and turned on the author of their confusion. The story of Christy Mahon, who becomes heroic when people believe his fiction that he has killed his father, is dangerously subversive, and critics in 1907 sought for some obvious immorality in the play which they could accuse. Some seized on the use of the word 'shift' [petticoat] as particularly offensive. A letter to a Dublin newspaper signed 'A Western Girl' complained: 'Miss Allgood [who acted the part of Widow Quin] is forced, before the most fashionable audience in Dublin, to use a word indicating an essential article of female attire, which the lady would probably never utter in ordinary circumstances, even to herself.' And a cleaner at the Theatre was overheard protesting that she would never use that word and asking rhetorically, 'Isn't Mr Synge a bloody old snot to write such a play?' Whether he was or not, his play caused a huge commotion on its first production not only in Dublin but in England and in the United States. It is said that no one from Synge's own family ever attended any of his plays.

Synge died in 1909 before he could complete his beautiful play *Deirdre of the Sorrows*. Unlike Yeats's version, which concentrates on the climax of the legend, his version covers the beginning of the love affair, the exile in Scotland and the tragic conclusion. Also Synge uses not verse but a lilting prose. For Yeats there was an overlap in the Irish English of Douglas Hyde's translations of *The Love Songs of Connacht* (1893), Lady Gregory's Kiltartan and Synge's dialect in the plays. *Deirdre of the Sorrows* probably represented the high point of Yeats's aspirations for the Abbey for, despite later successes and the firmer financial establishment of the Theatre, Irish drama did not follow Yeats's lead. At the end of his life, writing in *On the Boiler*, he looks back:

> The success of the Abbey Theatre has grown out of a single con-
> viction of its founders.... . 'Not what you [the public] want but
> what we [the dramatists] want'... . Yet the theatre has not, apart
> from this one quality, gone my way or in any way I wanted it to
> go, and often, looking back, I have wondered if I did right in giv-
> ing so much of my life to the expression of other men's genius.
> According to the Indians a man may do much good yet lose his
> own soul. Then I say to myself, I have had greater luck than any
> other modern English-speaking dramatist; I have aimed at tragic
> ecstasy, and here and there in my own work and in the work of
> my friends I have seen it greatly played... I am haunted by certain
> moments... .

The first of these moments to which he refers takes place just before Deirdre takes her own life in the final act of *Deirdre of the Sorrows*. The opening decade of the new century was largely devoted to theatrical work, and in this period Yeats wrote only a handful of poems. However, his experience in drama certainly fed into his poetry and his diction and rhythms changed markedly in this period. We must also remember that between its foundation in 1904 and 1920 the Abbey produced an average of eight new Irish plays annually and encouraged a wide range of fresh talent.

Although gradually he handed over many administrative duties to other people, Yeats retained a substantial say in the policies of the Abbey Theatre and fought tirelessly for its independence. Miss Horniman's financial support became increasingly suspect as a result of various clashes and disagreements. Because he was not prepared to concede any control in the choice of plays or in political attitude to the Theatre benefactor, her subsidy was withdrawn in 1910 and the building was subsequently bought from her. After the foundation of the Irish Free State, the Abbey was granted a state subsidy. Seldom has a theatre company had to struggle for its survival through so many non-theatrical controversies. From the earliest religious difficulties encountered with Yeats's *The Countess Cathleen*, through the granting of a patent, the riots caused by Synge's *The Playboy of the Western World*, the confrontation with the Castle authorities over the staging of Shaw's *Blanco Posnet* and storms of protest at O'Casey's *The Plough and the Stars* in 1926 – apart from all the internal squabbles and problems with plays and audiences – the Abbey had a rough passage.

The sad story of the split between O'Casey and Yeats does not impinge greatly on Yeats's theatrical practice but the incident demands a brief comment. With the popularity of *The Shadow of a Gunman* (1923) and *Juno and the Paycock* (1924) and the vast publicity attached to *The Plough and the Stars* (1926), O'Casey brought commercial success to the Abbey and enlarged the appeal of the Theatre, partly by breaking away from any suggestion that the Abbey existed only for Anglo-Irish with a taste for quaint peasants and old legends. O'Casey had been brought up in working-class Dublin by Protestant parents and he succeeded in giving a voice to the urban poor. Although the plays were not in line with his earlier ideals for the Abbey, Yeats recognised the dramatic quality of the writing. When O'Casey submitted *The Silver Tassie* in 1928, Yeats had his reasons for finding the play unacceptable. Since that rejection Yeats has been generally condemned for his meanness and blinkered attitude and O'Casey has been supported in his 'desire to experiment' beyond the naturalism of the Dublin trilogy. I happen to agree with most of Yeats's criticisms of the play but the subsequent self-imposed exile of O'Casey was not good for the Abbey.

Yeats's own development as a dramatist was certainly experimental and he tried out various methods to create a radically different kind of play, a play not, in fact, particularly suited to a theatre space such as the Abbey. In 1913 he first encountered examples of the Japanese Noh tradition when his new friend, the American poet Ezra Pound, was polishing and editing translations done by Ernest Fenellosa. He was fascinated by the severe formality of this aristocratic drama which had its great period about the same time as Shakespeare. In his intriguing essay, 'Certain Noble Plays of Japan', written in 1916, he explores his researches in this very alien idea of theatre and finds that it accords with many elements in his own notion of drama. There is a condensed quality in Noh which operates through the wearing of masks, a vocabulary of stylised gestures and movements, extreme economy of evocative language, music and dance, and set patterns of traditional characters and stories. Noh was handed down through certain families whose sons received a strenuous training in voice, movement and the religious teaching which underlies the plays. The plays concentrate on an unresolved dilemma, often involving an interaction between the living and the dead or the material and the spiritual. It is difficult to describe a performance of a Noh play (they were performed in cycles of different types in a fixed order) and it is difficult to imagine the performance of a Yeats Noh play by merely reading the text. He wrote four plays for dancers which show the influence of his understanding of Noh: *At the Hawk's Well*, *The Only Jealousy of Emer*, *The Dreaming of the Bones* and *Calvary* but many of his later plays contain elements of Noh. (Yeats himself had no opportunity to see a Noh play and learned relatively little from Japanese contacts.) He wished for a theatrical performance which does not require elaborate buildings, scenery and large audiences and the model of the Noh brought together inspirations he had gathered from his interest in myth and ritual, and from Florence Farr, Gordon Craig, the dancers Ninette de Valois and Ito and the painter Edmund Dulac:

All imaginative art remains at a distance and this distance, once chosen, must be firmly held against a pushing world. Verse, ritual, music and dance in association with action require that gesture, costume, facial expression, stage arrangement must help in keeping the door.... The arts which interest me, while seeming to separate from the world and us a group of figures, images, symbols, enable us to pass for a few moments into a deep of the mind that had hitherto been too subtle for our habitation. As a deep of the mind can only be approached through what is most human, most delicate, we should distrust bodily distance, mechanism, and loud noise.

5

Friends and Loves

Yeats quotes a comment made by the French poet Paul Verlaine, on Tennyson's *In Memoriam*, the long elegy prompted by the early death of his best friend, Arthur Hallam: '"Tennyson is too noble, too *anglais*; when he should have been broken-hearted, he had many reminiscences".' It is difficult to be sure what Verlaine intended to say. Should Tennyson not have written a poem at all? Did he dishonour his friend? Or did he misjudge his poem for Hallam? It is hard to conceive of a personal elegy which does not contain reminiscences, particularly a long poem written over a period of about seventeen years after Hallam's death. Is Verlaine making a moral point or an aesthetic one? These same questions arise over and over again in a consideration of Yeats's poetry. Few poets have so used or abused their friendships and loves as much as Yeats. Most readers, at some point, resent his exploitation of private material and query his apparent assumption that the reader should be interested in such material. Two apparently contradictory observations are appropriate. The poetry is often dense with proper names – frequently the names, as it turns out, of contemporaries; the uninitiated reader feels at a loss without a glossary. However, in some areas of the poetry names are curiously absent and the reader is at the mercy of unidentified pronouns: 'you', 'she', 'one', 'we', or undisclosed characters such as 'Red Rose', 'the Lover' and 'Friends'. Maud Gonne, a dominant presence in his life and poetry for almost fifty years, has her first named appearance in a poem written in 1937, two years before his death. Does Yeats wish us to identify her earlier? And what is the correlation between the figure in a poem and the biographical gloss provided by a scholar?

First, we must go back to beginnings. Yeats's relationships with his parents and siblings were delineated in Chapter 1. From this distance in time it would be presumptuous to erect any large theories on the evidence available. However, the powerful, sometimes overpowering, pressure of his father and the absence of pressure from his mother must have had an effect on the growing boy's expectations of friendship and his notions of male and female roles in society and in sexual relationships. Oddly enough, Yeats was attracted to forceful women and, certainly in the earlier years, he tended to be a very subservient male suitor. In Chapter 1 a quotation from his *Autobiography* describes his discovery about the age of 17 of specifically sexual feelings, a confusing situation he comments on in the public *Autobiographies*:

> The great event of a boy's life is the awakening of sex. He will bathe many times a day, or get up at dawn and having stripped leap to and fro over a stick laid upon two chairs, and hardly know, and never admit, that he had begun to take pleasure in his own nakedness, nor will he understand the change until some dream discovers it. He may never understand at all the greater change in his mind.

Sexually desirable women were imagined, 'modelled on those in my favourite poets and loved in brief tragedy, or like the girl in [Shelley's] *The Revolt of Islam*, [they] accompanied their lovers through all manner of wild places, lawless women without homes and without children'. He dreaded any talk about sex but confesses that in his early twenties women excited endless curiosity in him and his head was 'full of the mysterious women of Rossetti and those hesitating faces in the art of Burne-Jones which seemed always anxious for some Alastor [in Shelley's poem of that name] at the end of a long journey'. His vexing confusion about women and his sexual feelings is evident in his earliest relationships, with his cousin Laura Armstrong when he was 17, and with Katharine Tynan in his twenties (see Chapter 1). 'As prudish as an old maid', is his comment on himself at that stage. Physical sexual experience with a woman was delayed – as it was for many men of his generation – and he was 30 before anything happened. His poetry up to and including *The Wind Among the Reeds* (1899) reflects on something of his desire and his unease. Female figures and addressees are omnipresent but in a curiously unspecific way. There is a current of eroticism running through the poems but it is muted and insulated in swathes of limp adjectives; eyes, breasts, hair are offered and endlessly recede to be physically inaccessible. His Symbolist and esoteric aims operate through the incorporeality of the imagery. Looking back at the end of his life to the long poem *The Wanderings of Oisin* (1899), in which the warrior poet Oisin is spirited through realms of the other world by the beautiful Niamh, he mocks himself:

> that sea-rider Oisin led by the nose
> Through three enchanted islands, allegorical dreams,
> Vain gaiety, vain battle, vain repose,
> Themes of the embittered heart, or so it seems,
> That might adorn old songs or courtly shows;
> But what cared I that set him on to ride,
> I starved for the bosom of his fairy bride?
> ('The Circus Animals' Desertion')

We must remember that the young Yeats was often pathetically shy and gauche in social situations. As a young man he spent much more of his time with male friends than with females. The clubs and artistic groups to which he belonged were predominantly male and his models of writers were probably all men. Choice hardly entered into this situation and most of the acquaintances he made through his father were bound to be male. He learned much and developed in various directions in the company of his father, first of all, and of such as George Russell, John Todhunter, Edward Dowden, John O'Leary, Douglas Hyde, Edwin Ellis, William Morris, Lionel Johnson, William Henley, T. W. Rolleston, Oscar Wilde, Arthur Symons and Aubrey Beardsley. This list of men who were public figures could be hugely enlarged if we were to include family friends, neighbourhood friends in London, Sligo and Dublin, members of various societies and committees with whom he must have spent many hours. For a self-declared reticent person, he mixed with a large motley of people. For a young man with very little money, from a family with very little money, he managed to travel about and mix with people from all classes of society.

'I was twenty-three years old when the troubling of my life began.' So Yeats in his *Autobiography* announces the arrival of Maud Gonne in his consciousness. Actually he had heard of her before, when John O'Leary's sister wrote to him about a lovely girl who had forsaken English court and military circles in favour of Irish nationalism. The impression she made on him that day in 1889 was overwhelming and durable:

> I had never thought to see in a living woman so great beauty. It belonged to famous pictures, to poetry, to some legendary past. A

...arriage to MacBride did not last. Within months of the ...e was complaining to Yeats of her unhappiness, and ...n, Séan, being born in 1904, she sued successfully for a ...tion in 1905. She claimed that her husband was a violent ...nd that he had sexually assaulted her half-sister. Mac-...ater to be executed for his part in the Easter Rising in ...te bitter arguments and even breaches in their relation-...nd Maud Gonne maintained a friendship for fifty years. ...lism, according to him, narrowed as she grew older but ...considered that it had a dangerous and unscrupulous ...lt that Yeats had compromised his early ideals, had ...oney (particularly for the Abbey) from people who were ...d in Ireland's freedom, and promoted art which did not ...Irish people. In his *Journal* he records a visit to Maud in ...in 1910:

...r afternoon, there being much wind and rain, we all ...doors.... Maud Gonne and I got into the old argument ...n *Féin* and its attack on Synge, and the general circum-...at surrounded the first split in the Theatre. I notice that ...quarrel is the one difference about which she feels ...I for this reason let myself get drawn into it again and ...inking to convince her at last that apart from wrongs and ...possible to settle so long after, it was fundamental. I ...t have done otherwise. My whole movement, my integ-...man of letters, were alike involved. Thinking of her, as I ...a sense Ireland, a summing up in one mind of what is ...e romantic political Ireland of my youth and of the youth ...for some years yet, I must see to it that I close the Synge ...hich he was writing] with a statement of national litera-...would re-create it, and of its purpose. It is useless to ...one does not create....

...erature created out of a conscious political aim in the long ...ates weakness by creating a habit of unthinking obedi-...l a habit of distrust of spontaneous impulse. It makes a ...f slaves in the name of liberty.[3]

...ays that 'she feels strongly' we hear also his own strength ...Yeats genuinely admired her efforts on behalf of evicted ...olitical prisoners (as she saw them), and women's groups

complexion like the blossom of apples, and yet face and body had the beauty of lineaments which Blake calls the highest beauty because it changes least from youth to age, and a stature so great that she seemed of a divine race. Her movements were worthy of her form, and I understood at last why the poet of antiquity, where we would but speak of face and form, sings, loving some lady, that she paces like a goddess.... As I look backward, it seems to me that she brought into my life in those days – for as yet I saw only what lay upon the surface – the middle of the tint, a sound as of a Burmese gong, an overpowering tumult that had yet many pleasant secondary notes.

His description is in accord with the heroicising way in which she is represented in his poems. There are no actual physical details but from his sisters we learn that she wore slippers, had hazel eyes and kept a cab waiting while she visited the Yeatses. This extraordinary creature, hardly of the earth, and always travelling 'surrounded by cages of innumerable singing birds', was to exercise her power not just on Yeats but in many areas of Irish affairs.

Born in 1866 in Surrey, she was the daughter of a captain in the British Army. Her mother died when Maud was five and she and her sister grew up between Ireland, to which her father was posted for sizeable periods, and England and France. For a couple of years before her father, now a colonel, died in 1886, she attended functions with him and acted as his hostess; their relationship sounds curiously intimate. She always called him Tommy, and they both seem to have enjoyed being mistaken for lovers in public. Two years after her father's death and a year before she met Yeats, she became the mistress of a French lawyer and political journalist, Lucien Millevoye, who was involved in a reactionary plot against the French government of the day and was also fiercely hostile to everything English. She maintained an awkward association with Millevoye over ten years and had two children by him – all unbeknown to Yeats till she finally divulged the details in 1898. Her first child died after a year in 1891 and, when she returned to Dublin (on the boat carrying Parnell's body for burial), Yeats comforted her on the loss of what, she told him, was an adopted child, by talking to her of spiritualist matters and hopes of reincarnation. She was initiated by him into the Order of the Golden Dawn and together they worked hard on political, literary and occult projects. Always she threw herself into hectic activities, agitating for this and against that, and then collapsing exhausted and ill. The idea of reincarnation, backed by the belief of AE that a child who died could be reborn to the same parents, moved her to have intercourse with Millevoye in the very memorial chapel where her son had been buried. In 1894 she gave birth to a daughter, Iseult. After all their shared endeavours, the ups and downs of a relationship without consummation, a climax of sorts came in December 1898 when, after a vivid dream of mutual acceptance, Maud kissed Yeats sexually for the first time. She then told him something closer to the truth about her long affair with Millevoye, her children, and why she could not think of marrying Yeats except in a 'spiritual' way. Yeats was shattered. I do not think he wrote any publishable poems during the year following Maud's disclosures.

All his pleadings, proposals, adorations had failed to win her and although in 1898 she declared that she had loved him for some time, she was not prepared to accept him and give herself to him. Apparently, she had never enjoyed sex and had come to dread sexual intercourse. He was her best friend but .... In *The Wind Among the Reeds* (1899) there are two poems which, according to Yeats, illustrate how not to gain a woman's love and how to do so. One is 'He Wishes for the Cloths of Heaven':

> Had I the heavens' embroidered cloths,
> Enwrought with golden and silver light,
> Of night and light and the half-light,
> I would spread the cloths under your feet:
> But I being poor, have only my dreams;
> I have spread my dreams under your feet;
> Tread softly because you tread on my dreams.

The other poem, 'The Cap and Bells', is intricately patterned and enigmatic. In the end, the jester wins the love of the queen but his earlier attempts to gain her sympathy by giving his soul and then his heart are rebuffed. It is only when he gives her his cap and bells, his emblems as a jester, that she accepts him and then his heart and soul are included. I take the poems with Yeats's comment to mean that love is won not by solemnity and prostration but by a show of nonchalance, precisely what he found himself unable to do with Maud Gonne.

Her passionate anti-English, anti-colonialist feelings caused her to side with the Boers against the British in Southern Africa. Yeats

agreed with her sentiments in this and oth
organised alongside her. He could not inv
tancy, however, and came to detest her blin
ity which allowed her to say in her autob
Queen: 'I have always hated war and am b
pacifist, but it is the English who are forc
first principle is to kill the enemy. Unfort
been more successful in killing than we
Memoirs, confesses: 'I came to hate her po
One day when [she] spent all day playin
had sent her from Donegal I was delighte
that play a political caucus.'[2] Because of
the Boers she met Captain John MacBri
Brigade on the side of the Boers. In 1903
was later to describe as 'a drunken, vaing
verted to Roman Catholicism in 1897 and
confirmed. Her decision to marry MacBri
almost every conceivable way, nearly
Abbey Theatre and its problems diverte
after several years, he sees how close he

> Some may have blamed you that you t
> The verses that could move them on th
> When, the ears being deafened, the sig
> With lightning, you went from me, and
> Nothing to make a song about but kin
> Helmets, and swords, and half-forgott
> That were like memories of you – but
> We'll out, for the world lives as long a
> And while we're in our laughing, wee
> Hurl helmets, crowns, and swords int
> But, dear, cling close to me; since you
> My barren thoughts have chilled me t

This poem, 'Reconciliation', was probab
1908 and there is evidence to suggest
Maud Gonne at last consummated their
his letters to her have unfortunately be
to him demonstrate a marked increas
A. Norman Jeffares and Richard Ellma
widow confirmed that the two had bee

but he also saw a comic or daft side to her, as when he bracketed her with his friend Ezra Pound, another 'revolutionary simpleton'. (Pound, in turn, describes Yeats arriving from Paris with Maud Gonne, ten canaries, one parrot, one monkey, one cat and two members of her family.) Writing to the painter William Rothenstein in 1938, he laments that no artist has succeeded in drawing her and wishes that Rothenstein would try because 'she looks magnificent', aged 72. However, he continues, with grim irony, 'I cannot imagine anything but an air-raid that would bring her to London. She might come to see the spectacle.' In the earlier days her extravagantly beautiful appearance; her domineering manner in public, supported by the omnipresence of her Great Dane, Dagda; her energy and freedom of movement backed by financial independence; all these awed Yeats as if he moved in the company of Shelley's Witch of Atlas. Yeats himself became a commanding figure in any company and their relationship evened out to be a friendship of equals with fondness. Her autobiography, confusingly titled *A Servant of the Queen* (she meant Cathleen ni Houlihan, the spirit of Ireland), was published in 1938. Like many of her letters, it is rather dully mechanical and self-centred; she saw herself as a person of action, not as a writer. She died in 1953.

Through Yeats's poetry Maud Gonne is a pervasive and ambivalent presence. In his poems of the 1890s she, no doubt, lies behind the recurring female loved one but the identification of the female as Maud can be positively harmful to a full reading of those poems: the poems are concerned with emotional and spiritual conditions and are not about her as a person. 'The Two Trees' is a possible exception where a linkage with the biographical person adds a sharpness to the thoughts. With the new century, Yeats changes his manner of writing and, alongside his writing for the theatre, his poems have a stronger rooting in a world of actual people and events. His disappointment at unrequited love comes across with an immediacy in the straightforwardness of such poems as 'Adam's Curse' and 'The Folly of being Comforted'. This greater realism is spliced into adopted myths in poems related to Maud and she emerges as a version of Helen of Troy in 'No Second Troy', written in 1908. It begins:

Why should I blame her that she filled my days
With misery...

and ends:

> Why, what could she have done, being what she is?
> Was there another Troy for her to burn?

The logic of the poem provides an answer to these questions in that, without another Troy against which she can use her destructive power, Yeats himself becomes the thing to be destroyed or dis-Troyed. His ambivalence about Maud and his disagreements with her are explored in a group of poems in *The Wild Swans at Coole* (1919): 'Her Praise', 'The People', 'His Phoenix', 'Broken Dreams', 'A Deep Sworn Vow' and 'Presences', but his finest poem of appraisal, 'The Cold Heaven', came to him like a vision in 1912:

> Suddenly I saw the cold and rook-delighting heaven
> That seemed as though ice burned and was but the more ice,
> And thereupon imagination and heart were driven
> So wild that every casual thought of that and this
> Vanished, and left but memories, that should be out of season
> With the hot blood of youth, of love crossed long ago;
> And I took all the blame out of all sense and reason,
> Until I cried and trembled and rocked to and fro,
> Riddled with light. Ah! when the ghost begins to quicken
> Confusion of the death-bed over, is it sent
> Out naked on the roads, as the books say, and stricken
> By the injustice óf the skies for punishment?

Again there is no mention of Maud or any very specific reference to her but, in their unfolding love-torment, this has a remarkable place. The ferocity of judgement is concentrated in the multivocal 'riddled with light', containing 'puzzled', 'sifted' and 'shot through'. The final question takes us into Yeats's theory of the after-life.

Maud came to represent a misguided attitude to life, signalled as early as 'The Two Trees' (1892), but now for Yeats a warning about mistaking priorities. In 'A Prayer for my Daughter', written in 1919, at a time of international and Irish instability, he wishes to guard his newly-born daughter from the damaging attitudes he has encountered. In two stanzas he cites his experience of Maud:

> May she [his daughter] be granted beauty and yet not
> Beauty to make a stranger's eye distraught,

Or hers before a looking-glass, for such,
Being made beautiful overmuch,
Consider beauty a sufficient end,
Lose natural kindness and maybe
The heart-revealing intimacy
That chooses right, and never find a friend.

And:

An intellectual hatred is the worst,
So let her think opinions are accursed.
Have I not seen the loveliest woman born
Out of the mouth of Plenty's horn,
Because of her opinionated mind
Barter that horn and every good
By quiet natures understood
For an old bellows full of angry wind?

A more sympathetic picture of her is presented in 'Among School Children', where he remembers her youth and how he shared her experiences: 'it seemed that our two natures blent/Into a sphere from youthful sympathy'. Images, memories, aspects of her feed into the poetry in various guises, sometimes direct, sometimes very indirect. In his sequence-poems centred on women, particularly 'A Woman Young and Old' and the Crazy Jane group, Maud's nature and his experiences with her are ingredients in the mixture. The 'hysterical women' in 'Lapis Lazuli' who are antipathetic to what they see as the frivolous gaiety of art may be English society ladies but probably hark back to many bitter arguments between Maud and the poet. The late poem, 'A Bronze Head', re-examines the contradictory sides of her nature and his own contradictory feelings as he reviews, while he looks at a statue of her, his personal images gathered across their lives. For Yeats as a poet, there is always the nagging question with which this chapter opened:

Does the imagination dwell the most
Upon a woman won or woman lost?
If on the lost, admit you turned aside
From a great labyrinth out of pride,
Cowardice, some silly over-subtle thought
Or anything called conscience once;

And that if memory recur, the sun's
Under eclipse and the day blotted out.
('The Tower')

Maud had her own answer. She recounts how, when he had begged her yet again to marry him and live a peaceful life, she replied:

'Willie, are you not tired of asking that question? How often have I told you to thank the gods that I will not marry you. You would not be happy with me.'
   'I am not happy without you.'
   'Oh yes, you are, because you make beautiful poetry out of what you call your unhappiness and you are happy in that. Marriage would be such a dull affair. Poets should never marry. The world should thank me for not marrying you.'[4]

When, after John MacBride was executed by the British Army in 1916, Yeats yet again proposed to Maud and yet again was turned down, he switched his attention to her daughter (by Millevoye). Iseult was then 22, beautiful and talented, and fond of her mother's friend whom she called Uncle Willie. He had always taken a protective interest in her and several years earlier had written two poems about her: 'To a Child Dancing in the Wind' and 'Two Years Later'. The second expresses a worry that she will follow her mother's example:

Has no one said those daring
Kind eyes should be more learn'd?
Or warned you how despairing
The moths are when they are burned?
I could have warned you; but you are young,
So we speak a different tongue.

O you will take whatever's offered
And dream that all the world's a friend,
Suffer as your mother suffered,
Be as broken in the end.
But I am old and you are young,
And I speak a barbarous tongue.

In the collection, *The Wild Swans at Coole* (1919), there are three poems in similar vein: 'The Living Beauty', 'To a Young Beauty' and

'To a Young Girl'. A further poem, 'Owen Aherne and his Dancers', written in 1917 but not published for some years, looks back from his married position to his proposals to Iseult and wryly concedes a gap between himself and the young woman:

'How could she mate with fifty years that was so wildly bred?
Let the cage bird and the cage bird mate and the wild bird
      mate in the wild.'

In fact, after an affair with Ezra Pound, she married the novelist-to-be Francis Stuart, and encountered many problems, with some of which the old poet was asked to help.

In 1894, the year of Iseult's birth, Yeats first met Olivia Shakespear. She was a cousin of his friend, Lionel Johnson, and was eager to meet him because of her admiration for his work. Married but largely estranged from her husband, she had one daughter, Dorothy, who was later to marry Ezra Pound, and in 1894 she published her first novel. A correspondence developed into a friendship and then into an affair. He had told her about his hopeless love for Maud Gonne; at first he thought (wrongly) that she had some shameful past from which he might rescue her. 'Her beauty, dark and still, had the nobility of defeated things, and how could it help but wring my heart?' And, 'after all, if I could not get the woman I loved, it would be a comfort even but for a little while to devote myself to another'. His account of the affair's progress is given in his private *Autobiography* but, even with his pseudonym for her, Diana Vernon (the heroine of Scott's *Rob Roy*), she is not admitted to *Autobiographies*. From her, in a railway carriage, he received his first passionate kiss: 'I was startled and a little shocked.' They had assignations in museums, libraries and trains for some time but eventually they bought some meagre furnishings for his room and he recounts their buying a bed: 'I remember an embarrassed conversation in the presence of some Tottenham Court shop man upon the width of the bed – every inch increased the expense.'[5] She coaxed him through his chronic sexual nervousness and, after some difficulties, a year-long sexual relationship gave them both much pleasure. However, always in his mind was the pull of Maud Gonne, and a moment came when Olivia 'found my mood did not answer hers and burst into tears. "There is someone else in your heart", she said.' He confesses, 'It will always be a grief to me that I could not give the love that was her beauty's right, but she was too near my soul, too salutary and wholesome to my inmost being.' This is his strange way of saying that he had to follow the destructive suction of Maud Gonne. His poem 'The Lover Mourns for the Loss of Love' catches the collapse of his affair with Olivia Shakespear:

> Pale brows, still hands and dim hair,
> I had a beautiful friend
> And dreamed that the old despair
> Would end in love in the end:
> She looked in my heart one day
> And saw your image was there;
> She has gone weeping away.

Thirty years later he could still be vexed at the thought of what did not develop in their relationship:

> A crazy man that found a cup,
> When all but dead of thirst,
> Hardly dared to wet his mouth

Several poems were written with her in mind; for example, 'He bids his Beloved be at Peace', 'The Travail of Passion', 'The Empty Cup' (quoted above) and the 'Mermaid'. In 1929 he wrote the quiet piece of remembered love, 'After Long Silence':

> Speech after long silence; it is right,
> All other lovers being estranged or dead,
> Unfriendly lamplight hid under its shade,
> The curtains drawn upon unfriendly night,
> That we descant and yet again descant
> Upon the supreme theme of Art and Song:
> Bodily decrepitude is wisdom; young
> We loved each other and were ignorant.

In 1904 there had probably been a brief revival of their passion (the same year as his affair with Florence Farr) but their relationship settled down to a comfortable, confiding friendship which lasted till her death in 1938. Her charm, sophistication and straightforward-ness are apparent in her letters to him (and, in a remarkable letter, she wrote to her future son-in-law Ezra Pound in 1912). In 'Friends'

(1911), Yeats commended her along with Augusta Gregory and Maud Gonne, to be praised for the joy they had given him. When she died, he wrote to Dorothy Wellesley that 'for more than forty years she has been the centre of my life in London and during all that time we have never had a quarrel, sadness sometimes but never a difference.... For the moment I cannot bare [*sic*] the thought of London. I will find her memory everywhere.'

The easy cultured life which Olivia Shakespear represented, and in which Yeats, in the final twenty years of his life, fitted without nervousness, had in his early years intimidated him. A breakthrough for him came in 1894 when he was invited to spend some days at Lissadell House, the big house near Sligo and home to the Gore-Booths. The daughters, several years younger than Yeats, were interested in the local boy who had achieved some fame, and the poet was enchanted by their good looks and the style of their breeding. In a letter to Katharine Tynan, he makes two connected comments on them: 'These people are much better educated than our people and have a better instinct for excellence. It is very curious how the dying out of party feeling has nationalized the more thoughtful Unionists.' Writing these observations in 1895, he could hardly have imagined how far the nationalisation of Constance and Eva Gore-Booth would take them from their Georgian mansion. Both became deeply involved in politics, Eva in welfare work with the poor and in feminist groups, Constance in much more militant affairs. The latter became Countess Markiewicz through her marriage to a Polish count, but her commitment was to socialist republicanism and she became a follower of James Connolly and a member of the Citizen Army. For the leading part she played in the Rising in 1916 she was sentenced to death and, when spared, she entered politics and, although she refused to appear at Westminster, was the first elected female Member of Parliament. Eva, for whom the young Willie Yeats had entertained a small idea of marriage, died in 1926; Constance died in 1927. In 'Easter 1916', Yeats regrets how Constance had sacrificed herself in 'ignorant good will' until 'her voice grew shrill', and in 'On a Political Prisoner' contrasts her present situation and her youth in the confronting images of 'Blind and leader of the blind/Drinking the foul ditch where they lie' and 'clean and sweet/Like any rock-bred, sea-borne bird'. After their deaths he lamented the waste, as he saw it, of their lives in 'In Memory of Eva Gore-Booth and Con Markiewicz':

The light of evening, Lissadell,
Great windows open to the south,
Two girls in silk kimonos, both
Beautiful, one a gazelle.
But a raving autumn shears
Blossom from the summer's wreath.

The graciousness of accustomed affluence, the unostentatiousness
of inherited furnishings and family traditions, what he saw culminating in courtesy, appealed to Yeats and he considered Eva and Con
along with Maud Gonne as betraying something precious and
feminine. His own experience of such a life in such a household had
mainly been gained in his summers at Coole Park with Lady
Gregory. Her son Robert was to be the bearer-forward of this tradition but his early death led to the demise of the estate. In the previous year, 1917, Yeats bought the Tower at Ballylee, part of the Coole
estate, for £35 and, in restoring it, he felt that he was reviving five
centuries of habitation. Later in the same year he married Georgie
Hyde Lees. Ezra Pound was the best man.

Georgie, or George as Yeats was to call her, had been known by
him since 1911. Her stepfather was Olivia Shakespear's brother.
Some opposition from her mother had to be overcome before she
agreed to her daughter of 25 marrying the famous poet of 52. Lady
Gregory and Olivia Shakespear gave their important blessings.
Yeats had three years earlier initiated George into the Order of the
Golden Dawn and, on their honeymoon, apparently in the first
place to humour him because he was overcome with maudlin
thoughts about Maud and Iseult, she began to experiment with
automatic writing. It has been suggested that she practised a kind
hoax on him but the huge bulk of material which is now being tran-
scribed and edited renders this theory untenable. (Some admirers
and some attackers of Yeats are always seeking evidence to prove
either that he was not as foolish as he has been supposed or that he
was even more foolish.) The surprising marriage seems to have been
a satisfying and enhancing relationship for both Yeats and his wife.
Well-read and able to read in several languages, musical, intelligent,
kind and tolerant, she provided affection and a solid centre in his
life; she subtly steered him, defused certain situations, allowed him
space, and enjoyed his company. Their daughter Anne was born in
1919, and a son, Michael, two years later; the burden of bringing
them up rested mainly on George. Yeats had never been blessed

with consistent health and his wife had to cope with the ailments which frequently afflicted him, ranging from near-blindness and congestion of the lungs to measles and Malta fever. Her tact and good-humoured sense in complementing the celebrity in public were remarkable and, after his death, the early biographers, such as Hone, Jeffares, Ellmann and Henn, were full of praise for her handling of his papers.

Yeats's own appreciation is apparent in his poetry, particularly in the poems where she is presented as Sheba who brings unexpected gifts and a new kind of wisdom to old King Solomon: 'Solomon and Sheba', 'Solomon and the Witch' and in 'An Image from a Past Life' and 'The Gift of Harun Al-Raschid'. The rebuilt tower is dedicated to her in a dedication which can outlive the tower:

> I, the poet William Yeats,
> With old mill boards and sea-green slates,
> And smithy work from the Gort forge,
> Restored this tower for my wife George;
> And may these characters remain
> When all is ruin once again.

The main collaborative work was *A Vision*, published in 1926, and based to a substantial degree on what Mrs Yeats received in trance from the 'communicators' who spoke or wrote through her. More will be said about the contents of *A Vision* in Chapter 8 but here our attention is on Mrs Yeats's contribution to her husband's writing. In 'A Packet for Ezra Pound', first published in 1929 and included as an introduction to the second edition of *A Vision* in 1937, Yeats tells how the communicators 'have insisted that the whole system is the creation of my wife's Daimon and of mine, and that it is as startling to them as to us.... Much that has happened, much that has been said, suggests that the communicators are the personalities of a dream shared by my wife, by myself, occasionally by others.' Whatever the explanation is of her automatic writing, which continued in various forms over about seven years and occupies almost four thousand manuscript pages, she certainly had some psychological or psychic gift for bringing into the open a vast amount of material in her or his or someone else's mind.

In the 21 years of their married life, Yeats maintained a relationship with many of his female friends from earlier years – Maud, Iseult, Olivia, Lady Gregory – and developed new relationships.

Most of his new women friends were English, beginning with Lady
Ottoline Morrell, who gave lavish parties for literary figures at her
house, Garsington Manor in Oxfordshire. Her house, like Coole
Park, provided a model of good taste for Yeats, which he uses in the
opening section of 'Meditations in Time of Civil War'. It was in the
final few years of his life that he engaged in the intimate friendships
from which letters and reports survive. In 1934 he was sufficiently
worried about a diminution of vigour, including sexual, that he
arranged to undergo a surgical operation. The Steinach operation
was widely rumoured to transplant glands from monkeys into the
patient (hence the Dublin joke about Yeats as the Gland Old Man!);
in fact, what he had was a vasoligature and vasectomy of some sort.
Whatever the sort, he immediately felt a surge of physical and psychological energy. Although his health actually deteriorated during
his remaining six years it was in 1934 that he started two 'affairs'.
Margot Collis (or Ruddock) was an actress who was encouraged to
write poems and sing by Yeats, impressed as he was by her youth,
good looks and raw talent. She performed in his play *The Player
Queen*, and in 1936, when Yeats was recuperating from a heart condition in Majorca, she turned up in a desperate and delirious condition. She almost killed herself and Yeats had to pay for her transport
home to Britain. He wrote three poems about her: 'Margot' (unpublished until recently), 'Sweet Dancer' and 'A Crazed Girl'. He does
seem to have had qualms about his conduct with her and in the late
poem 'The Man and the Echo' asks:

> Did words of mine put too great strain
> On that woman's reeling brain?

Also in 1934 he began a friendship with the novelist Ethel Mannin
and, although there is no evidence of wildness in this case, he wrote
regularly to her, saw her when he was in London, and revealed a
considerable amount of what he was thinking and feeling. It is in a
letter to her that he copies his little poem 'The Spur', and it obviously connects with previous discussions:

> You think it horrible that lust and rage
> Should dance attention upon my old age;
> They were not such a plague when I was young;
> What else have I to spur me into song?

In 1935 Yeats was reading widely to choose material for *The Oxford Book of Modern Verse* when he chanced on some poems which pleased him by a Dorothy Wellesley. Dorothy Wellesley, Duchess of Wellington, was known to Ottoline Morrell and it was arranged that he would visit her at her splendid house, 'Penns in the Rocks', in Sussex. A friendship developed which continued in letters and sojourns at Penns till his death. Their correspondence is wide-ranging and intimate, often concerned with poetry and with projects they shared. His poem 'The Three Bushes' emerged from a collaboration commenced by her and she cooperated with him in his wish to promote the writing of ballads with musical settings. The poem 'To Dorothy Wellesley' was printed in his lifetime as 'To a Friend'. What their private relationship consisted of remains a mystery. He certainly had, for all his ailments, and they were many, strong sexual feelings or even inclinations and his letters have an open physical flavour. Although she was married, Dorothy's own preference seems to have been lesbian and there is an intriguing comment in a letter to her in December 1936: 'What makes your work so good is the masculine element allied to much feminine charm – your lines have the magnificent swing of your boyish body. I wish I could be a girl of nineteen, for certain hours that I might feel it even more acutely.' And he adds a *post scriptum*: 'Have you noticed that the Greek androgynous statue is always the woman in man, never the man in woman? It was made for men who loved men first.' He sent to her also 'The Spur' as his 'final apology'; in this letter 'Lust and Rage', with capitals, 'dance attendance'.

Dorothy Wellesley was in Cap Martin in the south of France when her friend died on 28 January 1939. Also there was Edith Shackleton (Heald) to whom, again, Yeats had written numerous intimate letters in the two years before his death. It seems that he first met her in 1906 when she was 21, but no evidence of a friendship is known before 1937. She was a very successful freelance journalist, from a family who had moved from Northern Ireland to Lancashire. She and her sister, who was also in journalism, worked hard and earned the money with which to buy luxuries and Chantry House in Sussex which they completely renovated. Yeats spent weeks there (as well as at Dorothy Wellesley's) and wrote many of his late poems and plays in Edith's company. He appreciated her intelligence, sharp wit and generosity; and, it appears, her friendship with him, often physically described in his letters to her, was accepted as helpful by Mrs Yeats. Five years after his death, Edith Shackleton entered into a new passionate relationship, this time with the woman painter Gluck.

In his poem 'On Woman' written in 1914, Yeats says:

> May God be praised for woman
> That gives up all her mind,
> A man may find in no man
> A friendship of her kind
> That covers all he has brought
> As with her flesh and bone,
> Nor quarrels with a thought
> Because it is not her own.

When the two ladies who wrote under the male name of Michael Field told him how they envied the conversation between men, Yeats retorted: 'Men don't talk well to each other – they talk well to women. There must be sex in good talk…. A man has no ideas among men – but he goes home to a cook or a countess and he is all right.'[6] His excitement in women, however, did not stem entirely from conversation but needed 'flesh and bone'. Sometimes in his later phase there seems to be a desperation, a need for some final assertion, in his emphasis on sex. In a letter to Olivia Shakespear in 1932 he proclaims: 'I shall be a sinful man to the end, and think upon my death-bed of all the nights I wasted in my youth'; and the following year in a letter to Mario Rossi he warns that, 'the man who ignores the poetry of sex… finds the bare facts written up on the walls of a privy, or himself is compelled to write them there'. He was very much in a line with Freud and Lawrence, who saw sex as central to creativity and well-being. Dorothy Wellesley relates how 'Sex, Philosophy and the Occult preoccupy him. He strangely intermingles the three', and recalls that he once said, despairingly, 'The tragedy of sexual intercourse is the perpetual virginity of the soul.'[7] And yet, perhaps, influenced by or following the example of Shelley, he enjoyed pursuing the unattainable; perhaps he liked to feel that there is always something unknowable in the other, and that is why Maud Gonne could hold him at arm's length and why he so often had liaisons with women who were married or are directed elsewhere. Is it a mere coincidence that two of his late 'lovers' were lesbian?

A crucial difference between Yeats's female and male friends in the first half of his career is that many of his male friends were considerably older than himself and died as he was maturing. His father, John O'Leary, William Morris, Edward Dowden, W. E. Henley, Edwin Ellis, George Pollexfen, all passed out of his life. A number of his other early male friends, such as Oscar Wilde, Lionel Johnson, Aubrey Beardsley, Hugh Lane and John Synge, died young. With a number he did fall out: for example, George Russell, George Moore and MacGregor Mathers. After his close friend Arthur Symons went mad in 1908–9, Yeats hardly mentions him in his autobiographical writings. There is only one of his female friends who springs to mind from whom he parted in anger – Mabel Dickinson, a masseuse (or 'medical gymnast') with whom he had a sexual affair between 1908 and 1913 and who alleged, falsely, that she was pregnant by him. Most of the exciting and personally informative letters were written to women correspondents. The conclusion to be drawn is that he established more lasting relationships with a number of female friends and it was often with them that he felt most comfortable in discussing his life and work.

Nonetheless, and although the bulk of this chapter concentrates on his friendships with women, he enjoyed a deep and rewarding companionship with a large number of men. Many of these men and their connections with him have been considered in earlier chapters and that material has to be fed into the present chapter by the reader in order to gain a more complete picture of Yeats's 'friends and loves'. When looking through Yeats's voluminous correspondence, one of the striking observations to be made by the person mainly interested in Yeats as a major literary figure is how many letters are addressed to unliterary people. The writer's other interests commanded large areas of his resources. Most specifically, his contacts with correspondents involved in the occult were certainly some of his most durable and demanding. He sustained a longlasting (1896–1918) correspondence with the cantankerous William T. Horton, for whose *Book of Images* he wrote an introduction in 1898. Horton, an artist obsessively intrigued with spiritual matters, delivered a series of rebukes to Yeats, usually for his non-Christian and occult practices, till his own final conversion to Roman Catholicism and death in 1919. Yeats commemorates him in 'All Souls' Night':

> He loved strange thought
> And knew that sweet extremity of pride
> That's called platonic love,
> And that to such a pitch of passion wrought

Nothing could bring him, when his lady died,
Anodyne for his love.
Words were but wasted breath;
One dear hope he had:
The inclemency
Of that or the next winter would be death.

I choose to mention Horton, not because he was a great artist or because he should be praised, but because, along with other, not very well-known, personages such as William F. Stead and Frank Sturm, he contributed to a context of human contact, experience and ideas which partly shaped Yeats's career.

Short biographies of writers sometimes encourage readers to believe that the writer's life consists largely of writing and advancing the art. In his introduction to the translation of *Gitanjali* by the Bengali poet Tagore, Yeats offers a different slant: 'Four-fifths of our energy is spent in the quarrel with bad taste, whether in our own minds or the minds of others.' An embodiment of what Yeats considered bad taste in another preoccupied him for some time in the person of George Moore: 'Moore had inherited a large Mayo estate, and no Mayo country gentleman had ever dressed the part so well. He lacked manners, but had manner; he could enter a room so as to draw your attention without seeming to, his French, his knowledge of painting, suggested travel and leisure. Yet nature had denied him the final touch: he had a coarse palate.' This was written in 1935, two years after Moore's death and almost thirty years after the paths of the two men had diverged. Their relationship from the time they first met in 1894 contained many ambivalences on both sides. Moore saw Yeats at a performance of the latter's *The Land of Heart's Desire*:

> a long black cloak drooped from his shoulders, a soft black sombrero on his head, a voluminous silk tie flowing from his collar, loose black trousers dragging untidily over his long heavy feet – a man of such excessive appearance that I could not do otherwise – could I? – than mistake him for an Irish parody of the poetry that I had seen all my life strutting its rhythmic way in the alleys of the Luxembourg Gardens, preening its rhymes by the fountains, excessive in habit and gait.[8]

The mannered parallels of double adjectives, the extravagance and the mock-innocence are all so typical of Moore that he is in danger of parodying himself. Later, in his autobiography *Hail and Farewell* (1911–14), there are two glorious chapters satirically questioning the achievements of the Revival manifested in Yeats, Lady Gregory and Synge. Despite all the sarcasm and cynical undermining of high-falutin' idealisms, he seems eventually to concede that Yeats did create something; according to him, Lady Gregory and Synge would have achieved nothing on their own and even in his own case, famous as a novelist before he even met Yeats, he might not have returned to Ireland in 1901 if Yeats had not persuaded him to do so, and if he had not returned he would not have written his classic short stories in *The Untilled Field* (1903), and the novel *The Lake* (1905). In his earlier novel *Evelyn Innes* (1898) the character Alick Dean represents a not unflattering version of Yeats but Moore altered the figure to someone more like George Russell in a revised edition three years later.

Although incensed by Moore's cavalier and unscrupulous presentation of himself and his friends in *Hail and Farewell*, Yeats could appreciate some good qualities in his attacker and he could also counter-attack with some brilliant cutting strokes. In *Dramatis Personae*, he describes Moore in Paris sitting among the intelligentsia as 'a man, carved out of a turnip, looking out of astonished eyes'. Moore's body was 'insinuating, upflowing, circulative, curvicular, pop-eyed'. This unprepossessing liar, lecher and betrayer of friends had, however, written several masterpieces in addition to *Esther Waters* and Yeats acknowledged that, without Moore's practical knowledge of the theatre, the idea of an Irish national theatre would have come to nothing. Moore's commitment to a Celtic vision of Irish culture did not last long but, while he was an ally, Yeats tolerated and even applauded the very qualities he later came to deplore. When *Hail and Farewell* was published, Yeats immediately responded with the poems which frame *Responsibilities* as introductory and closing pieces. The latter deplores a notoriety with which he has been branded when 'all my precious things / Are but a post the passing dogs defile'.

The poet had a sneaking regard for Moore's brashness, eagerness to shock, and insensitivity to people's feelings, even the feelings of friends: he seemed to enjoy an independence in his absence of loyalty or decency. According to Frank O'Connor, the short-story writer and later friend of Yeats, the poet was not one to harbour grudges against people he disliked; Moore, however, was his exception. The rough side which intrigued him in Moore he found also in the doctor and poet Oliver St John Gogarty (the character Buck Mulligan in Joyce's *Ulysses*) who removed his tonsils, dedicated a pair of swans to the Liffey in gratitude to the river by which he escaped from kidnappers, and was partly responsible for Yeats being made a Senator. Gogarty's poetry, his wit and a rapscallion bravado impressed the older poet. Younger friends of Yeats, such as Gogarty, Frank O'Connor, Thomas MacGreevy (who later became Director of the National Gallery in Dublin) and F. R. Higgins, poet and Managing Director of the Abbey, all comment in their reminiscences on his sense of fun and his delight in gossip. His wife considered him so indiscreet that she nicknamed him 'William Tell'. He loved bright conversation and an audience of sympathetic friends whom he could regale with lavishly-told stories. For all his sternness and often apparent remoteness from practicalities and people around him, he was loyal to the people he liked, often generous to young writers – for example, Joyce – and appreciative of the support given him by others.

One person, not particularly close to him emotionally or even geographically, to whom he owed a great deal was the American lawyer John Quinn. He first met Quinn in 1902 (the same year in which he met Joyce) and the American introduced him to the works of Nietzsche. This extraordinary self-made lawyer occupied an amazing position in relation to the development of the European arts in the first two decades of the century. He was a patron or a supporter to many writers and artists and, before his death in 1924, he had accumulated one of the largest collections of modern artworks and literary manuscripts in private hands in the United States. Among writers, he helped Joyce, Eliot, Pound, Conrad and Yeats and, at a crucial time, worked tirelessly to promote and protect Irish writing and the work of the Abbey Theatre. Without his financial, legal and administrative support would *The Waste Land* and *Ulysses* have been written? He helped to organise the tours of America which earned Yeats money which he desperately needed, he gave backing to many of the poet's projects and, almost in return for his giving, he found himself burdened with the poet's father when J. B. Yeats 'decided' to remain in New York from 1907 till his death in 1922. Yeats Senior was supported almost entirely by money sent by his son and by gifts and commissions from Quinn, who further supported the Yeats family by buying the poet's manuscripts. Pound reported that W. B. Yeats found Quinn 'the kindest, most generous, most irascible of men' and he was all three.

Quinn had no obvious personal influence on Yeats's work but he facilitated some things and provided space in which the poet could operate. They had their disagreements but Yeats acknowledged how much he owed to this benevolent patron and ally. At the end of his life, in 'The Municipal Gallery Revisited', the consummate writer and instigator of so many schemes, looking back through the portraits of his old associates, in particular Augusta Gregory and John Synge, but reviewing more inclusively than these two, turns to the reader and pronounces:

> You that would judge me, do not judge alone
> This book or that, come to this hallowed place
> Where my friends' portraits hang and look thereon;
> Ireland's history in their lineaments trace;
> Think where man's glory most begins and ends,
> And say my glory was I had such friends.

6
Masks and Development

The term 'Anglo-Irish', whatever else it may contain, suggests someone with a foot in two camps. Yeats's upbringing was divided between Dublin, London and Sligo and, for all his passionate nationalism, almost half of his life was spent outside Ireland. In England he was often perceived as heavily Irish, even something of a caricature in his manner of speaking and behaving; in Ireland he was in danger of being considered Anglified and of trying to impose on Ireland notions imported from elsewhere. His attempts to bring Catholic Ireland and Protestant Ireland closer together necessitated the adoption by him of characteristics of the former. In order to counter a colonial view of Ireland he needed to formulate images of Irish identity beyond those promoted by the dominant colonialist ideology. In all of these circumstances, he was forced to be aware of his stance and of how people reacted to it. Furthermore, according to his own account, as a young man he was very shy and awkward and, when he was in his early twenties, this condition caused him such pain that he felt obliged for the sake of his sanity to change his social manner by learning to act confidently. How plausible this account is of his maturation is open to question, but certainly he succeeded in impressing people with his apparent self-control and an air of authority. His explanation of his development was written many years on and by that time he had worked out a whole theory of personality. This chapter attempts to indicate something of the background to his theory and point to some of the manifestations of it in his work.

George Russell (AE) recalled how he had shown Yeats some drawings he had made:

> He was interested most of all in a drawing of a man on a hill-top, a man amazed at his own shadow cast gigantically on a mountain mist, for this drawing had not seemed to me the best. But I soon found his imagination was dominated by his own myth of a duality of self.[1]

126

This motif of a projected image of the self was popular in Romantic painting and poetry, for example, in Casper David Friedrich and Wordsworth, but Yeats was concerned with something more internal. He was impressed with a passage in the first act of Shelley's *Prometheus Unbound* where the Earth is reassuring Prometheus that there is a larger scheme into which temporal life fits:

> The Magus Zoroaster, my dead child,
> Met his own image walking in the garden.
> That apparition, sole of men, he saw.
> For know there are two worlds of life and death:
> One that which thou beholdest; but the other
> Is underneath the grave, where do inhabit
> The shadows of all forms that think and live
> Till death unite them and they part no more,
> Dreams and the light imaginings of men,
> And all that faith creates or love desires,
> Terrible, strange, sublime and beauteous shapes....

In the late 'Supernatural Songs' Yeats's invented hermit, Ribh, argues with St Patrick about the nature of existence and quotes the Smaragdine Tablet, on which Hermes Trismegistus (Egyptian Thoth) inscribed his wisdom: 'For things below are copies .... Yet all must copy copies.' There is an overlap between this notion and the idea of the *doppelganger* and *alter ego* so prevalent in nineteenth-century fiction. It is unlikely that Yeats knew of James Hogg's extraordinary psychological novel, *The Private Memoirs and Confessions of a Justified Sinner* (1824), but he was certainly familiar with *The Strange Case of Dr Jekyll and Mr Hyde* by R. L. Stevenson, which was published in 1886. Both of these, both by Scots, display an overtly moral orientation and explore aspects of schizophrenia (before the term came into use). The more Gothic tales of Mary Shelley's *Frankenstein* (1818), Maturin's *Melmoth the Wanderer* (1820) and Bram Stoker's *Dracula* (1897) investigate versions of shape-changing, a subject of recurring interest to Yeats. In 'Swedenborg, Mediums, Desolate Places', his strange disquisition on interactions between the living and the dead, or perhaps between the conscious and the unconscious mind, he writes:

> Yet we never long escape the phantasmagoria nor can long forget that we are among the shape-changers. Sometimes our own minds

shape that mysterious substance, which may be life itself, according to desire or constrained by memory, and the dead no longer remembering their own names become the characters in the drama we ourselves have invented.... Swedenborg has written that we are each in the midst of a group of associated spirits who sleep when we sleep and become the *dramatis personae* of our dreams, and are always the other will that wrestles with our thought, shaping it to our despite.

He was fascinated by stories of transformation, for example, seals becoming women, witches turning into hares, a trout becoming a beautiful girl (see 'The Song of Wandering Aengus'), and this fascination is apparent in his collections of tales gathered together in *Mythologies*; transitions between the natural and supernatural are a continuation of this process.

The main focus of his attention, however, was on the psychological constitution of the individual, on the specific stamp of character in action at a particular moment and on the nature of a whole personality. In 'Among School Children', one of his central poems, he presents himself in a number of guises: 'A sixty-year-old smiling public man'... 'Had pretty plumage once'... 'a comfortable kind of old scarecrow'... 'a shape upon her [mother's] lap'... 'that shape/With sixty or more winters on its head'. Maud Gonne is similarly presented: 'a Ledaean body, bent/Above a sinking fire'... 'She stands before me as a living child' ... 'Hollow of cheek as though it drank the wind/And took a mess of shadows for its meat.' One of the questions posed by the poem concerns the identity of a person. Is one phase of a person's life more definitive than another? Or is the person an accumulation or melting-down of these phases?

> O chestnut-tree, great-rooted blossomer,
> Are you the leaf, the blossom or the bole?

The poem concludes with questions rather than with answers. Various theories have been aired in the course of the poem. There is Plato's parable of how the original human condition of androgyny split into separate male and female genders, and Plato's other idea that life as we know it is insubstantial, a poor imitation of the reality that lies beyond. Aristotle tried to locate reality precisely in the physical world spurned by Plato. Pythagoras saw harmony or ratio as the basis of meaning. Lovers, mothers and religious people cultivate an image or icon on which to fix their passion. None of the theories seems to work and the very theories intensify a sense of ignorance and futility: 'self-born mockers of man's enterprise'. We cannot 'know the dancer from the dance' because we are in the dance; we are involved in a process and, therefore, are unable to see the whole shape dispassionately.

In his reference to Swedenborg above, Yeats speaks of the spirits or 'Presences' (the term used in 'Among School Children') as 'the *dramatis personae* of our dreams'. *Dramatis personae* means the characters in a drama and the Latin word *persona*, from which we derive our words 'person' and 'personality', meant a mask of the sort worn by actors playing certain characters. Yeats's theories of personality and poetry are both dramatic and they centre on a notion of masks. His father always insisted to him that all great poetry is dramatic but the young poet argued fiercely for lyrical self-expression. It was his father who took him when he was about 12 to see Henry Irving playing Hamlet and, as was mentioned in Chapter 1, the figure of Irving's Hamlet caused the boy to imitate his style. Yeats recalls that 'for many years Hamlet was an image of heroic self-possession for the poses of youth and childhood to copy, a combatant of the battle within myself'. Probably when he was in his early twenties he found himself forced to revise his simple faith in self-expression and learned 'that if a man is to write lyric poetry he must be shaped by nature and art to some one out of half a dozen traditional poses, and be lover or saint, sage or sensualist, or mere mocker of all life'. In ballads and myths he discovered a repertoire of traditional poses in which his personal emotions could be subsumed and cleared of egotism. To begin with, his choice of sources was promiscuous, and Arcadia or India was as appropriate as Ireland, and the recent past as suitable as a distant past. In *The Wanderings of Oisin* the journeys of the hero to the three islands of gaiety, fighting and torpor can be read as explorations of different attitudes or moods in Yeats's own mind. Similarly, different poems written in the 1890s focus on different aspects of the central symbol of the Rose; and many of the poems in *The Wind Among the Reeds* were originally allocated to three *personae*, Michael Robartes, Hanrahan and Aedh, who each stood for a psychological attitude as well as for an occult quality. Hanrahan is also the protagonist in the sequence of short stories called *Stories of Red Hanrahan* published in 1897 and reappears in the poetry as a lecherous scholar who accepts his instincts.

In the 1890s – but it is difficult to date some processes in his autobiography, and he revised not just his writings but also his life – some time in the 1890s, Yeats came to some new thoughts about himself:

My mind began drifting vaguely towards that doctrine of 'the mask' which has convinced me that every passionate man... is, as it were, linked with another age, historical or imaginary, where alone he finds images that rouse his energy. Napoleon was never of his own time... but had some Roman emperor's image in his head and some condottiere's blood in his heart.

Certainly in this period, which he entitled 'The Tragic Generation', he made the acquaintance of some people who lived their lives at such an extremity and with such intensity that they seemed possessed by a daimon or committed to playing an extraordinary part to the bitter end. Sometimes the disparity between the person and the part was so intense that, as in the case of William Sharp, an alter ego had to be invented to carry part of his life, or, in the case of Oscar Wilde, the dichotomy was fictionalised in *The Picture of Dorian Gray.* Yeats knew Wilde's family background and could see how he had diverged from it; he 'lived with no self-mockery at all an imaginary life; perpetually performed a play which was in all things the opposite of all that he had known in childhood and early youth'. In his dialogue *The Critic as Artist II* (1891), Wilde through his mouthpiece, Gilbert, replies to his interlocutor's claim that the critic/artist must needs be sincere:

A little sincerity is a dangerous thing, and a great deal of it is absolutely fatal. The true critic will, indeed, always be sincere in his devotion to the principle of beauty, but he will seek for beauty in every age and in each school, and will never suffer himself to be limited in any settled custom of thought, or stereotyped mode of looking at things. He will realise himself in many forms, and by a thousand different ways, and will ever be curious of new sensations and fresh points of view. Through constant change, and through constant change alone, he will find his true unity. He will not consent to be the slave of his own opinions. For what is mind but motion in the intellectual sphere? The essence of thought, as the essence of life, is growth. You must not be frightened by words, Ernest. What people call insincerity is simply a method by which we can multiply our personalities.[2]

The younger Yeats saw Wilde, Henley and Morris as cultivating an image 'always opposite to the natural self or the natural world' and he admired their experimental daring. He was unable at this stage to see his own direction so clearly:

I know very little about myself and much less of that anti-self: probably the woman who cooks my dinner or the woman who sweeps out my study knows more than I. It is perhaps because Nature made me a gregarious man, going hither and thither looking for conversation, and ready to deny from fear or favour his dearest conviction, that I love proud and lonely things.

Again, it is unclear as to which period of his life he is referring and it appears from his use of the present tense that his ignorance of himself continues. The passage was written in 1921 and comes from his account of the years 1887 to 1891. In any case, it sounds rather wilfully unknowing or even confusing. Was he not a timid person by nature? However, his point is clear that, in order to develop, he had to pursue an anti-self; to quote one of his favourite masters, Blake: 'Without Contraries is no progression. Attraction and Repulsion, Reason and Energy, Love and Hate, are necessary to Human existence.'

His most sustained exposition of his theory of the anti-self and Mask is in the long essay *Per Amica Silentia Lunae* published in 1917. The opening section consists of a poem 'Ego Dominus Tuus' in which two figures, Hic and Ille, argue about the nature of the self and how poetry has been used by some poets in order to extend the self. Hic makes a claim for straightforward self-expression. Ille refutes his citation of Dante and Keats and argues that their poetry emerged from the friction between the selves they were born with and the opposites they pursued. He concludes:

Those men that in their writings are most wise
Own nothing but their blind, stupefied hearts.

In his own life, Ille seeks an image which would

Look most like me, being indeed my double,
And prove of all imaginable things
The most unlike, being my anti-self....

The poem is less abstractly theoretical than my description suggests, and Dante with his lecherous life, and the poor boy Keats, 'With face and nose pressed to a sweet-shop window', are presented in vivid images. Ille (or Yeats) is not concerned with the people who accept the world and flourish in action, 'The struggle

of the fly in marmalade', but with the person whose self-awareness
has wakened him or her from 'the common dream'. Later in the
essay, Yeats offers the aphorism: 'We make out of the quarrel with
others, rhetoric, but of the quarrel with ourselves, poetry.' He
quotes his own earlier thoughts on the subject from his diaries of
1909:

> I think all happiness depends on the energy to assume the mask
> of some other life, on a re-birth as something not one's self, some-
> thing created in a moment and perpetually renewed; in playing a
> game like that of a child where one loses the infinite pain of self-
> realisation, in a grotesque or solemn painted face put on that one
> may hide from the terror of judgement....

and

> If we cannot imagine ourselves as different from what we are, and
> try to assume that second self, we cannot impose a discipline
> upon ourselves though we may accept one from others. Active
> virtue, as distinguished from the passive acceptance of a code, is
> therefore theatrical, consciously dramatic, the wearing of a
> mask.... Wordsworth, great poet though he be, is so often flat and
> heavy partly because his moral sense, being a discipline he had
> not created, a mere obedience, has no theatrical element.

This comment on Wordsworth is very perceptive but only partially
true; the Lyrical Ballads have a strong theatrical element which is
central to their moral force. The uncultivated figure challenges and
often abashes the staid poetical voice put forward by Wordsworth.
Curiously enough, in all his discussion of masks in poetry, Yeats
makes scant reference to the whole tradition of what we now call
dramatic monologues. One might have expected him to find models
in such poems as 'Holy Willie's Prayer' by Burns, *Maud* by Tennyson
and 'Caliban upon Setebos' and 'Fra Lippo Lippi' by Browning, but
he passed them by. In fact, apart from actual plays, he appears to
have favoured poetic narratives with a wide variety of characters –
for example, Chaucer's *Canterbury Tales*, Dante's *Divine Comedy*,
Spenser's *The Faerie Queene* and Morris's *The Earthly Paradise*. Much
more directly influential and in accord with his theory of an anti-self
was some of the work of Blake. *Songs of Innocence and of Experience*,
subtitled 'Showing the Two Contrary States of the Human Soul',

showed Yeats how, in a sequence, poems could enlarge on or contradict each other and make rival claims on the reader's agreement. From very early in his career, he organised his collections with the deliberate intention of involving the reader in a highly dramatic process. His expectation was that the reader would read the collection in the order of the list of contents and would read steadily through Yeats's work (probably including prose and plays) as it was published. Symbols and characters were introduced to the reader and a system of cross-reference and accretion or depletion was assumed. In reading Blake's Prophetic Books, Yeats had been disturbed by an arbitrary quality in the symbolic figures, and he determined to give the total structure of his work a coherence and an inevitability. This attempt at a total structure will be discussed again in the succeeding chapters.

Despite or resulting from his arguments with his father as to whether poetry is primarily 'dramatic' or 'lyrical', Yeats came to see his writing of plays and his writing of poems as vitally interconnected. His earliest plays, written before he possessed any close knowledge of the actual workings of a theatre, are static, literary and hopelessly untheatrical. He gradually learned that for a play to be theatrically viable it has to be more than a tableau of good speeches operating parallel to each other; there must be conflict, confrontation, motifs developed and recalled, overlap and interruption of one character on another. His reading of Balzac's novels taught him much along these lines. This awareness of dramatic texture helped him to shape a new kind of poetry. It is significant how many of Yeats's poems, even as titles, suggest a dialogue: 'Fergus and the Druid', 'Shepherd and Goatherd', 'The Saint and the Hunchback', 'Youth and Age', 'Leda and the Swan', 'A Dialogue of Self and Soul', 'Blood and the Moon', 'Crazy Jane and the Bishop'. Some poems invite comparison and seem to address each other. This is very obvious in two poems written concurrently in the late 1920s, 'A Man Young and Old' and 'A Woman Young and Old': both are in eleven sections, both conclude with a passage translated from Sophocles, both trace a rough chronology, and they share images. In 'A Woman Young and Old', sections of the sequence match each other, for example, 'A First Confession' and 'A Last Confession', 'Parting' and 'Meeting', 'Her Triumph' and 'Consolation', as if they follow the ups and downs of a drama.

Some plays consist of characters who behave and interact in accordance with the forward movement of the plot. Some other plays, however, consist of characters who represent or comment on aspects of a central consciousness or problem. Classic examples of this second kind are Milton's *Samson Agonistes*, some morality plays and O'Neill's *The Emperor Jones*. Yeats often inclined towards a rather Manichean view of the world, and a number of his plays from as early as *The Countess Cathleen*, itself a morality play, present a struggle for balance or dominance between antagonistic forces. Characters, often masked to fix their stance, are like the counters in an argument or game: in The *Resurrection* (1925), for example, the Greek, the Syrian and the Hebrew represent metaphysical attitudes to the mystery of existence as manifested in the life, death and resurrection of Jesus Christ. In *Purgatory*, written in 1938, the distinctions between past and present, death and life, the actual and the imagined, are so uncertain that the whole play could be taking place inside the consciousness of the Old Man. A much earlier play, *On Baile's Strand*, first performed in 1904, offers a different use of characters but there is something in common. The play concerns a tussle between the High King, Conchubar, and the greatest warrior in Ireland, Cuchulain, and the tragic outcome of their argument about authority. However, the subject is introduced to the audience by a half-farcical scene between a Fool and a Blind Man, 'both ragged, and their features made grotesque and extravagant by masks' and they return at the end to complete the frame round the serious business of the play. The Fool and the Blind Man, in their interdependence and complementary qualities, mimic and also mock the relationship of the King with his anxiousness about rules and order, and the anarchic, belligerent Cuchulain. Conchubar is like a superego to Cuchulain's id and the two forces are temporarily united in the ritual of fire enacted by a Chorus of Women at the centre of the play. This union against the disruptive power of the Shape-Changers is immediately subverted by the arrival of Cuchulain's disguised son and the warrior is obliged, against his instinct, to abide by his oath to the King and to fight and kill his own only son. Yeats was primarily interested, not in reconstituting a heroic story, but in utilising a mythic action in order to explore a psychological dilemma: Can impulse be harnessed with obedience to rules?

Blake, in one of the Proverbs of Hell, pronounces that, 'The tigers of wrath are wiser than the horses of instruction', and at the time that Yeats was writing the play he was investigating Nietzsche's distinction between the Dionysian and the Apollonian types. These terms have proved elusive to many people partly because, in his development from *The Birth of Tragedy* (1872), where he first deploys them, to *Twilight of the Idols* (1888), Nietzsche alters their meaning and 'Dionysian' comes to be an inclusive term for the creative urge to weld all material into an artistic whole. In the earlier work, however, Apollonian and Dionysian are contraries, albeit necessary to each other as parts of the process of life and art. The Apollonian is concerned with form, rationality, order; the Dionysian deals in dangerous, imaginative intuition. Nietzsche offers a fascinating study not just of Greek Tragedy, not just of tragedy but also of individual and social self-knowledge and wellbeing. It is the Dionysian side, expressed in Greek Tragedy through the Chorus, that plugs the story of individuals into the myth, in a frightening but thrilling way. Dionysus was the god of ecstasy and intoxication and worship of him could induce these states or it could lead to wanton destructiveness. The surrender of the devotee's will to the god was symbolised in a mask, often featureless. Euripides' play *The Bacchae* shows how the force represented by Dionysus must be accommodated by individuals and societies: the dark, anarchic side of our nature, if repressed, will erupt with dire consequences. In Greek tragedy a balance has to be achieved by a shift effected by an act of Dionysian daring:

> Such magic transformation is the presupposition of all dramatic art. In this magic transformation the Dionysian reveller sees himself as a satyr, *and as a satyr, in turn, he sees the god*, which means that in his metamorphosis he beholds another vision outside himself, as the Apollonian complement of his own state. With this new vision the drama is complete.[3]

Nietzsche sees the relationship between the dialogue or surface and the chorus or depth of the play as a dialectic:

> Suppose we penetrate into the myth that projects itself in these lucid reflections: then we suddenly experience a phenomenon that is just the opposite of a familiar optical phenomenon. When after a forceful attempt to gaze on the sun we turn away blinded, we see dark-coloured spots before our eyes, as a cure, as it were. Conversely, the bright image projections of the Sophoclean hero – in short, the Apollonian aspect of the mask – are necessary effects of a glance into the inside and terrors of nature; as it were, luminous spots to cure eyes damaged by gruesome night. Only in this

sense may we believe that we properly comprehend the serious and important concept of 'Greek cheerfulness'.[4]

In 'Lapis Lazuli' Yeats points to a very similar cheerfulness in the face of death in Shakespeare's tragedies and describes it in images reminiscent of Nietzsche:

> They [the actors] know that Hamlet and Lear are gay;
> Gaiety transfiguring all that dread.
> All men have aimed at, found and lost;
> Black out; Heaven blazing into the head:
> Tragedy wrought to its uttermost.

There is a passage in *Twilight of the Idols*, written in the year before Nietzsche's mind broke down, which declares his later use of the term 'Dionysian' and also anticipates Yeats's espousal of a total flexibility in the creative personality:

> In the Dionysian state ...the entire emotional system is alerted and intensified so that it discharges all its powers of representation, imitation, transfiguration, transmutation, every kind of mimicry and play-acting, conjointly. The essential thing remains the facility of the metamorphosis, the incapacity *not* to react.... It is impossible for the Dionysian man not to understand any suggestion of whatever kind, he ignores no signal from the emotions, he possesses to the highest degree the instinct for understanding and divining, just as he possesses the art of communication to the highest degree. He enters into every skin, into every emotion; he is continually transforming himself.[5]

Nietzsche's inflated rhetoric may remind us more of Walt Whitman but Yeats found much in 'that strong enchanter' to corroborate his developing concept of the Mask and he saw the same necessity of 'continually transforming himself'. When he was 71 he wrote 'An Acre of Grass' in which he acknowledges how the weakness of age circumscribes most of his life:

> Picture and book remain,
> An acre of green grass
> For air and exercise,
> Now strength of body goes;

Midnight, an old house
Where nothing stirs but a mouse.

My temptation is quiet.
Here at life's end
Neither loose imagination,
Nor the mill of the mind
Consuming its rag and bone,
Can make the truth known.

He turns on himself with bitterness and some desperation, adopting that imprecatory mood so characteristic of him:

Grant me an old man's frenzy,
Myself must I remake
Till I am Timon and Lear
Or that William Blake
Who beat upon the wall
Till truth obeyed his call;

A mind Michael Angelo knew
That can pierce the clouds,
Or inspired by frenzy
Shake the dead in their shrouds;
Forgotten else by mankind,
An old man's eagle mind.

Much earlier, in 1912, he had written 'A Coat' in which he announced that he was discarding his Celtic mythological guise of the early period:

I made my song a coat
Covered with embroideries
Out of old mythologies
From heel to throat;
But the fools caught it,
Wore it in the world's eyes
As though they'd wrought it.
Song, let them take it,
For there's more enterprise
In walking naked.

It has often been noted that Yeats did not go naked: he changed his clothes and style. One area of life where openness or nakedness might be expected is in sexual relationships but in Yeats's poetry concerned with this area, masks are particularly apparent. In his *Journal* he writes: 'In wise love each divines the high secret self of the other and, refusing to believe in the mere daily self, creates a mirror where the lover or the beloved sees an image to copy in daily life. Love also creates the mask.'[6] It is a commonplace of literary criticism, although discussed by some recent theorists as if they had just invented the notion, that all the people in a literary work, including the narrating 'I', are constructs which have their existence, not in the actual world, but in the literary work itself. (Put in this way, the commonplace is itself a gross simplification and, reading through a collection of poems, the sensitive reader can recognise the voices in poems and identify them with a figure called W. B. Yeats.) Granted this problem, however, we are often perplexed at the variety of stance and of addressed *persona* in his love poetry. I have in mind, not the obvious guises in which he presents a woman, based on Maud Gonne, as Helen of Troy, Leda and Pallas Athene, but poems seemingly narrated by a woman or highlighting a peculiarly feminine side of a woman. An obvious example is 'The Mask', derived from a song in the play *The Player Queen* (begun in 1907 but first performed only in 1919), a complicated farce of plays within plays and characters acting parts and wearing masks. The poem, published in 1912, is in the form of a dialogue in which the man speaks first:

> 'Put off that mask of burning gold
> With emerald eyes.'
> 'O no, my dear, you make so bold
> To find if hearts be wild and wise,
> And yet not cold.'

> 'I would but find what's there to find,
> Love or deceit.'
> 'It was the mask engaged your mind,
> And after set your heart to beat,
> Not what's behind.'

> 'But lest you are my enemy,
> I must enquire.'

'O no, my dear, let all that be;
What matter, so there is but fire
In you, in me?'

In *The Player Queen* the exchange has a mocking context which makes the song heavily ironic but, as a poem, 'The Mask' is a straight confrontation of two attitudes: the man looking for the woman's 'true self', the woman trusting in what is shown by each and in the response to what is shown. Neither attitude is habitual to Yeats; he swings about between them and finds satisfaction and dissatisfaction in either one. In his own life, he had believed Maud Gonne's account of herself, and loved her as she presented herself, only to discover that her mask concealed many layers of otherness. He was almost broken by the discovery of what lay behind her mask but he had loved her as he had known her. In 1928 he wrote 'Before the World Was Made', the second section of 'A Woman Young and Old'; the idea of a public image constructed by a person is given a Platonic twist:

If I make the lashes dark
And the eyes more bright
And the lips more scarlet,
Or ask if all be right
From mirror after mirror,
No vanity's displayed:
I'm looking for the face I had
Before the world was made.
What if I look upon a man
As though on my beloved,
And my blood be cold the while
And my heart unmoved?
Why should he think me cruel
Or that he is betrayed?
I'd have him love the thing that was
Before the world was made.

Often in his love poetry, a dualistic debate is conducted regarding the claims of the body and of the soul. 'A Last Confession' in the sequence 'A Woman Young and Old' articulates the debate most clearly, and should be read in conjunction with Sections VIII, IX and X of the same poem.

In 'The Three Bushes' with its six satellite songs, however, the claims are given an odd development in a *ménage-à-trois*. The lady is to sleep with him but she cannot tolerate the idea that she should lose her virginity. She arranges with her chambermaid that she shall take the lady's place and go to the lover's bed in the darkness. All three appear to enjoy contentment although the two women speculate as to what they are missing in their partial love for the man and the lady's very chastity leads her mind to think of love in bestial images. The man, enjoying both women in their different ways, seems to feel a balance:

> Bird sighs for the air,
> Thought for I know not where,
> For the womb the seed sighs,
> Now sinks the same rest
> On mind, on nest
> On straining thighs.

'The Lady's Third Song' shows the acutest awareness of the unsatisfactoriness of dualism:

> When you and my true lover meet
> And he plays tunes between your feet,
> Speak no evil of the soul
> Nor think the body is the whole,
> For I that am his daylight lady
> Know worse evil of the body;
> But in honour split his love
> Till either neither have enough,
> That I may hear if he should kiss
> A contrapuntal serpent hiss,
> You, should hand explore a thigh,
> All the labouring heavens sigh.

The chambermaid, who is obliged to do the 'dirty' work for her lady, feels the lack of something spiritual in her relationship with the man and in her second verbless song she complains:

> From pleasure of the bed,
> Dull as a worm,
> His rod and its butting head

Limp as a worm,
His spirit that has fled
Blind as a worm.

Only after their deaths is a unity achieved, when the three rose-
bushes planted over their adjoining graves have such intermingled roots that nobody can ascertain from which individual grave
the bush has emerged and the rose of love blossomed. Yeats's
interest was not in any historical incident and his ballad was written in response to an attempt by Dorothy Wellesley to develop an
idea of her own (the note added to his title attributing the subject
to a French source is sheer invention). One of the aspects in traditional ballads which appealed to him was that the story is jumped
into and the reader is asked to accept characters and situations
without explanations or justifications and concentrate on a dramatic *dénouement*.

Thus, even in the midst of passion, perhaps particularly in the
midst of passion, we cannot be sure that we behave as ourselves. It
may be that we are taken out of ourselves or that we try to maintain
some control in the situation by choosing a role, adopting a mask. In
a larger perspective we might see how we played a part, given or
chosen, but in the turmoil of the moment we cannot stand back and
observe whether we take the lead or are led. In 'Whence had they
come?', Section VIII of 'Supernatural Songs', Yeats explores this
problem against a background of vast historical cycles:

Eternity is passion, girl or boy
Cry at the onset of their sexual joy
'For ever and for ever'; then awake
Ignorant what Dramatis Personae spake;
A passion-driven exultant man sings out
Sentences that he has never thought;
The Flagellant lashes those submissive loins
Ignorant what that dramatist enjoins,
What master made the lash. Whence had they come,
The hand and lash that beat down frigid Rome?
What sacred drama through her body heaved
When world-transforming Charlemagne was conceived?

Of course, for the individual the problem is of a much more local
nature and seems more closely related to Dale Carnegie's *How to*

Make Friends and Influence People, where it is recommended that different smiles should be practised in order to impress different kinds of people, or as Yeats describes himself in 'Coole Park, 1929': 'one that ruffled in a manly pose/For all his timid heart'. Across his collected poems, an exploration and enlargement of self take place in adopted poses which include kings, heroes, women, hermits, saints, beggars, pilgrims and wild, old, wicked men. Dualities are presented of love and hate, youth and old age, reason and intuition, male and female, life and art, public and private.

If someone follows Yeats's advice to explore masks, anti-selves, contrary images, how do the antinomies adjust to each other? Do they co-exist uneasily, take turns in prominence, melt into some harmony? The poet recalls how, when he was about 24, he became obsessed by a sentence ringing in his head: 'Hammer your thoughts into unity.' 'Unity of being' came to be a central aim of his activities and, writing in 1919, he saw it as not just a philosophy of personal development but as the gospel for a new age in Ireland, just as Douglas Hyde's lecture, 'The De-anglicization of Ireland', had instigated a new epoch in 1894. Unity of being came to be seen by him as integral with unity of culture:

> Have not all races had their first unity from a mythology that marries them to rock and hill? ...Nations, races, and individual men are unified by an image, or bundle of related images, symbolical or evocative of the state of mind which is, of all states of mind not impossible, the most difficult to that man, race, or nation; because only the greatest obstacle that can be contemplated without despair rouses the will to full intensity.

Just as his theory of personality and masks, and his exploration of the feminine side of his consciousness seem parallel with Jung's theory of personality and his notion of the *anima/animus*, so his ambition of unity of being and his related concept of *Anima Mundi* remind one strongly of Jung's collective or racial unconscious. It appears that the only direct acquaintance Yeats had of Jung's work occurred in 1931 when he read *The Secret of the Golden Flower*, a book on Chinese systems of meditation with a commentary by Jung. The clearest description of what he means by *Anima Mundi* is provided in *Hodos Chameliontos*, written in 1922. He asks the question: 'Is there nation-wide multiform reverie, every mind passing through a stream of suggestion, and all streams acting and reacting upon one another, no matter how distant the minds, how dumb the lips?' And he goes on to pose and answer a further question:

> When a man writes any work of genius, or invents some creative action, is it not because some knowledge or power has come into his mind? It is called up by an image ...but our images must be given to us, we cannot choose them deliberately. ...I know now that revelation is from the self, but from that age-long memoried self, that shapes the elaborate shell of the mollusc and the child in the womb... that genius is a crisis that joins that buried self for certain moments to our trivial daily mind. There are, indeed, personifying spirits that we had best call but Gates and Gatekeepers, because through their dramatic power they bring our souls to crisis, to Mask and Image, caring not a straw whether we be Juliet going to her wedding, or Cleopatra to her death; for in their eyes nothing has weight but passion.

There is a connection between the ideas outlined here and Yeats's earlier adherence to Symbolism.

As he moved into old age he came to accept that his optimism for a unity of being in Ireland was misplaced but he retained his belief in the source of such a unity in the *Anima Mundi*, that reservoir of archetypes of images or myths of the central experiences of the tribe. Since Yeats's death, research and speculation in this area have increased and, for example, Bruce Chatwin's *Songlines*, on Australian aboriginal race memories, would have delighted the poet. Equally, he moderated his advocacy of the Mask as a mechanism for advancement for everyone. He came to acknowledge that, for some people, the pursuit of an anti-self could be dangerous and that some types of people have their strength in building on the self they have been given by circumstances beyond their control. The importance granted by Yeats to the Mask in his work turns out, when we consider the art of the twentieth-century in retrospect, to have been consonant with a major thematic concern beyond literature. Various psychological theories opened up thinking about the nature of the self and prominence was given to role-play, role-models, fantasy, defence mechanisms, schizophrenia. Anthropologists researched areas of tribal behaviour previously unknown to Europeans, recording and analysing ritual performances as sacred dramas. In these rituals, where a human being has to play the part of a god or an animal, masks are crucial and seem to impart special power to the participant. Tribal masks fascinated a number of painters, including Rouault, Picasso and Gauguin. Facets of personality can be explored through masks and a picture of 'Man with mask' prompts a dual interpretation of what the man is 'in himself' and what he is as represented by the mask. Fiction and drama, almost by their nature, exploit various kinds of masks and charades, from Thurber's *The Secret Life of Walter Mitty* to Joyce's *Ulysses* and the extraordinary plays of the Flemish dramatist Michel de Ghelderode (1898–1962), and Brecht. Synge's *The Playboy of the Western World* delivers a fascinating package of character-shifts and transformations. So convincing is Christy Mahon's adoption of the role as the wild, poetic hero, the Playboy, that even his father believes that he cannot be the spineless son brought up by him. In the shifts of gears in actions and language, every stability of the community and the self is called into question, and the usual distinctions between fiction and actuality are made to look very suspect. The writer whom Yeats recognised as a fellow-thinker was his contemporary Luigi Pirandello (1867–1936). Pirandello, through the bitter experience of his marriage to a woman whose mind collapsed into delusion, learned the relativity of truth according to viewpoints and how often a solid fiction or delusion can be more comfortable than the messy arbitrariness of ordinary life. His plays have the feel of labyrinthine games but a pulse of desperation and longing for security throbs through the drama. *Henry IV* appeared in 1922, the same year as Yeats's *Hodos Chameliontos*. It probes the boundary between society's normality and madness in the figure of a man fixed in playing the historical Holy Roman Emperor Henry IV. In some of the speeches the positive and negative sides of adopting a mask are wonderfully scrutinised. In the opening Act a warning is uttered: 'Woe to him who doesn't know how to wear his mask' and, towards the end of the play, Henry consoles himself by saying that he is aware that he plays at being a madman but those around him do not see their madness. *Six Characters in Search of an Author* appeared in 1921 and *Right You Are (If You Think So)* in 1917; all three were translated into English in 1929. The perplexing mixture of intense, even tragic, emotion and the manoeuvres of a farce is often difficult to absorb; the reader or spectator is constantly outflanked and made to feel emotionally inept. It anticipates much of what later emerged in the Theatre of the Absurd and yet it has an immaculate quality. Yeats, in trying to catch something of the fusion of the individual and the general, the emotional and the intellectual, comes close to describing the plays of Pirandello which he admired:

Does not all art come when a nature, that never ceases to judge itself, exhausts personal emotion in action or desire so completely that something impersonal, something that has nothing to do with action or desire, suddenly starts into its place, something which is as unforeseen, as completely organized, even as unique, as the images that pass before the mind between sleeping and waking?

7

A Vision of Byzantium

From very early in his life Yeats was fascinated with systems of thought, orderings of ideas. The very sequence of events in his life appeared to some contemporaries as planned by him, and his life and art appear in retrospect as so intermingled that they form parts of a contrived pattern. He admired people who had devised comprehensive systems, people such as Plato, Dante, Boehme, Vico, Swedenborg, Blake, Goethe, and contemporaries such as Spengler, Toynbee and Henry Adams. However, he never seemed conclusively satisfied with his grand plans, and the question asked by the Syrian sceptic in the play *The Resurrection* recurs: 'What if there is always something that lies outside knowledge, outside order? What if at the moment when knowledge and order seem complete that something appears?' In a similar way, the final lines of *The Words Upon the Window-pane*, uttered in the voice of the long-dead Dean Swift, usurp the tidy explanation offered by rationalism.

In Chapter 2, his involvement with the Symbolist Movement and the Order of the Golden Dawn was outlined. His major effort in the 1890s to create an inclusive scheme was directed towards the proposed Celtic Order of Mysteries to be centred in the castle on the island in Lough Key:

> For ten years to come my most impassioned thought was a vain attempt to find philosophy and to create ritual for that Order. I had an unshakable conviction, arising how or whence I cannot tell, that invisible gates would open as they opened for Blake, as they opened for Swedenborg, as they opened for Boehme, and that this philosophy would find its manuals of devotion in all imaginative literature, and set before Irishmen for special manual an Irish literature which, though made by many minds, would seem the work of a single mind, and turn our places of beauty or legendary association into holy symbols. I did not think this philosophy would be altogether pagan, for it was plain that its

symbols must be selected from all those things that had moved men most during many, mainly Christian, centuries.

The pivotal symbols of the Order were to be the Four Jewels of the Tuatha de Danaan (half-legendary inhabitants of ancient Ireland) which, according to his collaborator Maud Gonne, Yeats believed were universal symbols which appeared also in the Tarot pack, thought to have been used for divination by the Egyptians, and in the Christian emblems of the Grail. In a number of the earlier poems he culls elements from various mythic strata and treats them as interchangeable manifestations of these universal symbols, often connected in his mind in the rose, the 'far-off, most secret, and inviolate Rose'. For example, in the poem, 'The Secret Rose', he alludes to the Holy Sepulchre, the Magi, Conchubar, Fand, King Eochaid Airim, Fergus and a farmer from a folk-tale as bearing a revelation of the truth of the Rose. 'The Blessed' and 'Red Hanrahan's Song about Ireland' offer similar cases of grafted myths in the early poetry and, in his final phase, he returned to the practice with a fresh excitement but the same conviction that although the Quest can take many routes and forms, the heart of the mystery remains constant.

During the first decade of the new century Yeats read with considerable thoroughness two authors whose influence he always acknowledged, Balzac and Nietzsche. He returned repeatedly to the massive *Comédie Humaine* of 91 volumes, grouped in the three main categories of the study of daily life, philosophy and analytical studies. The sheer diversity and meshing of two thousand characters across the novels gave the poet a sense of life whole and heightened and filled him with wonder at Balzac, 'the bull-necked man, the great eater, whose work resembles his body, the mechanist and materialist who wrote upon the darkness with a burnt stick such sacred and exciting symbols'. In his essay (1934) on Balzac's novel, *Louis Lambert*, Yeats writes:

Something more profound, more rooted in the blood than mere speculation... constrained him to think of the human mind as capable, during some emotional crisis, or, as in the case of Louis Lambert by an accident of genius, of containing within itself all that is significant in human history and of relating that history to timeless reality.

Further on in the same essay he declares that, for Balzac, the people in all their variety are his 'readers and theme, seen with his eyes they have become philosophy without ceasing to be history'. In the *Comédie Humaine*, a complement to Dante's *Divina Commedia*, this ability to generalise or create patterns, apparently without distorting the raw material, deeply impressed Yeats who all his life worried away at the question: Can fixity and flux coexist?

He was first introduced to the works of Nietzsche by John Quinn in 1902, two years after the author's death, although he had read essays on his ideas some years earlier. Something has been said in the previous chapter about the German philosopher's Apollonian and Dionysian types and their relevance to Yeats's theory of the Mask; the connection he established between the types as psychological traits and as phases in societies also proved stimulating to the poet's thinking about the mechanisms of change in history. On the crucial question as to whether history is an accumulation of individual actions, indicating choice, or the imprint of huge, disinterested forces, Yeats swings about and advances different positions. He can come down on one side sometimes, as when he writes in his diary in 1930: 'History seems to me a human drama, keeping the classical unities by the clear division of its epochs, turning one way or the other because this man hates or that man loves'. However, he concludes his paragraph with, 'Yet the drama has its plot, and this plot ordains character and passions and exists for their sake.' Nietzsche is no more consistent but in his insistence, certainly in his earlier works, on going beyond the human, on living dangerously, on aspiring to be Superman, he imparted a positive impetus to Yeats. Yeats's cyclical theory of change contains some elements of Nietzsche's theory of the eternal recurrence, in part a counter to the latter's earlier nihilism. Towards the end of *Thus Spake Zarathustra* the doctrine is ecstatically proclaimed:

> Pain is also joy, a curse is also a blessing, the night is also a sun – be gone, or you will learn: a wise man is also a fool.
>
> Did you ever say Yes to one joy? O my friends, then you said Yes to *all* woe as well. And things are chained and entwined together, all things are in love;
>
> if ever you wanted one moment twice, if ever you said: 'You please me, happiness, instant, moment!' then you wanted *everything* to return!

You wanted everything anew, everything eternal, everything
chained, entwined together, everything in love, O that is how you
loved the world,
    you everlasting men, loved it eternally, and for all time: and
you say even to woe: 'Go, but return!' *For all joy wants – eternity!*[1]

The Self figure in 'A Dialogue of Self and Soul', written in 1928, succeeds in declaring Yeats's parallel affirmation in a more memorable
manner than that of Nietzsche; he first concedes the stupidities and
humiliations in his life and then declares:

I am content to live it all again
And yet again, if it be life to pitch
Into the frog-spawn of a blind man's ditch,
A blind man battering blind men;
Or into that most fecund ditch of all,
The folly that man does
Or must suffer, if he woos
A proud woman not kindred of his soul.
I am content to follow to its source
Every event in action or in thought;
Measure the lot; forgive myself the lot!
When such as I cast out remorse
So great a sweetness flows into the breast
We must laugh and we must sing,
We are blest by everything,
Everything we look upon is blest.

Although Nietzsche's writings are dense with references to periods
across history and although he often shows a pontifical confidence
in his assessment of these periods, he is distrustful of any system
which suggests a plan or direction. Yeats was provoked by the
philosopher's call to go beyond good and evil now that God had
been pronounced dead, but it may be significant that Yeats called
the book of essays he published in 1903 *Essays on Good and Evil*, as if
he had not quite jumped beyond. From Nietzsche, however, more
than from Blake, he learned to dare ideas to the uttermost, even
when they were inconsistent or unsavoury, to nurture hatred as well
as love as a positive emotion in his writing, and accommodate
violence as an inevitable, necessary part of the cycle of change.

Thus, whatever else he may have contributed to Yeats's thinking, Nietzsche could not answer the poet's question about fixity and flux. In his diary for 1930, Yeats writes:

> I think that two conceptions, that of reality as a congeries of beings, that of reality as a single being, alternate in our emotion and in history, and must always remain something that human reason, because subject always to one or the other, cannot reconcile. I am always, in all that I do, driven to a moment which is the realisation of myself as unique and free, or to a moment which is the surrender to God of all that I am.

What did he mean by 'God'? After his youth was over, he felt no inclination towards any kind of Christianity and was remarkably unperturbed by the fact. The name 'God' occurs throughout his work but usually in relation to an invented character or in an impersonal way. For example, in 'To the Rose Upon the Rood of Time', he worries that he may

> seek alone to hear the strange things said
> By God to the bright hearts of those long dead,
> And learn to chaunt a tongue men do not know.

Here God seems merely to represent that other dimension of archetype and the occult as distinct from the world of actuality. Often the name is indicative of a superior judgement, as in 'For Anne Gregory':

> only God, my dear,
> Could love you for yourself alone
> And not your yellow hair.

For a non-believer, Yeats is remarkable for the frequency of prayers in his poems but they are seldom addressed to a personal or identifiable deity, even in 'A Prayer for My Daughter' and 'A Prayer for My Son'. An exception can be found in 'At Algeciras – A Meditation Upon Death', written in 1928 after a bout of serious illness, when God is much closer:

> Greater glory in the sun,
> An evening chill upon the air,

Bid imagination run
Much on the Great Questioner;
What He can question, what if questioned I
Can with a fitting confidence reply.

In *A Vision* (1926), the scheme of change is peculiarly deterministic but a presiding will or God seems absent, and the culmination of all development is the Thirteenth Cone, 'which is in every man and called by every man his freedom. Doubtless, for it can do all things and know all things, it knows what it will do with its own freedom but it has kept the secret.' This enigmatic black hole into which everything sinks but which has the instigative function in the continuation of the process leaves godhead as undefined as before. The closest parallel, although Yeats expresses reservations about it, is in Shelley's *Prometheus Unbound*, where the equally enigmatic force of Demogorgon appears to be the agent of change for the ultimate power which is 'imageless'. Sometimes Yeats asserts a defiant reaction to certain traditional claims about divinity and the Christian vision of ultimate rewards and punishments. The concluding stanza of 'All Souls' Night' expresses a power and wisdom:

such thought have I that hold it tight
Till meditation master all its parts,
Nothing can stay my glance
Until that glance run in the world's despite
To where the damned have howled away their hearts,
And where the blessed dance;
Such thought, that in it bound
I need no other thing,
Wound in mind's wandering
As mummies in the mummy-cloth are wound.

Even the philosophers whose thoughts he has found sympathetic can at times be discarded in favour of a simpler, more direct faith, which he states in 'The Tower':

And I declare my faith:
I mock Plotinus' thought
And cry in Plato's teeth,
Death and life were not
Till man made up the whole,

Made lock, stock and barrel
Out of his bitter soul,
Aye, sun and moon and star, all,
And further add to that
That, being dead, we rise
Dream and so create
Translunar Paradise.

His cyclical view of existence and his belief in reincarnation, it can
be argued, preclude him from any creation myth and he is much
less speculative about beginnings than he is about continuities.

In June 1917, after the publication of *Per Amica Silentia Lunae*
(originally entitled *An Alphabet*), he wrote an explanatory letter to
his father, knowing that he would look at the work with a very
sceptical eye. The son claims that in much of his thought he
resembles his father, but

> mine is part of a religious system more or less logically worked
> out, a system which will I hope interest you as a form of poetry. I
> find the setting it all in order has helped my verse, has given me a
> new framework and new patterns. One goes on year after year
> getting the disorder of one's mind in order and this is the real
> impulse to create.

J.B Yeats was not impressed, and complained that, despite all his
fatherly efforts, the work was an unfortunate return to mysticism,
which he saw as 'a sentimentalism of the intellect'. He could not
have foreseen his son's *A Vision* and, dying in 1922, he never had the
chance to see it but the following sentence in his letter of 1918 does
anticipate such a book when he mimics such an author: '"I will
make the unknown known, for I will present it under such sym-
metrical forms that everyone will be convinced – and what is more
important I shall convince myself"'.[2] Although *Per Amica Silentia
Lunae* is a short piece of about thirty pages, it is framed with a rather
defensive Prologue and Epilogue addressed to 'Maurice' (a private
name for Iseult Gonne), and seeks corroboration for its ideas not just
in the seventeenth-century Neo-Platonist Henry More, but in a
strange mixture including Japanese poets, mediums in Soho, and
old women in Connacht.

When *A Vision* was published in 1926 (dated as 1925), it was
similarly hedged about with odd introductory accounts of authors

and authorities, as if Yeats was reluctant to acknowledge the work as his own. We know that his wife wished her part in the matter to be kept secret; in fact, he was apprehensive about possible reactions to the book and it was published originally for private subscribers. He was later to revise the book and devise a different introduction, and the new version emerged in 1937; the substance remains the same. *Per Amica Silentia Lunae* is concerned with the overlapping area of the conscious and unconscious mind and of the living and the dead. *A Vision* extends this base and constructs a very elaborate model of the process of development in individuals and cultures (in the anthropological sense). The Communicators who spoke through Mrs Yeats inhabit a collective mind, the *Anima Mundi*, of which we, the 'living', are also components. In *Per Amica Silentia Lunae* Yeats describes this dimension as the 'condition of fire' and the one we ordinarily inhabit as the 'terrestrial'. The interchange between the two is never simple and, in their communications, the Yeatses were sometimes bothered by Frustrators who seemed eager to mislead them but who were often indistinguishable from the Communicators.

One of the problems for a reader of *A Vision* is that abstract ideas are often presented in geometric terms. The most basic ideas or images are a wheel of 28 phases, identified as the phases of the lunar cycle, and pairs of cones or gyres expanding and contracting on a shared axis. These two shapes or movements have to be envisaged as interacting simultaneously. The two cones are contraries, tending, in Yeats's terms, towards the primary or the antithetical; the cones possess in any one phase different proportions or alignments of four faculties: the Mask and the Body of Fate, on one hand, and Will and Creative Mind, on the other. At any one time, in any one person or culture, there is a tendency towards either the primary or the anti-thetical, and this gives a defining character to the person or culture in the particular phase (of the 28). However, the contrary tendency is also present, so that as one tendency increases, its opposite is already apparent. In historical time and in individuals, there are climactic points where the previously dominant gyre yields the position of dominance to the contrary gyre. In history such a radical change occurs every two thousand years with lesser shifts of emphasis appearing every five hundred years. For all the permuta-tions in the system to be enacted, a period of about 26 000 years would be needed, a period similar to the Great or Platonic Year talked of in the Ancient World.

It is difficult, first of all, to understand fully what Yeats is constructing and it is also difficult to do justice, in a brief account, to the complexity and inclusiveness of the system. In 'A Packet for Ezra Pound' which formed an introduction to the second edition in 1937, he concedes that, 'Some, perhaps all, of those readers I most value, those who have read me many years, will be repelled by what must seem an arbitrary, harsh, difficult symbolism.' Shortly after the sessions of automatic writing began, Yeats was informed by the Communicators that what they were giving him was 'metaphors for poetry', but *A Vision* goes far beyond this. His claims for it ('a book which will, when finished, proclaim a new divinity') are balanced with a diffidence:

> Some will ask whether I believe in the actual existence of my circuits of sun and moon. Those that include, now all recorded time in one circuit, now what Blake called 'the pulsation of an artery', are plainly symbolical, but what of those that fixed, like a butterfly upon a pin, to our central date, the first day of our Era, divide actual history into periods of equal length? To such a question I can but answer that if sometimes, overwhelmed by miracle as all men must be when in the midst of it, I have taken such periods literally, my reason has soon recovered; and now that the system stands out clearly in my imagination I regard them as stylistic arrangements of experience comparable to the cubes in the drawing of Wyndham Lewis and to the ovoids in the sculpture of Brancusi. They have helped me to hold in a single thought reality and justice.

This final sentence affirms a bold confidence, a god-like vantage point. What he learned from the Communicators encouraged him to read widely in history and philosophy and he freely confesses his previous ignorance of both these areas of knowledge. Of course, he was already well-read in esoteric literature, some of the neo-Platonist writers from Plotinus to Henry More, occult or mystical authors such as Boehme, Cornelius Agrippa (d.1535), Swedenborg and Blake, and the tradition of knowledge handed down through groups engaged in the occult. In the 1920s and 1930s he searched out large-scale historians whose patterns might corroborate his system. Among the histories were some essays by Henry Adams, including 'A Dynamic Theory of History' (1904), Giambattista Vico's *Principles of a New Science concerning the Nature of Nations* (1725; described in some detail by Croce), Flinders Petrie's *Revolutions of Civilisation* (1922) and Spengler's *Decline of the West* (published in German, 1918 and 1922).

After the first version of *A Vision* was completed in 1925, he embarked on a serious study of philosophy in the works of Berkeley, Plato, Kant, Hegel and modern philosophers such as Whitehead, G. E. Moore, McTaggart, Bergson, Croce and Gentile. How accurate a reader of philosophy he was is open to question; his correspondence with Sturge Moore, the brother of G. E. Moore, suggests that he was inaccurate, but he took sustenance from his reading and was fond of quoting Goethe, who said that the poet needs to know all philosophy but must keep it out of his work. Some of the poems associated with *A Vision*, or stemming from it, are programmatic – poems such as 'The Phases of the Moon', 'The Double Vision of Michael Robartes' and 'The Saint and the Hunchback'.

The two collections published during the seven years after *A Vision* contain some of Yeats's most powerful poems and are closely linked to the system outlined there. However, whatever credence we give to the scheme in *A Vision* or to the account of the genesis of the book, many of the thoughts in it are developments of earlier ideas rather than ideas original to the poet in the early 1920s, or even in 1917 when his wife began her automatic writing. Certainly as early as 1919, when he wrote 'The Second Coming', he moves with confidence among notions to be explicated in *A Vision*. The opening lines announce his theory of gyres in an image of the trained bird of prey reverting to its wild state:

> Turning and turning in the widening gyre
> The falcon cannot hear the falconer;
> Things fall apart; the centre cannot hold;

The revelation granted to the poet is not the millennial vision of St John the Divine but a 'rough beast', the anti-Christ who embodies the reverse of the now-spent Christian gyre. The poet-prophet looks back and forward in time through the 2000 year cycles:

> now I know
> That twenty centuries of stony sleep
> Were vexed to nightmare by a rocking cradle,
> And what rough beast, its hour come round at last,
> Slouches towards Bethlehem to be born?

The new cycle is already imminent in our present cycle, hence the beast being able to slouch before it is born. In 1936, at the height of totalitarianism in Germany and the Soviet Union, he cited 'The Second Coming' as his foretelling of what was to come. It is precisely the horror of his vision that helps to explain and perhaps justify the paternalist concern of 'A Prayer for my Daughter' which immediately follows 'A Second Coming' in *Collected Poems*:

> Imagining in excited reverie
> That the future years had come,
> Dancing to a frenzied drum,
> Out of the murderous innocence of the sea.

The reverse stage of the cycle, when the next epoch announces itself is, in Yeats's view, cataclysmic and, in his scheme, seems to centre on a crucial sexual act involving the human and the superhuman. This Annunciation of a new era is the subject of 'Leda and the Swan', in which the rape of the girl by Zeus in the form of the bird initiates a sequence of momentous and destructive happenings in Greek civilisation:

> A sudden blow: the great wings beating still
> Above the staggering girl, her thighs caressed
> By the dark webs, her nape caught in his bill,
> He holds her helpless breast upon his breast.
>
> How can those terrified vague fingers push
> The feathered glory from her loosening thighs?
> And how can body, laid in that white rush,
> But feel the strange heart beating where it lies?
>
> A shudder in the loins engenders there
> The broken wall, the burning roof and tower
> And Agamemnon dead.
>   Being so caught up,
> So mastered by the brute blood of the air,
> Did she put on his knowledge with his power
> Before the indifferent beak could let her drop?

The space between the octave and the sestet carries the unspeakable, sexual union of god and human, and the human story forks out from there through Helen and Clytemnestra to the destruction of Troy and the murder of Agamemnon. In her experience of the power of the divine, was the human Leda granted access to the foreknowledge of Zeus? In the poem 'The Magi', written ten years earlier, in 1913, Yeats engaged in a similar enquiry about the repercussions of Christ's birth:

> Now as at all times I can see in the mind's eye,
> In their stiff, painted clothes, the pale unsatisfied ones
> Appear and disappear in the blue depth of the sky
> With all their ancient faces like rain-beaten stones,
> And all their helms of silver hovering side by side,
> And all their eyes still fixed, hoping to find once more,
> Being by Calvary's turbulence unsatisfied,
> The uncontrollable mystery on the bestial floor.

The Wise Men here represent the awareness of a continuous cycle without conclusion. In *A Vision* he describes the same process in the prosaic terms of his system: 'When the old primary [gyre] becomes the new *antithetical* [gyre], the old realisation of an objective moral law is changed into a subconscious turbulent instinct. The world of rigid custom and law is broken up by "the uncontrollable mystery on the bestial floor".' His cyclical view, presented most explicitly in historical epochs, appears in the two songs which introduce and conclude his play *The Resurrection*; the view is obviously related to Nietzsche's doctrine of the Eternal Recurrence but is also close to the thoughts expressed in the Chorus to Shelley's *Hellas*:

> The world's great age begins anew,
> The golden years return,
> The earth doth like a snake renew,
> Her winter weeds outworn;
> Heaven smiles, and faiths and empires gleam
> Like wrecks of a dissolving dream.

In *The Resurrection* itself, at the very moment when, in the room, the risen Christ Jesus (God-man) shows himself to his disciples, outside in the street the followers of Dionysus celebrate his annual resurrection with the cry, 'God has arisen.' In Yeats's scheme the coinciding of the two myths is inevitable.

Often he seems so attracted to the heroic stance, in history or in fiction, whether adopted by Cuchulain or Hamlet or Parnell, that it is difficult to reconcile this admiration with his system which would appear to roll on regardless of individual gestures. This apparent discrepancy is the subject of 'Long-Legged Fly', which focuses on three pivotal figures: Caesar (unspecified but most probably Julius); Helen of Troy; and Michelangelo. One of his most geometrically arranged poems, it consists of three stanzas each culminating in the refrain:

Like a long-legged fly upon the stream
His [or her] mind moves upon silence.

Through a replication in each stanza of metre, rhyme scheme, punctuation units and syntax, he effects such a symmetry that the ideas seem bound to obey the same ordering. In each stanza, the opening two lines point to a momentous event. For it to take place, certain conditions of quietness and solitude have to be established (lines 3–4), and in this area of stillness a famous person is set (lines 5–6). In the remaining two lines before the refrain, this person's actions are described in a way which makes them seem trivial or inconsequential. To the observer, the reader, there is no obvious connection between the individual activity of the central figure and the great event. However, in the refrain, we learn that, just as the fly, for all its apparent randomness, feeds on the stream, so the mind of the person of destiny learns to attend to silence or the unconscious; it is precisely this talent for receptive vacancy that makes a particular individual the conduit for the movements in civilisation and the psyche.

From the age of 20 when he became acquainted with Buddhism, Madame Blavatsky's teaching based on Tibetan masters, and the Brahmin Theosophist Mohini Chatterjee, who lectured at the Dublin Hermetic Society, Yeats was fascinated by Oriental traditions of meditation and wisdom. In 1931 he met an Indian monk, Shri Purohit Swāmi, and over the following few years learned much from him. Yeats wrote introductions for some of the Swāmi's translations, including an account of a pilgrimage to Mount Meru, which provided the poet with material for his 'Supernatural Songs' (1934). He helped the Swāmi to translate The Ten Principal Upanishads (1937), partly because of the exasperation he had felt with earlier translations of Indian texts which were a 'polyglot, hyphenated, latinised, muddied muddle of distortion that froze belief'. He found in Indian texts a parallel to the Western questers who 'postulate an individual self possessed of such power and knowledge that they seem at every moment about to identify it with that Self without limitation and sorrow, containing and contained by all, and to seek there not only the living but the dead'. In the essay he wrote about the Swāmi's autobiography, Yeats connects some of the lore that he and Lady Gregory collected in the west of Ireland (and which went into her *Visions and Beliefs*) with stories told of holy men by the Swāmi and with the practices of Byzantine mystical theologians. He had become fascinated with the history of Byzantium (Constantinople or Istanbul) and during the 1920s had read whatever he could find on the subject. As so often in his life, he was seeking to locate a place or point in history where unity of being was a possibility. Byzantium, geographically and spiritually straddling the West (Europe) and the East (Asia), seemed to offer something very sympathetic to Yeats's spiritual search. In Part IV of the section of *A Vision* entitled 'Dove and Swan' he explains what attracted him to that city when it was, in terms of his system, approaching its fifteenth phase:

> I think if I could be given a month of Antiquity and leave to spend it where I chose, I would spend it in Byzantium a little before Justinian opened St Sophia and closed the Academy of Plato [about AD 520]. I think I would find in some little wine-shop some philosophical worker in mosaic who could answer all my questions, the supernatural descending nearer to him than to Plotinus even, for the pride of his delicate skill would make what was an instrument of power to princes and clerics, a murderous madness in the mob, show as a lovely flexible presence like that of a perfect human body.
>
> I think that in early Byzantium, maybe never before or since in recorded history, religious, aesthetic and practical life were one, that architects and artificers – though not, it may be, poets, for language had been the instrument of controversy and must have grown abstract – spoke to the multitude and the few alike. The painter, the mosaic worker, the worker in gold and silver, the illuminator of sacred books, were almost impersonal, almost perhaps unconscious of individual design, absorbed in their subject-matter and that the vision of a whole people.

Two of his poems explore this special dimension: 'Sailing to Byzantium', written in 1926, and 'Byzantium', written in 1930. The first sets up a contrast between his present condition as part of the 'dying generations' of sensuality and 'the holy city' with its 'Monuments of unaging intellect'. For all Yeats's aspirations to be gathered 'Into the artifice of eternity', many readers have found his description of the matters of the flesh, despite his lavishly-expressed contempt, more appealing than his ambition to be a golden bird singing, like Blake's Bard in *Songs of Experience*, 'Of what is past, or passing, or to come'. In a comment written for a radio programme in 1931, he described his intentions:

> Now I am trying to write about the state of my soul, for it is right for an old man to make his soul [Irish idiom meaning to prepare for death and meeting one's maker], and some of my thoughts upon that subject I have put into a poem called 'Sailing to Byzantium'. When Irishmen were illuminating the Book of Kells and making the jewelled croziers in the National Museum, Byzantium was the centre of European civilisation and the source of its spiritual philosophy, so I symbolise the search for the spiritual life by a journey to that city.

The symbolism is clearer if more elaborate in the second poem, 'Byzantium'. Yeats recognised that there was an artificial and willed quality in the vision in his earlier poem, and he enlarged the scope of Byzantium. It now represents that dimension beyond life and change, a purification and fixity as is found in the supreme works of art, which defeats mutability. The poem's duration is the sounding of the midnight gong in the church of St Sophia, marking the transition from day to night and from life to death:

> The unpurged images of day recede;
> The Emperor's drunken soldiery are abed;
> Night resonance recedes, night-walkers' song
> After great cathedral gong;
> A starlit or a moonlit dome disdains
> All that man is,
> All mere complexities,
> The fury and the mire of human veins.

And yet, again, for all his assertions of 'glory of changeless metal', of 'Dying into a dance,/An agony of trance', the poem, in the end, cannot take off in the purely spiritual and we are left with the wonderfully resonant and unresolved finale:

Those images that yet
Fresh images beget,
That dolphin-torn, that gong-tormented sea.

In the poem Yeats hails 'the superhuman;/I call it death-in-life and
life-in-death'. Elsewhere in his work, he describes the continuous
interaction and transaction between the living and the dead,
between the human and the superhuman. He was fond of quoting a
saying of the Greek philosopher, Heraclitus: 'God and man die each
other's life, live each other's death.' Probably at no time as an adult
did he consider death as a finality; some kind of continuity or
reincarnation always made sense to him. Not that he could find a
glib acceptance of death, not that he did not lament the termination
of friends and the horror of killings, not that he did not rage against
old age and infirmity, but he did believe that something of our print
on life could survive somewhere. One of the prompts to 'Byzantium'
was the death of a friend but, as is so characteristic of Yeats, any individual instance is merged in with the general meditation. Immediately before 'Byzantium' in the *Collected Poems* is 'Mohini Chatterjee',
written in 1929 but looking back to the Brahmin from Bengal who
visited the Dublin Hermetic Society when the poet was only 20. The
Brahmin's teaching that each soul has multiple lives appealed to the
poet and, in the poem, he takes comfort in believing that 'Old lovers
yet may have/All that time denied' and declares that 'Grave is
heaped on grave... Birth is heaped on birth... Men dance on death-
less feet'. Whatever belief an individual entertains, emotions are
bound to be complex at the approach of the end, but Yeats admired
arrogant stoicism. In 1927, Kevin O'Higgins, Minister for Justice, was
murdered. He had signed the death-warrants of 77 men found guilty
of defying a ban on the carrying of firearms and his assassination
was carried out as revenge for these executions. Yeats, who had
known and supported O'Higgins, wrote an assertive, defiant poem,
called 'Death':

Nor dread nor hope attend
A dying animal;
A man awaits his end
Dreading and hoping all;
Many times he died,
Many times rose again.
A great man in his pride

Confronting murderous men
Casts derision upon
Supersession of breath;
He knows death to the bone –
Man has created death.

There is, in the defiant last line, something of the histrionic flourish
sounded in the final lines of Donne's Sonnet 10:

One short sleep past, we wake eternally
And death shall be no more; Death, thou shalt die.

In 'The Three Hermits', written in 1913, two of the hermits argue
about what lies beyond death, but Yeats appears to favour the third,
who takes no part in the debate, who, 'Giddy with his hundredth
year,/Sang unnoticed like a bird'. The insouciance of the hermit was
an attitude admired by the poet, the attitude of the truly heroic who
'have lived in joy and laughed into the face of Death', who come
'Proud, open-eyed and laughing to the tomb'. Such a stance is
central to his notion of tragedy: in 'Lapis Lazuli' he points to Hamlet
and Lear with their 'Gaiety transfiguring all that dread'.

Yeats's idea of death, however, is complex and rather forbidding
although it contains hope as well as dread. 'When we are dead,
according to my belief', he writes in *Autobiographies*, 'we live our
lives backward for a certain number of years, treading the paths that
we have trodden, growing young again, even childish again, till
some attain an innocence that is no longer a mere accident of nature,
but the human intellect's crowning achievement.' Often he presents
the prospect in more purgatorial terms, as when he describes the
process of Dreaming Back in *A Vision* (first edition):

The [dead] man must dream the event to its consequence as far as
his intensity permit; not that consequence only which occurred
while he lived, and was known to him, but those that were
unknown, or have occurred after his death. The more complete
the exploration, the more fortunate will be his future life, but he is
concerned with events only, and with the emotions that accompanied events. Every event so dreamed is the expression of some
knot, some concentration of feeling separating off a period of
time, or portion of the being, from the being as a whole and the
life as a whole, and the dream is as it were a smoothing out or an

unwinding. Yet it is said that if his nature had great intensity, and the consequence of the event affected multitudes, he may dream with slowly lessening pain and joy for centuries.[3]

This notion, and Yeats outlines the various stages or phases of death in considerable detail in *A Vision*, occurs in many poems, elaborated on in poems such as 'Shepherd and Goatherd', and working most poignantly in 'The Cold Heaven'. In the latter case, after the poet has experienced the agony of remembered, unrequited love and he feels 'riddled' and 'I cried and trembled and rocked to and fro', he asks in anguish if the process of recrimination and scrutiny will continue:

> Ah! when the ghost begins to quicken,
> Confusion of the death-bed over, is it sent
> Out naked on the roads, as the books say, and stricken
> By the injustice of the skies for punishment?

If 'the books' are correct, he has reason to dread his old age, 'Because of the increasing Night/That opens her mystery and fright' ('The Apparitions').

In a number of the plays, a Dreaming Back process is crucial to the drama, and this is one of the elements of his theatre which allies him with the Japanese Noh tradition. The process has an expiatory function for a ghost still tormented by an unresolved dilemma from his or her life but it is more particularly in the interaction between the living and the dead that the dramatic force is manifest. In the appropriately-named *The Dreaming of the Bones* (1917), a young revolutionary on the run from the English authorities, after taking part in the Easter Rising, encounters in the wilds of County Clare a Stranger and a Young Girl who, it emerges, are the ghosts of Diarmuid and Dervorgilla whose behaviour in the twelfth century had led to the English occupation of Ireland. Their betrayal of their country has wedged them apart as lovers and after all these years they still seek the forgiveness which would allow them a completion of their love and peace. Such a forgiveness the young nationalist is not prepared to grant although he is deeply moved, as we are, by their story. *The Words upon the Window-pane*, written in 1930, is not such an obvious example of Dreaming Back, but this ingenious exploration of Jonathan Swift does posit the persistence of his unsatisfied spirit and challenges the declaration in his famous epitaph: 'He has gone where fierce indignation can lacerate his heart no more.'

Purgatory, written in the year before Yeats's death, offers the most condensed, dramatic presentation of his idea of the repetition necessary in death. The Old Man voices the theory:

> The souls in Purgatory that come back
> To habitations and familiar spots...
> re-live
> Their transgressions, and that not once
> But many times; they know at last
> The consequence of those transgressions
> Whether upon others or upon themselves;
> Upon others, others may bring help,
> For when the consequence is at an end
> The dream must end; if upon themselves,
> There is no help but in themselves
> And in the mercy of God.

The Old Man's aristocratic mother had married a drunken groom. After she died in giving birth to her son, the great house and estate were brought to ruin by the husband. The Old Man remembers how he killed his father in the house, set fire to when he was drunk, and now he kills his own bastard son in an attempt to halt the process of degradation and terminate his mother's ghost's reliving of her mistake. With the first part of his purpose he can achieve some success but, as the tape of the past begins to re-play in the ruined house, he realises his impotence to aid his mother:

> Her mind cannot hold up that dream.
> Twice a murderer and all for nothing,
> And she must animate that dead night
> Not once but many times!
> O God,
> Release my mother's soul from its dream!
> Mankind can do no more. Appease
> The misery of the living and the remorse of the dead.

Despite the bleakness of such a view – and Yeats certainly shared something of it – and despite his raging against old age, he was also capable, as always, of seeing another side to the matter, a side where 'Bodily decrepitude is wisdom' and, in the words of his *persona* Tom O'Roughley, 'What's dying but a second wind?' It seems appro-

priate for a poet who revised his work obsessively and who proclaimed repeatedly, 'Myself must I remake', that his vision of death
should consist so substantially of retracing and editing his entire
life. Of course, Yeats's theories on what happens to individuals
beyond death are not peculiar to him. He belongs to a central
tradition of thinking which is not exclusive to one culture or one
time. What is special about him in a context of twentieth-century
European writers is the elaborateness of his categories in describing
what lies beyond the grave and the pervasiveness of his ideas on the
subject throughout his work. Some similar notion of dreaming back,
but with a less labyrinthine thoroughness, is utilised in such works
as William Golding's *Pincher Martin*, Beckett's *Play* and even Sartre's
Huis Clos. Yeats was never bull-headedly dogmatic on such large
and unprovable topics; he worked out a theory which offered
some coherence and likeliness, but was always aware of counter-
arguments and even worried about ridicule. When the revised
edition of *A Vision* was completed in 1937 he wrote to his friend
Edith Shackleton Heald:

> This book is the skeleton in my cupboard. I do not know whether
> I want my friends to see it or not to see it. I think 'Will so-and-so
> think me a crazed fanatic?' but one goes on in blind faith. The
> public does not matter – only one's friends matter. Friends die, are
> estranged, or turn out but a dream in the mind, and we are
> poisoned by the ungiven friendship that we hide in our bones.

8

Yeats and Modern Poetry

In a memorial lecture delivered in the Abbey Theatre, a year after Yeats's death in 1939, T. S. Eliot made several claims concerning the status of the dead poet. The first, and we must remember that Eliot's influential criticism made 'impersonality' a central criterion of poetry, is stated as follows:

> There are two kinds of impersonality: that which is natural to a mere skilful craftsman, and that which is more and more achieved by the maturing artist ... The second impersonality is that of the poet who, out of intense and personal experience, is able to express a general truth; retaining all the particularity of his experience, to make of it a general symbol. And the strange thing is that Yeats, having been a great craftsman in the first kind, became a great poet in the second.[1]

Any poet whose pre-eminence is so accepted that his *Collected Works* can be published when he is 43 and who continues to write excitingly for a further thirty years, poses a particular problem for the critic who wishes to evaluate this total output. Furthermore, Yeats's proclamation in 1936: 'Myself must I remake' could have been made at any stage of his restless career and no poet could provide a less compartmented answer to the question asked in the final stanza of 'Among School Children':

O chestnut-tree, great-rooted blossomer,
Are you the leaf, the blossom or the bole?

Although he often seemed out of sympathy with much of the writing that travelled under the label of Modernism, his own poetry cannot be described as static; he protests defensively in his Introduction to *The Oxford Book of Modern Verse*: 'I too have tried to be modern.'

166

When he was only 22, he was already revising and reassessing his poems:

> It is almost all a flight into fairyland from the real world, and a summons to that flight. The Chorus to the 'Stolen Child' sums it up – that it is not the poetry of insight and knowledge, but of longing and complaint – the cry of the heart against necessity. I hope some day to alter that and write poetry of insight and knowledge.

His revisions and reshapings have created enormous problems for his subsequent editors. Even his late work, written when one might think that the mature artist would have delivered a text with his decisive imprimatur, has presented difficulties. Earlier, when he worked with so many publishers and in so many varied publications, and then altered his texts repeatedly over many years, the difficulties he has bequeathed to scholars are immense. At least from his point of view, however, Yeats from very early on found reasonably sympathetic publishers who were eager to print his writings and his work was reviewed and reprinted.

In earlier chapters I have attempted to describe some of the influences on and models for his poetry as he developed. Not surprisingly, it is in his early phase, to the end of the nineteenth century, that the pressure of other writers is most evident, that he writes in the accents he borrowed from these others. It is interesting to consider what he was not open to, what he failed to hear around him. For example, although he met Hopkins, nothing of significance happened between the two poets and even when Hopkins's poems were eventually published in 1918 they meant little to Yeats. Equally, when he was looking for examples of Celtic poetry, in his early phase he searched mainly in a remote past and neglected to see some fascinating poems written in his own lifetime by the Scottish Gaelic poet Mary Macpherson (Màiri Mhór nan Òran, 1821–98); the blend of satirical sharpness, love of the land and personal commitment which made her songs populist anthems in the land reform movement in the Highlands would, if he had known them, have seemed irrelevant to his poetic education. Both Hopkins and Màiri Mhór showed that contemplative poetry and poetry of political involvement could take new directions, away from some of the more orthodox modes of the nineteenth century but, although Yeats wished to depart from these same orthodoxies, he could not follow in their directions. To use his own image in the quotation above, he was obliged to travel through the very fairyland about which he sounded so apprehensive.

How did Yeats become a 'Modern' poet? In the early years of the new century and at a time when he was most preoccupied with the theatre and writing very few poems, he realigned himself poetically. In a letter to George Russell in 1904 he accepts the force of some of his 'stupidest critics' and complains that 'the region of shadows' in his poems 'is full of false images of the spirit and the body'. He explains that he is trying to deal with the problem: 'I have been fighting the prevalent decadence for years, and have just got it under foot in my own heart – it is sentiment and sentimental sadness, a womanly introspection.' Perhaps the rather confused idiom 'under foot in my heart' suggests that he has not eliminated the problem. In an earlier letter (1900) he shows an awareness of his difficulty with diction: 'I avoid every kind of word that seems to me either "poetical" or "modern"'. But by 1905, in a letter to John Quinn, he can boast, '[I] have very joyfully got "creaking shoes" and "liquorice-root" into what had been a very abstract passage. I believe more strongly every day that the element of strength in poetic language is common idiom, just as the element of strength in poetic construction is common passion.' One can detect clearly over the following decade the influence of his work in drama on his thinking about poetry. There is a repeated emphasis on 'personality' and 'dramatic'. In a letter to his father, who was constantly advocating these very qualities, he writes:

> Of recent years instead of 'vision', meaning by vision the intense realization of a state of ecstatic emotion symbolized in a definite imagined region, I have tried for more self portraiture. I have tried to make my work convincing with a speech so natural and dramatic that the hearer would feel the presence of a man thinking and feeling.

In the previous year, 1912, he had received from Professor H. J. C. Grierson a copy of his new edition of Donne's poems and he wrote gratefully of the help afforded by Grierson's notes and text: 'I notice that the more precise and learned the thought the greater the beauty, the passion; the intricacy and subtleties of his imagination are the length and depths of the furrow made by his passion.'

This emphasis on the personal and the passionate does not seem to fit easily with Eliot's praise for the impersonality in Yeats quoted at the opening of this chapter. And, indeed, this discrepancy was an area of disagreement between Yeats and an influential new friend in this period. He first met Ezra Pound in 1908 when the American was only 23 and had just published his first book of poems, *A Lume Spento*, showing some influence of the Irish poet. Pound's contribution to modern literature and Modernism was to be immense, not simply through his own writings but through his propagandising and his vigorous promotion of innovative talent in such people as Eliot, Frost, Carlos Williams, Joyce, Wyndham Lewis, T. E. Hulme and Gaudier-Brzeska. No two people seemed less likely to get on with each other than Yeats and Pound. Yeats was twenty years older, famous and, according to many observers, arrogantly set in his ways; Pound was brash, irreverent, and bristling with a revolutionary fervour against artistic orthodoxies and determined to 'Make it new'. The two came from utterly different cultural backgrounds. Their friendship, however, and a mutual respect which outweighed their disagreements, lasted till Yeats's death. Yeats had a very limited regard for his friend's poetry and often deplored his taste. He probably agreed with his father's view of the kind of poets associated with Pound, 'I am tired of Beauty my wife, says the Poet [favoured by Pound], but here is that enchanting mistress Ugliness. With her will I live, and what a riot we shall have – not a day shall pass without a fresh horror.'[2] What the established figure looked for from Pound was not necessarily approval but the response and even criticism of one who represented 'the most aggressive contemporary school of the young'. In particular, he wished for advice in removing poetical fustian and abstractions from his writing; he could not have found a sounder ear. The process of modernisation begun by him around the turn of the century was accelerated with Pound's help, the same tough-minded editorial Pound who later hacked out and patched together Eliot's bits and pieces into the unified poem, *The Waste Land*. Yeats admired the caustic brutality of Pound's judgement even when a draft of his play, *The King of the Great Clock Tower* (1934), elicited the abrupt response, 'Putrid!' In the years before his marriage, at which Pound was best man, they spent many months together and although, after Pound's departure from England in 1920, they saw each other infrequently, they remained on excellent terms. In the *Cantos*, Yeats, often called Uncle William, features prominently as a mockable but exemplary figure. In the 1930s an obsessive tendency in Pound developed into a fanatical, political narrowness and even Yeats found him dangerously cantankerous and intolerant. In a letter to Dorothy Wellesley, he complains: 'I am tired, I have spent a day reading Ezra Pound for the Anthology – a single strained attitude instead of passion, the sexless American professor for all his violence.'

During the first decade of their relationship, Pound was a leading member of the Imagist movement and then of Vorticism. In both, he advocated concreteness, objectivity, surfaces, lack of 'emotional slither'. Some of this advocacy did rub off on Yeats, although the desired attributes are not very obviously descriptive of Yeats's work. Pound's own poems are not quite as clean as he wished them to be; and his experiments in social satire (for example, *Hugh Selwyn Mauberley*), in historical reconstruction (for example, 'Near Perigord'), in translations and imitations, and in the vast cultural tableau of the *Cantos*, did not impinge on Yeats's development. Nonetheless, Pound's craftsmanship, his obstinate insistence that 'the natural object is the adequate symbol', and the epic ambition of the *Cantos*, did operate as correctives or sounding-boards or modes for Yeats's own self-definition.

In his actual writing of poetry Yeats was always laborious but his struggles to improve his writing were all designed to make the result feel more natural. In 'Adam's Curse', written in 1902, he quotes himself:

> A line will take us hours maybe
> Yet if it does not seem a moment's thought,
> Our stitching and unstitching has been naught.

For all the reputation he enjoys as a master of sounds, he was bashful and hesitant throughout his life about the technicalities of verse. In *Reveries over Childhood and Youth* he describes his early efforts: 'My lines but seldom scanned, for I could not understand the prosody in the books .... [I] discovered when I read them to somebody else that there was no common music, no prosody.' In a letter in 1937 he expresses a mixture of confidence and diffidence: 'You will notice how bothered I am when I get to prosody – because it is the most certain of my instincts, it is the subject of which I am most ignorant. I do not even know if I should write the mark of accent or stress thus ' or thus `.' He had absolutely no ear for music but became fascinated by the tradition of Irish unaccompanied singing and wrote a number of poems specifically to be sung. From 1935 till his death, he cooperated with various poets and musicians to produce a series of Cuala Press Broadsheets containing new poems set to music. For him there was a continuity running from his experiments in the incantation of verse with Florence Farr, through what he learned about the Provençal Troubadours from Pound, to his rediscovery of the very wealthy Irish tradition in which,

> stories that live longest
> Are sung above the glass.

Gradually over his life he accumulated a reasonable knowledge of the literary tradition in Irish and, in working with Frank O'Connor on his translations, he learned much more intimately about such poets as Egan O'Rahilly, Anthony Raftery, Eileen O'Leary, Bryan Merryman (of the sensational poem *The Midnight Court*) and the work of many anonymous poets. He delighted in a rumbustious satire and an unsentimental directness of emotion in the older ballads and he wished to devise a similar 'simplicity', as he called it, in his late songs:

> Come gather round me, Parnellites,
> And praise our chosen man;
> Stand upright on your legs awhile,
> Stand upright while you can,
> For soon we lie where he is laid,
> And he is underground;
> Come fill up all those glasses
> And pass the bottle round.

In 'A General Introduction for my Work' (1937) he looks back over twenty years and reflects on the changes in the writing of his poetry:

> Style is almost unconscious. I know what I have tried to do, little what I have done .... I tried to make the language of poetry coincide with that of passionate, normal speech. I wanted to write in whatever language comes most naturally when we soliloquise .... It was a long time before I had made a language to my liking ... a powerful and passionate syntax, and a complete coincidence between period [sentence] and stanza. Because I need a passionate syntax for passionate subject-matter I compel myself to accept those traditional metres that have developed with the language.

The 'coincidence between period and stanza' is, indeed, one of the characteristics of Yeats's later poetry and he succeeds in accommodating most dexterously some extraordinarily involved thoughts and emotions in a stanza form with its metrical requirements all satisfied.

Looking at Yeats's thinking on style makes us aware how he shares many of the problems and questions confronting other contemporary poets and theorists. He vacillates between, or seeks to balance, options which can be balanced or chosen only as a temporary measure. The personal vies with the impersonal, the individual asserts itself against the collective, the original or new challenges the traditional, spontaneous speech usurps the formal, the randomness of life's flux mocks the formulaic systems. One way, among others, of categorising poetry in the twentieth century is to see some poems as offered material and others as tending towards a formulated statement. Certainly, since some of Wordsworth's 'simple' poems were considered to be not poor poems but not poems at all, and since Whitman's dissolution of the conventional boundaries, there has emerged a kind of poem which seems to attempt not to be a Poem but, at the same time, to be real poetry.

Practitioners of such writing often claim that what is offered is immediate to life, freed from the museum of a frozen culture, and democratic in that the reader is invited to cooperate in deriving a poetic experience from the offered material. An extreme example of this type is the found poem or *objet trouvé*. William Carlos Williams is the poet most crucially identified with this notion of the poem. On the other hand, the poem as formulated statement is characterised by complexity of thought, intricacy of verbal and metrical pattern, and in or through it the poet presents the reader with an exploration of, or findings on, a problem or situation. Keats's Odes, Hopkins's poems and Yeats's 'Byzantium' and 'Among School Children' can be taken as examples of this type. D. H. Lawrence, in the Preface to the American edition of *New Poems* (1918), spells out the features of the poem as offered material and obviously sees it as a poetry appropriate to the twentieth century in contrast to an earlier mode:

[There are] the gem-like lyrics of Shelley and Keats. But there is another kind of poetry: the poetry of that which is at hand: the immediate present. In the immediate present there is no perfection, no consummation, nothing finished .... Life, the ever-present, knows no finality, no finished crystallisation .... Give me nothing fixed, set, static .... Give me ... the moment, the quick of all change and haste and opposition: the moment, the immediate present, the Now. The poetry of now is never finished, and it is not like the ouraboros, the serpent of eternity with its tail in its own mouth, with a rhythm that returns upon itself. There is no static perfection, none of that finality which we find so satisfying because we are so frightened.

If one thinks of 'The Lake Isle of Innisfree', 'The Cap and Bells', 'The Wild Swans at Coole' or 'Lapis Lazuli', it is apparent that Yeats's inclination is towards the ouraboros. When the reader analyses 'Long-legged Fly' what is being unpacked is a highly compressed view of the world and a pattern of sound and syntax which suggests completeness. Contrast such a poem with William Carlos Williams's poem, 'The Artist':

Mr T.
   bareheaded
      in a soiled undershirt
his hair standing out
   on all sides
      stood on his toes
heels together
   arms gracefully
      for the moment
curled above his head.
   Then he whirled about
      bounded
into the air
   and with an *entrechat*
      perfectly achieved
completed the figure.
   My mother
      taken by surprise
where she sat
   in her invalid's chair
      was left speechless.
Bravo! she cried at last
   and clapped her hands.
      The man's wife

came from the kitchen:
> What goes on here? she said
> But the show was over.

Many readers finish the piece and ask the same question, 'What goes on here?' It is immediate, ordinary, continuous with life; it resists explication just as 'Long-legged Fly' demands it. It seems not to need historical or cultural knowledge in its readers (although *'entrechat'* may be unfamiliar to some). And yet, it has a suggestive title and a very obvious arrangement on the page: it is not a section of uncontrolled, random rambling.

In pointing to the distinction in modern poetry between poems as formulated statements and poems of offered material, I am indicating tendencies, rival claims, rather than totally separate entities or schools of poets who can write in only one of these modes. Yeats gives his central allegiance to the poem as formulated statement and his collected poems operate in a similar inter-referential manner as a completed corpus. Of course, he is never totally pinned down in a hermetically sealed system, the *fait* is never absolutely *accompli*. Throughout his career, he was attracted to the aberrant, the exceptional, the character standing out from the multitude, the apparently random shape-changer, 'zig-zag wantonness', but in his writing of poetry he favours strict form, controlled syntax, and a line of thought reaching a conclusion. His notion of poetry is centred on tension and a rather desperate control, as he describes in 'The Balloon of the Mind':

> Hands, do what you're bid:
> Bring the balloon of the mind
> That bellies and drags in the wind
> Into its narrow shed.

In a letter to Dorothy Wellesley in 1936 he reiterates this idea:

> We have all something within ourselves to batter [did he intend 'batten'?] down and get our power from this fighting. I have never 'produced' a play in verse without showing the actors that the passion of the verse comes from the fact that the speakers are holding down violence or madness – 'down Hysterica passio'. All depends on the completeness of the holding down, on the stirring of the beast underneath.[3]

His taste in the poetry of his contemporaries declares itself most openly in his *Oxford Book of Modern Verse* (1936) with its justificatory introduction. Yeats was an odd choice as editor and he produced a very odd anthology. Oxford University Press had some difficulty in settling on an editor and Yeats was certainly not their first choice. He was not a person who made attempts to keep up with what was happening in poetry and even went so far as to say in a letter to James Stephens: 'I'm not interested in poetry, I'm only interested in what I'm trying to do myself ... out of ten poets who are pushed on you by literary ladies, nine are no good, and the tenth isn't much good.'[4] In reading for the anthology, he set himself the task of establishing whether or not he liked the poetry of, what he called, the 'Ezra, Eliot, Auden School' and why younger poets were following this direction with such relish. During 1935 he read widely and often, inevitably, without much pleasure. He was impressed at how many good lyrics had been written by contemporaries and in his correspondence with Dorothy Wellesley we have an interesting running commentary on his reading and thinking in the final years of his life. To say he read 'widely' may be misleading in that his efforts to read beyond poets he already knew about were not strenuous. The final selection is decidedly eccentric and rather ignorant. He was partly aware of its oddity and partial nature: in a letter to Dorothy Wellesley he comments on the number of pages given to certain poets but adds that 'nobody will count'. Of course, readers have counted and the figures are very revealing. Taking space allocated as a gauge of significance, we discover that the big poets are Edith Sitwell, Herbert Read, W. J. Turner, Dorothy Wellesley and Lawrence Binyon. Next in importance come Eliot, T. Sturge Moore, Oliver St John Gogarty and Yeats himself. An almost token appearance is granted to Hardy, Auden and MacDiarmid. Notoriously, he refused, notwithstanding pleas from his friends, to include any poems by Wilfred Owen and there is nothing by Austin Clarke, Basil Bunting, Edwin Muir or Dylan Thomas. His discussion about including American poets sounds defensive and, for any editor, rather ridiculous:

A distinguished American poet urged me not to attempt a representative selection of American poetry; he pointed out that I could not hope to acquire the necessary knowledge: 'If your selection looks representative it will commit acts of injustice'. I have therefore, though with a sense of loss, confined my selection to those

American poets who by subject, or by long residence in Europe, seem to English readers a part of their own literature.

Only Pound and Eliot, in fact, are granted some space. On the other hand, he chooses translations of numerous poems from sundry places and times, including ancient Irish, medieval Chinese, nineteenth-century French and contemporary Bengali. A comparison of the *Oxford Book* and Robert Lynd's *Anthology of Modern Verse* (Nelson, 1939) indicates that, in his choice of poets, Yeats was not unusual at the time. A comparison, however, with *The Faber Book of Modern Verse* (1936), edited by Michael Roberts, does show that poetry was travelling away from the orthodoxies represented by Yeats and Lynd.

Yeats's selection begins with a move which is both in character and extremely bold, even Modernistic. He takes the description of Leonardo da Vinci's *La Gioconda* in Walter Pater's *Studies in the History of the Renaissance* and lineates the prose into free verse:

MONA LISA

She is older than the rocks among which she sits;
Like the Vampire,
She has been dead many times,
And learned the secrets of the grave;
And has been a diver in deep seas,
And keeps their fallen day about her;
And trafficked for strange webs with Eastern merchants;
And, as Leda,
Was the mother of Helen of Troy,
And, as St Anne,
Was the mother of Mary;
And all this has been to her but as the sound of lyres
    and flutes,
And lives
Only in the delicacy
With which it has moulded the changing lineaments,
And tinged the eyelids and the hands.

Although his prose-master published *The Renaissance* in 1873, Yeats saw this description of the *Mona Lisa* as an essential archetype and anticipation of a development of modern art of which he felt a part. The 'poem' can speak for itself; Yeats did not include Pater's summing up which makes its point explicit:

The fancy of a perpetual life, sweeping together ten thousand experiences, is an old one; and modern thought has conceived the idea of humanity as wrought upon by, and summing up in itself, all modes of thought and life. Certainly Lady Lisa might stand as the embodiment of the old fancy, the symbol of the modern idea.[5]

At the beginning of his literary career, Yeats had found confirmation in Pater for a religious or sacramental vision of life and this vision was sustained as the centre of his aesthetic values. In his autobiographical piece, 'The Child in the House' (1878), later reprinted as *An Imaginary Portrait*, Pater declares something about himself and, in effect, about Yeats:

A place adumbrated itself in his thoughts, wherein those sacred personalities, which are at once the reflex and the pattern of our nobler phases of life, housed themselves; and this region in his intellectual scheme all subsequent experience did but tend still further to realise and define. Some ideal, hieratic persons he would always need to occupy it and keep a warmth there. And he could hardly understand those who felt no such need at all, finding themselves quite happy without such heavenly companionship, and sacred double of their life, beside them.[6]

Such an attitude was bound to be antipathetic to what Yeats saw as a dissipated, secular and temporal quality in much of Modernist verse. In his radio lecture, 'Modern Poetry' (1936), he comments on T. S. Eliot, 'the most revolutionary man in poetry during my lifetime, though his revolution was stylistic alone':

No romantic word or sound, nothing reminiscent … could be permitted henceforth. Poetry must resemble prose, and both must accept the vocabulary of their time; nor must there be any special subject-matter. Tristram and Isoult were not a more suitable theme than Paddington Railway Station. The past had deceived us: let us accept the worthless present.

As a description of Eliot's poetry, this is totally wrong in every detail but it is indicative of Yeats's way of seeing the new poets. He was quite partial to Edith Sitwell, and obviously thought that his liking for her was very daring:

Her language is the traditional language of literature, but twisted, torn, complicated, jerked here and there by strained resemblances, unnatural contacts, forced upon it by terror or by some violence beating in her blood, some primitive obsession that civilisation can no longer exorcise. I find her obscure, exasperating, delightful.

Incidentally, although he did attend some exhibitions of modern French paintings and even expressed an interest in one by Gauguin, and although he gave his energetic support to attempts, including Hugh Lane's, to bring post-Impressionist art to Dublin, he showed no enthusiasm for the new art of such artists as Picasso, Cezanne and Matisse. His taste in modern art was again firmly rooted in the art he had come to enjoy as a young man, and in his choice of designers for his book covers and theatrical sets he favoured what can be seen as developers of the symbolist art of the 1890s. Althea Gyles and Gordon Craig gave way to Sturge Moore and Edmund Dulac.

His view of the poet manifested different emphases during his career but, overall, it remained remarkably consistent. In common with other poets in the first half of the twentieth century, he gave much thought to the relation between the individual writer and some notion of a tradition. An assertion in 'A General Introduction for my Work' (1937) can be put alongside some of Eliot's argument in 'Tradition and the Individual Talent' (1919); Yeats writes: 'Talk to me of originality and I will turn on you with rage. I am a crowd, I am a lonely man, I am nothing. Ancient salt is best packing.' When he read through the rival *Faber Book of Modern Verse* he appreciated that the fashion was moving away from his kind of poetry but he proclaims his poetic lineage in a letter to Dorothy Wellesley:

This difficult work, which is being written everywhere (a professor from Barcelona tells me they have it there) has the substance of philosophy and is a delight to the poet with his professional pattern; but it is not your road or mine, and ours is the main road, the road of naturalness and swiftness and we have thirty centuries on our side. We alone can 'think like a wise man, yet express ourselves like the common people'. These new men are goldsmiths working with a glass screwed into one eye, whereas we stride ahead of the crowd, its swordsmen, its jugglers, looking to right and left. 'To right and left' by which I mean that we need like

Milton, Shakespeare, Shelley, vast sentiments, generalizations supported by tradition.

Some poets seem to fit their writing into otherwise unoccupied corners of their lives or are practising poets in one phase, usually earlier; it is very difficult to think of Yeats not being a poet. He had, of course, recurring doubts about the usefulness or happiness of such an activity. In 'The Choice' he accepts that the dedication to his work as a poet has its bleak consequences:

The intellect of man is forced to choose
Perfection of the life, or of the work,
And if it take the second must refuse
A heavenly mansion, raging in the dark.

When all that story's finished, what's the news?
In luck or out the toil has left its mark:
The old perplexity an empty purse,
Or the day's vanity, the night's remorse.

Deconstructionist critics sometimes seem to suggest that they have discovered the instability and inadequacy of language. In one of Yeats's final letters he declares that 'Man can embody truth but he cannot know it' – much less express it. And much earlier, in exasperation at 'this blind bitter land' of Ireland and his inability to win Maud Gonne or even to make her understand what he wished for Ireland, he concludes that if she had realised what he desired,

who can say
What would have shaken from the sieve?
I might have thrown poor words away
And been content to live.

No one, however, could have a higher sense of vocation and commitment to the craft than Yeats showed. The little poem 'The Choice' was originally the final stanza of 'Coole Park and Ballylee, 1931' but now stands apart from the ringing conclusion of that poem:

We were the last romantics – chose for theme
Traditional sanctity and loveliness;
Whatever's written in what poets name

The book of the people; whatever most can bless
The mind of man or elevate a rhyme;

Then, recognising the new poetic climate of Modernism, and antici-
pating Lady Gregory's death in the following year, and sensing the
demise of his aspirations for art, he laments:

But all is changed, that high horse riderless,
Though mounted in that saddle Homer rode
Where the swan drifts upon a darkening flood.

Because Yeats possessed little ability as a linguist his knowledge
of twentieth-century poets in other languages was bound to be very
limited. We know that he read in 1916, with the help of Iseult
Gonne, some of the poems of the French poets Péguy, Claudel and
Jammes and that he knew some poems by Paul Valéry. He also
knew something of the work of Rilke and D'Annunzio and his own
work was known by Rilke, von Hoffmansthal and Montale. When,
in 1923, he was awarded the Nobel Prize, only the second English-
language writer to be thus honoured (Kipling won it in 1907) since
the Prize's inception in 1901, his stature was certainly recognised
internationally but he was not during his lifetime an influential
figure beyond English in the way that Eliot certainly was and
Yeats's poetry was not translated very quickly into other languages.
Possibly in the Indian subcontinent and Japan, his work has met
with a warmer welcome.

To innovation in poetry in English he was neither alert nor sympathetic. He did, at least, read Eliot and Pound but dismissed them
with suspicious ease. Eliot – 'I think of him as satirist rather than
poet' – is credited with only eight lines in 'the great manner': the
final two stanzas of 'Sweeney Among the Nightingales'. Pound, his
friend, fares little better and is cudgelled with a hefty sentence:

When I consider his work as a whole I find more style than form;
at moments more style, more deliberate nobility and the means to
convey it than in any contemporary poet known to me, but it is
constantly interrupted, broken, twisted into nothing by its direct
opposite, nervous obsession, nightmare, stammering confusion;
he is an economist, poet, politician, raging at malignants with
inexplicable characters and motives, grotesque figures out of a
child's book of beasts.

It could be argued that in common with many other major modern poets, Yeats needed a system of thought as his poetic foundation. For example, Eliot had his Christianity; Pound had his Usury; MacDiarmid had his nationalism and materialism; Rilke had his Angels; Stevens had his Supreme Fiction. Yeats's system, however, is more comprehensive than that of most other poets and this comprehensiveness has, in itself, limited his influence. In the Introduction to *The Oxford Book of Modern Verse* he quotes Stephen Spender as having said that 'the poetry of belief must supersede that of personality'. His poetry is resolutely of personality; beliefs and styles can be imitated, personality cannot. I am talking not of Yeats as a tricky human being but as an extraordinarily complex poetic personality. When we try to trace that personality to some source or sources there is no simple origin or point of literary departure. In the early 1930s a member of his audience in the United States asked him which six books he would keep to re-read, when Yeats quoted his early friend Lionel Johnson as having advocated that 'a man should have read through all good books before he was forty and after that be satisfied with six'. He declared:

> First comes Shakespeare.... Then the *Arabian Nights* in its latest English version, then William Morris, who gives me all the great stories, Homer and the Sagas included, then Balzac, who saved me from Jacobin and Jacobite.

He claimed that he had forgotten the names of the other two, and such a curious fit of amnesia should make us suspect that his reply was either particular to the context or was not entirely serious. Nonetheless, it was not unserious and we are left wondering how to locate a poet who offers such a list. Where are his sacred books? What the four choices have in common is that they offer to the reader a wide range of diverse characters, and Yeats, in answer to questions about his identity, retreats into the camouflage of a multitude.

His considerable influence is clearly discernible in a number of writers. Even if they cannot imitate his personality they use aspects of him as a model for, or challenge to their own work. Gradually his work has become available in translation into all the major languages, so that something of his stature can be recognised by non-Anglophones. The political stance in his poetry and his symbology have proved exciting to a variety of writers; interesting comparisons can be drawn between Yeats and such poets as Neruda, Milosz, Bonnefoy and Montale.

I offer here some samples of Yeats's influence on poets using English to illustrate the different uses which his example has served for different poets. What attracted the American poet Robinson Jeffers to him is his solitary sternness, his declared disdain for general opinion and fashion, his castigation of Paudeen. Jeffers built his granite tower on the wild Big Sur coast of California and from this detachment lambasted the servile, ingrown gregariousness of urbanised Western civilisation, particularly in the United States. His ferocity against timidity far exceeds Yeats's directed hate but certainly he felt a reinforcement from the older poet's stance and he extended an imagery of tower, stone and hawks to be found in Yeats's work. Such elements were not what appealed to Theodore Roethke, who confessed to having an imitative tendency and could not resist the cadences of Yeats's verse. He openly acknowledged a debt and his love poems sometimes slip into a Yeatsian turn of phrase with recurring images of dancing, music and sexual play. Incidentally, Roethke does not always receive the credit he deserves for being, in effect, one of the founding members of the Confessional group of poets, and some of his apparent frankness in dealing with his personal problems looks back to Yeats's habit of making public poems around his friends, members of his family and his personal dramas. This mingling of private and public, personal and political, also appealed to Robert Lowell. The poems in his *Life Studies* (1959) could never be confused with poems by Yeats, but the confrontation of himself and the exploration of his family are reminiscent of some of the Irish poet's poems; *Life Studies* marks a turning point in Lowell's poetic career quite similar to a pivotal point in Yeats's career marked by *Responsibilities*. Furthermore, Lowell's great political poems, 'For the Union Dead' and 'Waking Early Sunday Morning', show some of the same poetic eloquence and sweep of mind as 'Easter 1916' or 'Nineteen Hundred and Nineteen'. When, in 1960, Lowell read the just-completed 'For the Union Dead' to an audience of 4000 in the Public Garden, Boston, and used local names and history to raise a political question in the minds of contemporary Americans, this was as close as a poet in English has come, allowing for differences in time and country, to the way in which Yeats could address his fellow Irish in the 1920s.

In Britain I wish to glance at an effect which he exerted on three very different Scottish poets. Edwin Muir, himself a manipulator of symbols, admired Yeats's reanimation of ancient myths to demonstrate the recurring patterns in human behaviour. The archetypes of the Great Memory are a guarantee for both poets of a shared humanity across time and culture. Muir's greater contemporary, Hugh MacDiarmid, was acquainted with Yeats and was included briefly in the Oxford anthology. MacDiarmid, who never saw much virtue in modesty, rather exaggerated his friendship with Yeats and represented himself as a figure in Scotland parallel with him in Ireland. To be fair to him, his contribution to the realignment of Scottish culture in this century was enormous and certain major comparisons can be drawn between the two men. Born in 1892, MacDiarmid (or, to give him his non-literary name, C. M. Grieve) published his first book of poems, *Sangshaw*, in 1925, by which time Yeats had entered the period of his full poetic power and had achieved a number of his goals in the cultural–political regeneration of Ireland. In MacDiarmid's view, Scotland and Ireland, allied Celtic countries, had suffered a similar colonisation at the hands of the English. Yeats provided for him (as he did for the young Saunders Lewis in Wales) a model of how to fight back and assert a distinctive national identity; his poems and plays in themselves were not what excited him but they were an essential part of the nationalist programme. Scotland's linguistic situation was more complicated than Ireland's in that there were three literary languages – English, Gaelic and Scots – to Ireland's two. MacDiarmid's wonderful early collections, including *A Drunk Man Looks at the Thistle* (1926), are written in a 'synthetic Scots' devised, in part, to insist on the distinctness of the Scottish tradition. Later on, in the 1930s, he moved towards a pan-Celtic idea in which Ireland and Scotland would recover their shared past and character in the Gaelic language: like Yeats, he could not speak or read Gaelic but his vision was not to be wobbled by such a small consideration. In the later long poems (for example, *In Memoriam of James Joyce*), he moves beyond Yeats's horizons of poetry and joins the deliverers of 'offered material' on an encyclopaedic scale. The third Scottish poet, Sorley Maclean, in fact writes exclusively in Gaelic. His poetic education has drawn on three main sources: a Gaelic oral tradition which was robust in the island community of his youth and in his own family; a Gaelic literary tradition, some of which was common to Scotland and Ireland; and an English literary tradition extending to Classical and Continental literatures. Although Yeats needed to study and collect Irish folklore, he did show how such material could be grafted on to a modern sensibility and Maclean wished to do something similar, even if his starting-point was markedly different. When he was writing his earlier poems in the 1930s, Maclean was conscious of an affiliation to Symbolism and found Yeats his most readily accessible model. Towards the end of the 1930s and into the 1940s he experienced a strong conflict between his love for a woman, called Eimhir, and his sense of political duty. Some of these poems, published in 1943 as *Dàin do Eimhir* (Songs to Eimhir), owe a great deal to Yeats's poetic presentation of his vexed love for Maud Gonne. Both Maclean and MacDiarmid, although very much on the Left in politics and suspicious of Yeats's tendencies to the Right, felt an identification with his public courage, his straightness and his apparent contempt for bought popularity.

These samples of Yeats's influence beyond Ireland are chosen because they are evident and because they demonstrate how different poets have followed very different aspects of him. Obviously there are many poets who absorb or conceal an influence more completely or where the 'anxiety of influence', to use Harold Bloom's phrase, would have to be decoded. In Ireland itself, it seems almost impossible for a poet not to be aware of his huge shadow or dazzling light, and some go to extraordinary lengths to deny or disguise his lingering presence. From as early as 1892 he sets out to declare a solidarity with aspiring Ireland. In 'To Ireland in the Coming Times' he writes:

> Know, that I would accounted be
> True brother of a company
> That sang to sweeten Ireland's wrong....

He identifies himself 'With Davis, Mangan, Ferguson', and dedicates his career to his country:

> While still I may, I write for you
> The love I lived, the dream I knew.

In 1938 he is still insisting on a solidarity. In section V of 'Under Ben Bulben', he gives his counsel:

> Irish poets, learn your trade,
> Sing whatever is well made,
> Scorn the sort now growing up

All out of shape from toe to top,
...
Cast your mind on other days
That we in coming days may be
Still the indomitable Irishry.

During his lifetime, his attitudes, public involvements and writings divided his compatriots and many of them felt that he was no compatriot. After his death – and few poets have shown such an awareness of posterity – he continued to prompt fierce loyalty or antagonism. For some, his work had not healed divisions, had not helped to unify Ireland, had not furthered the struggle for independence from England, but had emphasised a political Anglo-Irishism and promoted an Anglophone, West Brit mentality, a new form of subservience to the colonial master. Daniel Corkery's contention in *The Hidden Ireland* (1925), that Yeats had constructed a false notion of Irish culture, was supported by later writers who resented the way in which Yeats, according to them, claimed to feel for and speak for the quintessential Ireland. Louis MacNeice, who published a sceptical but appreciative book on Yeats in 1941, the first full appraisal of him, seems in his autobiographical poem 'Carrickfergus' (1937) to write deliberately in a style opposed to Yeatsian magniloquence. Although he was often supportive of young writers, he also appeared to other aspiring poets to be concerned only with his own image. Patrick Kavanagh is a crucial figure in any attempt to chart the influence of Yeats in Ireland. He did not find the older poet a sympathetic figure and he saw him, for all his insistence on Irish soil and its peasantry, as ignorant of the rough, 'real' peasant Ireland of County Monaghan where Kavanagh had been brought up and where he had to labour to survive. Kavanagh's major poem *The Great Hunger* (1942) can be seen as a bitter rejoinder to Yeats's cultivated idea of rural Ireland and, for many, it expressed the blighting force of poverty, religious repression, particularly of sexuality, and familial conformism. For a large number of poets growing up after the First World War, Kavanagh represented the truth about their communities and offered a more acceptably indigenous model of the Irish poet than did Yeats. His poetry has not travelled well beyond Ireland and, for some of his supporters, this fact bears out their distrust of Yeats's campaign to make Irish writing known outside Ireland: if a writer does not adapt to middle-class English and liberal American requirements, his or her voice will be ignored.

Seamus Heaney, shackled with Robert Lowell's commendation as the best Irish poet since Yeats, has recently suffered a backlash in Ireland because of his popularity outside the island. Heaney has on many occasions stated his admiration for both Yeats and Kavanagh but some of his adverse critics seem to demand of him an undivided loyalty to the poet closer to his own background. Contemporary poets often seem more balanced than the theorists in handling Yeats. It is difficult, particularly in a small country, to have such a dominating presence looming over subsequent poets and there is a temptation to try to ignore him, denounce him, or demote his authority by exposing frailties, flaws and inconsistencies. Some of the Deconstructionist critics have moved out of their depth by probing for shallows in the poetry. Poets as varied as Thomas Kinsella, Richard Murphy, John Montague, Brendan Kennelly, Michael Longley and Derek Mahon have all managed to digest some nourishment from Yeats without appearing imitative or partisan. A more recent generation of writers, such as Paul Durcan, Ciaron Carson, Paul Muldoon, Nuala Ni Dhomhnaill and Medbh McGuckian, have gone in their own directions without special reference or reverence to him. It is probably true that outside Ireland and in anthologies of poetry in English, Yeats has sometimes been granted a prominence to the virtual exclusion of other Irish poets – for example, Austin Clarke, Patrick Kavanagh and even Louis MacNeice; and something similar has happened in the case of Seamus Heaney. It is, however, unfair to blame Yeats or Heaney for this disproportion or tokenism on the part of publishers, programme producers and editors.

Half a century after his death, how does Yeats emerge in the perspective of modern poetry? His stature as a literary phenomenon has seldom been seriously queried by critics of note although the nature and scale of his stature have been challenged by the stimulating and usually wrongheaded American critic Yvor Winters and the less stimulating but equally wrongheaded English critic F. R. Leavis. Poets such as Auden and Larkin have expressed reservations about aspects of his work. It must be stated that Yeats is not – no poet can be – the complete poet of the twentieth century in sensibility and expression. Often, in fact, he seems to be peculiarly out of touch with this century. The bulk of the populations in developed countries live in conurbations with all the attendant stresses and opportunities. Yeats not only does not write out of this situation, he barely refers to it. Not only are there no factories or offices in the poems, there is scarcely a wheel. With hardly an exception, scientific and technological developments seem arrested at about the time of Galileo. The economic and social condition of his country's populace, and the large-scale emigration, rarely impinge on his verse and, for all his endless travelling, a mere handful of poems have locations outside Ireland, and then mainly in Byzantium. His visual awareness is not strong and there are few descriptions of buildings, animals and the natural world. There is little wit and even less humour: and there are virtually no poems about childhood. The major international events during his long career are prominently absent; he sneered at Wilfred Owen as 'all blood, dirt and sucked sugar stick' and considered the First World War, with all its suffering, as irrelevant to him. Would he have felt the same about the Second World War, though it was an utterly different conflict? Ireland in his poetry is not considered in relation to contemporary Europe but more to Urbino, Athens and ancient Tara. His endless editing and modernising did not lead to anything markedly modern in his diction, verse forms and syntax. The bulk of his poetry in style and subject could have been written before the twentieth century.

In spite of all these omissions and doubtful commissions, Yeats is, in my view, the greatest poet to write in English in the twentieth century. Much of the detail of the justification for my view is apparent in the earlier parts of this book. Few poets ever have evolved such a comprehensive vision of existence, a vision which allows for contradictions and yet has a grand consistency. His is a poetry of large concepts but they are anchored and explored in specific circumstances: people, locations, incidents humanise and localise the ideas. He wished all his poems to be recited aloud, and they are memorable, resonant and aurally seductive. The rhetorical control is deeply satisfying and in it we feel a balancing of the conscious and the unconscious, the rational and the emotional, what is lived and what is imagined, the individual and the general. His growth as a poet does not have an ultimate point, nor does a new development cancel out an earlier one. A recurring image of his growth is the tree, with the 'holy tree' growing in 'thine own heart' ('The Two Trees') and the 'flourishing hidden tree' ('Prayer for My Daughter'), to his late request to Dorothy Wellesley, 'Stretch towards the moonless midnight of the trees'. In the third section of 'The Tower' he offers his testament to the solitary 'upstanding men' earlier described in 'The Fisherman' as his ideal audience:

I declare
They shall inherit my pride,
The pride of people that were
Bound neither to Cause nor to State,
Neither to slaves that were spat on
Nor to the tyrants that spat,
The people of Burke and of Grattan
That gave though free to refuse –
...
And I declare my faith:
I mock Plotinus' thought
And cry in Plato's teeth,
Death and life were not
Till man made up the whole,
Made lock, stock and barrel
Out of his bitter soul,
Aye, sun and moon and star, all
And further add to that
That, being dead, we rise,
Dream and so create
Translunar Paradise.
I have prepared my peace
With learned Italian things
And the proud stones of Greece,
Poet's imaginings
And memories of love,
Memories of the words of women,
All those things whereof
Man makes a superhuman
Mirror-resembling dream.

Here we have the courage and defiance of one who has looked at life, history, love and death and has put his own thoughts in a poetic order.

Notes

Introduction

1. Quoted in Ellmann, *Yeats: The Man and the Masks*, pp. 5–6.
2. Quoted in Jeffares, *A New Commentary on The Poems of W. B. Yeats*, p. vi.
3. Quoted in Tuohy, *Yeats*, p. 89.
4. T. S. Eliot, *On Poetry and Poets* (London: Faber, 1957), p. 262.

1   Family and Place

1. J. B. Yeats, *Letters to his Son W. B. Yeats and Others*, p. 78.
2. John Butler Yeats, *Early Memories* (Dublin: Cuala, 1923), pp. 13, 18.
3. Quoted in Murphy, *Prodigal Father*, p. 51.
4. Hilary Pyle, *Jack B. Yeats: A Biography*, Revised edition (London: André Deutsch, 1989), p. 58.
5. Quoted in Jeffares, *A New Biography*, p. 258.
6. J. B. Yeats, *Letters*, pp. 280–1.
7. J. B. Yeats, *Letters*, p. 210.
8. J. B. Yeats, *Letters*, p. 229.
9. Quoted in Murphy, *Prodigal Father*, p. 425.
10. Quoted in Murphy, *Prodigal Father*, p. 437.
11. Quoted in Murphy, *Prodigal Father*, p. 437.
12. Quoted in a note in *Collected Letters of W. B. Yeats*, Vol. I, p. 123.
13. Written in 1948, quoted in Hilary Pyle, *Jack B. Yeats: A Biography* p. 156.
14. *Memoirs* pp. 71–2.
15. Quoted by Kuch in *Yeats and AE: 'The Antagonism That Unites Friends'*, p. 5.
16. *Uncollected Prose I*, p. 380.
17. *Memoirs*, p. 32.
18. K. Tynan, *Twenty-five Years: Reminiscences* (London: Smith, Elder and Co., 1913), p. 145.
19. *Further Letters of Gerard Manley Hopkins* quoted by Ellmann, *Yeats: The Man and the Masks*, p. 50.

2   Yeats and the 1890s: Celtic Twilight and Golden Dawn

1. *Selected Writings of Walter Pater*, ed. Harold Bloom (New York: New American Library, 1974), p. 60.
2. Fiona Macleod, *The Winged Destiny, and Studies in the Spiritual History of the Gael* (London: Heinemann, 1922), p. 325.
3. *Memoirs*, pp. 128–9.
4. Maud Gonne in *Scattering Branches*, ed. Stephen Gwynn, pp. 22–3.

3   Yeats and Politics

1.   Quoted in note in *Memoirs*, p. 82.
2.   *Joseph Holloway's Abbey Theatre*, ed. Hogan and O'Neill (Southern Illinois University Press, 1967), p. 81.
3.   Standish O'Grady, *Selected Essays and Passages*, introduced by E. A. Boyd (1918), p. 180.
4.   G. B. Shaw, *Irish Statesman*, September 1923.
5.   Quoted in F. S. L. Lyons, *Culture and Anarchy in Ireland 1890–1939*, p. 96.
6.   Quoted in F. S. L. Lyons, *Culture and Anarchy in Ireland 1890–1939*, p. 12.
7.   Maud Gonne MacBride, *A Servant of the Queen: Reminiscences*, p. 7.
8.   Quoted in Nancy Cardozo, *Maud Gonne: Lucky Eyes and a High Heart* (London: Victor Gollancz, 1979), p. 220.
9.   Quoted in Murphy, *Prodigal Father*, p. 317.

4   Yeats and the Theatre : 'Baptism of the Gutter'

1.   *John Bull's Other Island* with its various prefaces is included in *Landmarks of Irish Drama*, ed. Brendan Kennelly (London: Methuen, 1988).
2.   Sean O'Casey, *Autobiographies*, Vol. II (London: Macmillan, 1963; originally written, 1949), pp. 102–3.

5   Friends and Loves

1.   Maud Gonne MacBride, *A Servant of the Queen*, p. 115.
2.   *Memoirs*, p. 63.
3.   *Memoirs*, p. 247.
4.   Maud Gonne MacBride, *A Servant of the Queen*, p. 329.
5.   *Memoirs*, pp. 88–9.
6.   Quoted in Frank Tuohy, *Yeats*, p. 85.
7.   Dorothy Wellesley, *Letters on Poetry from W. B. Yeats to Dorothy Wellesley*, p. 174.
8.   George Moore, *Hail and Farewell*, ed. R. Cave (*Ave* originally published 1911), pp. 78–9.

6   Masks and Development

1.   AE, *Song and Its Fountains* (London: Macmillan, 1932), pp. 9–10.
2.   Oscar Wilde, *Selected Writings*, ed. R. Ellmann (Oxford: Oxford University Press, 1961), pp. 101–2.
3.   Friedrich Nietzsche, *'The Birth of Tragedy'* and *'The Case of Wagner'*, translated Walter Kaufmann (New York: Random House, 1967), p. 64.
4.   Ibid., p. 67.
5.   Nietzsche, *'Twilight of the Idols'* and *'The Anti-Christ'*, translated R. J. Hollingdale (Harmondsworth: Penguin, 1968), p. 73.
6.   *Memoirs*, p. 145.

7   A Vision of Byzantium

1.   Nietzsche, *Thus Spake Zarathustra*, translated by R. J. Hollingdale (Harmondsworth: Penguin, 1961), pp. 331–2.
2.   Letter to W.B. Yeats, quoted in Murphy, *Prodigal Father*, p. 485.
3.   *A Vision*, first edition (London: T. Werner Laurie, 1925), p. 227.

8   Yeats and Modern Poetry

1.   T. S. Eliot, *On Poetry and Poets*, p. 255.
2.   J. B. Yeats, *Letters to his Son W. B. Yeats and Others*, p. 245.
3.   *Letters on Poetry from W. B. Yeats to Dorothy Wellesley*, p. 86.
4.   Letter to James Stephens, quoted in Frank Tuohy, *Yeats*, p. 209.
5.   *Selected Writings of Walter Pater*, ed. H. Bloom (New York: New American Library, 1974), p. 47.
6.   Ibid., p. 13.

Select Bibliography

The purpose of the list of books is to enlarge the reader's knowledge of Yeats and to open up discussion of his work. Inclusion of a title does not betoken my approval of the contents.

WORKS OF W. B. YEATS

Autobiographies (London: Macmillan, 1955).
Collected Plays (London: Macmillan, 1953).
Donoghue, Denis (ed.), *Memoirs* (London: Macmillan, 1972).
Essays and Introductions (London: Macmillan, 1961).
Explorations (London: Macmillan, 1962).
Frayne, John P. and Colton Johnson (eds), *Uncollected Prose of W. B. Yeats*, Vol. 1 (London: Macmillan, 1970).
Frayne, John P. (ed.), *Uncollected Prose of W. B. Yeats*, Vol. 2 (London: Macmillan, 1975).
Jeffares, A. Norman (ed.), *Yeats's Poems* (London: Macmillan, 1989).
Kelly, John S. and Eric Domville (eds), *Collected Letters of W. B. Yeats*, Vol. 1, 1865–1895 (Oxford: Oxford University Press, 1986).
Letters on Poetry from W. B. Yeats to Dorothy Wellesley (Oxford: Oxford University Press, 1940).
Martin, Augustine (ed.), *Collected Poems* (London: Arrow Books, 1990).
Mythologies (London: Macmillan, 1959).
Pearce, Donald R. (ed.), *The Senate Speeches of W. B. Yeats* (London: Faber and Faber, 1961).
A Vision, Revised by the Author (London: Macmillan, 1937).
Wade, Allan (ed.), *Letters of W. B. Yeats* (London: Rupert Hart-Davis, 1954).

BACKGROUND AND BIOGRAPHICAL MATERIAL

Bowra, C. M., *The Heritage of Symbolism* (London: Macmillan, 1943).
Boyce, D. G. (ed.), *The Revolution in Ireland 1879–1923* (London: Macmillan, 1988).
Brown, Malcolm, *The Politics of Irish Literature: From Thomas Davis to W. B. Yeats* (London: Allen and Unwin, 1972).
Eglinton, John, *Irish Literary Portraits* (London: Macmillan, 1935).
Ellmann, Richard, *a long the riverrun* (London: Hamish Hamilton, 1988).
Ellmann, Richard, *Yeats: The Man and the Masks* (London: Macmillan, 1949).
Fallis, Richard, *The Irish Renaissance: An Introduction to Anglo-Irish Literature* (New York: Syracuse University Press, 1977).

Fletcher, Ian, *W. B. Yeats and his Contemporaries* (Brighton: The Harvester Press, 1987).

Foster, R. F. (ed.), *The Oxford Illustrated History of Ireland* (Oxford: Oxford University Press, 1989).

Gonne MacBride, Maud, *A Servant of the Queen: Reminiscences* (London: Victor Gollancz, 1938).

Gregory, Augusta, *Our Irish Theatre* (London: Putnam, 1914).

Gwynn, Stephen, *Scattering Branches: Tributes to the Memory of W. B. Yeats* (London: Macmillan, 1940).

Hamburger, Michael, *The Truth of Poetry: Tensions in Modern Poetry from Baudelaire to the 1960s* (London: Weidenfeld and Nicolson, 1969).

Henn, T. R., *The Lonely Tower* (London: Methuen, 1950; Revised edition 1965).

Hough, Graham, *The Last Romantics* (London: Duckworth, 1949).

Jeffares, A. Norman, *W. B. Yeats: Man and Poet* (London: Routledge and Kegan Paul, 1949).

Jeffares, A. Norman, *W. B. Yeats: A New Biography* (London: Hutchinson, 1988).

Jeffares, A. Norman (ed.), *Yeats the European* (Gerrards Cross: Colin Smythe, 1989).

Kermode, Frank, *Romantic Image* (London: Routledge and Kegan Paul, 1957).

Kuch, Peter, *Yeats and AE: 'The Antagonism that Unites Friends'* (Gerrards Cross: Colin Smythe, 1986).

Lyons, F. S. L., *Culture and Anarchy in Ireland 1890–1939* (Oxford: Clarendon Press, 1979).

Martin, Augustine, *W. B. Yeats* (Gerrards Cross: Colin Smythe, 1983; Revised edition, 1990).

Moore, George, *Hail and Farewell*, ed. Richard Cave (Gerrards Cross: Colin Smythe, 1976).

Murphy, William M., *Prodigal Father: The Life of John Butler Yeats (1839–1922)* (Ithaca and London: Cornell University Press, 1978).

Raine, Kathleen, *Defending Ancient Springs* (Oxford: Oxford University Press, 1967).

Reid, B. L., *The Man from New York: John Quinn and his Friends* (New York: Oxford University Press, 1968).

Saddlemyer, Ann, and Colin Smythe (eds), *Lady Gregory: Fifty Years After* (Gerrards Cross: Colin Smythe, 1982).

Smith, Stan, *Inviolable Voice* (Dublin: Gill and Macmillan, 1982).

Stead, C. K., *The New Poetic: Yeats to Eliot* (London: Hutchinson, 1964).

Storey, Mark (ed.), *Poetry and Ireland since 1800: A Source Book* (London: Routledge, 1988).

Tuohy, Frank, *Yeats* (London: Macmillan, 1976).

Watson, G. J., *Irish Identity and the Literary Revival* (London: Croom Helm, 1979).

Wilson, Edmund, *Axel's Castle: A Study in the Imaginative Literature of 1870–1930* (New York: Charles Scribner's Sons, 1931).

Worth, Katherine, *The Irish Drama of Europe from Yeats to Beckett* (Atlantic Highlands: Humanities Press, 1978).

Yeats, J. B., *Letters to his Son W. B. Yeats and Others 1869–1922*, ed. Joseph Hone (London: Faber and Faber, 1944).

ON THE WORKS OF YEATS

Cullingford, Elizabeth, *Yeats, Ireland and Fascism* (London: Macmillan, 1981).

Donoghue, D. and J. R. Mulryne (eds), *An Honoured Guest* (London: Macmillan, 1965).

Harper, George M. (ed.), *Yeats and the Occult* (London: Macmillan, 1976).

Hoffman, Daniel, *Barbarous Knowledge: Myth in the Poetry of Yeats, Graves and Muir* (New York: Oxford University Press, 1967).

Jeffares, A. Norman, *A New Commentary on the Poems of W. B. Yeats* (London: Macmillan, 1984).

Jeffares, A. Norman and K. G. W. Cross (eds), *In Excited Reverie* (London: Macmillan, 1965).

Lynch, David, *The Poetics of the Self* (Chicago: University of Chicago Press, 1979).

Miller, Liam, *The Noble Drama of W. B. Yeats* (Dublin: The Dolmen Press, 1977).

Moore, Virginia, *The Unicorn* (New York: Macmillan, 1954).

O'Driscoll, Robert and Lorna Reynolds (eds), *Yeats and the Theatre* (London: Macmillan, 1975).

Parkin, Andrew, *The Dramatic Imagination of W. B. Yeats* (Dublin: Gill and Macmillan, 1978).

Pritchard, William H. (ed.), *W. B. Yeats: A Critical Anthology* (Harmondsworth: Penguin Books, 1972).

Skelton, Robin and Ann Saddlemyer (eds), *The World of W. B. Yeats* (British Columbia: University of Victoria, 1965).

Stallworthy, Jon, *Between the Lines: Yeats's Poetry in the Making* (Oxford: Oxford University Press, 1963).

Stock, A. G., *W. B. Yeats: His Poetry and Thought* (Cambridge: Cambridge University Press, 1961).

Unterecker, John (ed.), *Yeats: A Collection of Critical Essays* (Englewood Cliffs, N. J.: Prentice Hall, 1963).

Unterecker, John, *A Reader's Guide to W. B. Yeats* (London: Thames and Hudson, 1959).

Vendler, Helen Hennessy, *Yeats's Vision and the Later Plays* (Cambridge, Mass.: Harvard University Press, 1963).

Webster, Brenda, *Yeats: A Psychoanalytic Study* (London: Macmillan, 1974).

Wilson, F.A.C., *W. B. Yeats and Tradition* (London: Victor Gollancz, 1958).

Zwerdling, Alex, *Yeats and the Heroic Ideal* (New York: New York University Press, 1965).

General Index

Index of References to Yeats's Works

DATE			